EAST INDIA
Publishing Company

THE SECRET HISTORY of the COURT of SPAIN
Rachel Challice

Published by the
EAST INDIA PUBLISHING COMPANY
Ottawa, Canada

© 2023 East India Publishing Company

Cover Design by EIPC © 2023
9781778941672

www.eastindiapublishing.com

Contents

I.

INTRIGUES OF FERDINAND, PRINCE OF ASTURIAS, AGAINST HIS PARENTS AND GODOY
1800–1804

The history of Spain during the nineteenth century is synonymous with that of favourites at the Court of Madrid, for as the country, in spite of all its struggles, had practically no voice in the election of the Parliaments, the main events of the land had their rise in the royal palace, where self-interested persons blinded the eyes of the rulers for their own purposes.

Thus the fall of Spain into the hands of the French evidently resulted from the dissensions of those environing the Royal Family, and the hopes entertained by the optimistic Spaniards at the return of Ferdinand VII. were destroyed by the flattering courtiers encouraging the Sovereign in his despotic ideas.

The evils of the reign of Isabel II., and the revolution and republic which followed, can all be traced to the same intriguing spirit of the Court, and from the death of Charles III., who is still spoken of as the "great Charles," the government of the country was, in reality, in the invisible hands of those who ruled the Sovereign; and hence the disastrous influence exercised in the land by Queen Maria Luisa, whose feeble, good-natured consort, Carlos IV., let her pursue her self-willed course, whilst falling himself an easy prey to the overweening ambition of Godoy, her favourite. This daughter of Philip, Duke of Parma, had shown from her childhood signs of great intelligence, and her education had given full scope for her talents. Without being absolutely beautiful, her features had a charm of their own from their expression, and her fine eyes, elegant figure, and pleasant manners, soon exercised a sway at the Court of Spain when she made her appearance as the bride of the Prince of Asturias.

Albeit generous and warm-hearted, Maria Luisa was of a somewhat arrogant disposition. This was seen when she was only twelve years old, in the tone of superiority she adopted in her home after the contract of her marriage to the heir of the Spanish throne had been signed. Her brother Ferdinand resented this assumption of superiority, and remonstrated with his sister on the subject. Upon this the Princess promptly lost her temper, and said: "I will teach you to pay me the attention which you owe me, because I shall finally be Queen of Spain, whilst you will never be more than a little Duke of Parma!" "Well, the Duke of Parma will have the honour of slapping the Queen of Spain," was the reply, and Ferdinand promptly gave his sister a slap in the face.

The Duke was then arrested by order of his father, and he was only released at the plea of his sister, who was sorry when the quarrel assumed such a serious aspect.

When crowned Queen of Spain, in 1789, as the wife of Charles IV., twenty-four years after her marriage, Maria Luisa soon showed that her impulsive nature, which knew no check from her husband, would bring her country to grief.

Captivated by the young Godoy, she surprised and alarmed the nation by the swift way she exalted him to the highest position in the realm. As the favourite had known how to dominate the will of the King, as well as to subjugate the heart of the Queen, there was no limit to his power, and when he was given the title of "The Prince of the Peace," for the alliance he made with the French, the animosity of the nation was so much excited that public interest was soon centred in Prince Ferdinand as one who might free the Court from the favourite, and thus save the country from the disastrous effect of an undue submission to France.

As Alcalá Galiano says in his "Memorias," "The title of 'Prince' conferred on Godoy seemed to detract from the dignity of the Royal Family." The Prince of Asturias was at this time eleven years of age.

2

It must be remembered that the Queen had never gained any real hold on her son's love. She was naturally disinclined to any efforts dictated by maternal love, and she had taken no pains to overcome the constitutional defects of her son, which were repellent to her lively imagination and quick temperament.

In a letter to the Grand Duke of Berg, the Prince is described by the royal mother as peculiarly deficient in sensibility, and she remarks that his torpid nerves indeed required strong stimulants for their exercise. He spoke little, rarely smiled, and found a sardonic satisfaction in all kinds of petty acts of cruelty. He liked to crush a little bird if it fell into his hands, and, indeed, pity was a quality to which he was a stranger.

As the education of the young Prince was entrusted to Don Juan Escoiquiz, it was soon seen that he exercised a great power over the royal pupil, and he sought to use him as an instrument for thwarting the schemes of the Queen's favourite—which boded ill for the land.

Escoiquiz was certainly clever. He had translated Young's poems and Milton's "Paradise Lost," and when he was summoned to the royal palace in his capacity of tutor to the young Prince, he exclaimed: "I shall be happy if my instruction of my royal pupil leads to his being the most humane of Princes."

However, time did not show that he guided the Prince in this direction, for the intrigue of the Queen with Godoy so aroused his malicious envy that his one idea was to instigate his pupil to courses tending to the overthrow of the favourite. Classics and mathematics were foregone by the cleric, who devoted the time to teaching the Prince that the one great secret of a ruler was to trust nobody entirely, but to oppose one man to another man and one party against the other.

This lesson of distrust the royal boy learnt to perfection, and as his cold eyes watched his mother's deceitful conduct, and he saw how easily his father fell a prey to the artifice and design of the lovers, his heart was a fruitful soil for the poisonous words of his preceptor.

Escoiquiz soon determined to use the lad more effectually as an

3

instrument against Godoy, and so he inspired him with the desire to have a seat in the Cabinet Ministry, and he wrote discourses and treatises which he gave the Prince to publish as his own, so that the lad might pose as a statesman of a wisdom and foresight beyond his years.

But although Carlos IV. was an easy tool for an unprincipled wife, he was not inclined to fall a prey to the machinations of his son, and to give his son a place that had been denied to himself at a like age; so the artifice of the tutor was discovered, and he was dismissed from Court with the appointment of Archdeacon of Alcaraz, in the Chapter of Toledo.

But albeit banished from his post as tutor, the cleric still retained his influence over the Prince, and he seized every opportunity of going to the royal palace to foster the ideas which he had instilled in the mind of his former pupil.

The picture given by Manuel Godoy in his "Mémoires" of the daily life of the young royal people at this time shows that parental affection played little part in the lives of the young Princes and Princesses. After the morning Mass was over, the young people were allowed to receive visits till half-past eleven, when they went to their parents' room, and there remained till lunch-time, and each Infante and Infanta had his or her meal in a separate apartment. The afternoon drive was generally taken in the same direction every day, and the carriage was accompanied by a royal guard. In the evening the Infantes and Infantas spent half an hour with their parents, and then returned to their own quarters, where they were sometimes allowed to have their friends.

Whenever the Infantes and Infantas went from one part of the palace to another, they were accompanied by a gentil hombre, and they were treated very much like State prisoners.

This monotonous life of the Royal Family was suddenly disturbed by the Mission from the Court of France in which the proposal was made by Napoleon to unite his brother Lucien in marriage with Isabel, daughter of Carlos IV. The King was alarmed at the idea of such a close connection with the warrior who treated Europe like a chess-board, but, not wishing openly to refuse the

4

powerful ruler, he promptly arranged for the marriage of the Princess with his nephew, who was heir to the throne of Naples, and he also made arrangements for the marriage of Ferdinand with Princess Maria Antonia of Naples.

Godoy was strongly opposed to the Prince's marriage, declaring that eighteen was too tender an age for this step, and that it would be better for the young man to improve his mind by travelling, and fit himself for his future task of governing the nation before he married. However, the King listened to the Marquis of Caballero, who was in favour of the alliance, and the wedding of Ferdinand took place in Barcelona in October, 1802, at the same time as that of his sister.

When Ferdinand subsequently heard how Godoy had tried to prevent his marriage, he thought it was with a desire to prevent the succession being established in his favour, and his hatred of the favourite increased accordingly.

Godoy writes very emphatically in his "Mémoires" of the evil influence exercised by Escoiquiz on the mind of Prince Ferdinand:

"The master seized upon the moral faculties of his pupil like an unclean insect which sticks to the bud of a rose and stops the growth by the web it weaves. Ferdinand, doomed at an early age to feel no affection for anyone, was a prey to fear and dissimulation. His youth, his manhood—in short, his whole life—was passed in a state of uninterrupted suspicion. He did not believe in virtue, not even in that of Escoiquiz, and at last the tutor received the due reward of the instructions he had imparted to his pupil.

"He died, loaded with contempt, ejected and banished from his pupil."

Godoy declared that his enemies paralyzed his endeavours to free Spain from the dominion of the French. He writes in the same "Mémoires":

"Determined to impose upon the young Prince that I wished to deprive him of the natural affection of his august parents, my enemies so far succeeded in alarming him that the Prince was brought to look upon me as a dangerous rival who aspired to seat himself on the throne. To such perfidious insinuations they added other indirect practices.

"They made Charles IV. tremble at the bare idea of a war with France, when I had in September, 1806, firmly resolved upon proclaiming it."

The account of Manuel Godoy's last visit to the ex-Queen Maria Luisa is characteristic of the devotion of the courtier:

"It was in May, 1808, that my old King, his august lady, and the young infant Francisco, the unhappy victims of the iniquitous faction that called Napoleon to interfere in the matters of Spain, were transported from that country to France, and they remained in the dull, lonely dwelling of Fontainebleau.

"The Queen, a stranger in the royal palace of her ancestors, was in a grand bed. Her eyes were full of sadness but of majesty; her grave and venerable face was stamped with virtue. As she was able to speak openly without the presence of any importunate witnesses, she evidently wished to give expression to her feelings when her eyes fell on those who were with her, and she noted the tears which they vainly strove to stop. At last she broke the silence, and said:

"'And you (tu), Manuel, my loyal friend, from whom I have had so many proofs that you would always remain so till the end—you will have your customary patience and listen to what I have to say!'"

And then the Queen once more poured into her friend's ears her doubts and fears as to her future and that of Charles IV.

From the time Maria Antonia of Naples married the eighteen-year-old Prince of Asturias in 1802, she proved herself an active partisan of her husband and his tutor Escoiquiz, and if she had lived longer her clear-sightedness might have prevented the surrender of Spain to Bonaparte.

In obedience to her mother, Queen Caroline of Naples, the Princess of Asturias was unremitting in her efforts to contravert the plans of her irreconcilable enemy Napoleon, which were subsequently furthered by the short-sighted policy of Godoy and Maria Luisa. Secret and almost daily were the letters which passed between Princess Maria Antonia and Queen Caroline, and, as the correspondence was conducted in cipher, it entered the Court of

Naples without attracting any attention, and thus many diplomatic secrets from Madrid travelled thence to England. In the bitter warfare of personal hatred and political intrigue no accusations were too bad to be levelled by one part of the Spanish Royal Family against the other.

The partisans of the Prince and Princess of Asturias declared that Godoy and Maria Luisa filled the King's mind with suspicions against Ferdinand, even to the point of attributing parricidal thoughts to him, so that the King might disinherit him and put Godoy in his place. And the followers of Godoy declared that the Princess of Asturias not only had designs against the Prince of the Peace, but against the Sovereigns themselves.

The secret correspondence between Queen Caroline and her daughter was found years afterwards in the house of the Duke of Infantado, and it showed the hatred of the Prince and his wife towards the Queen's favourite, whilst speaking of the King as if he already had one foot in the grave. One of these letters to Naples was intercepted by Napoleon, and it fully convinced him of the part played by Prince Ferdinand and his wife with regard to France.

The people's discontent with Godoy was fostered by Ferdinand's followers, and, indeed, the government of the turbulent country required a more expert hand than that of the favourite.

The clergy were also enraged when they heard that the Minister had received a Bull from Rome for the reform of the monastic institutions, and they exalted Ferdinand to the sky as a patron and protector of the altars, whilst they circulated exaggerated stories with regard to those in power, and his mother was the chief object of these attacks.

When Queen Maria Luisa found the love which the people had formerly professed for her and her husband was now turned into hatred, she said that "Madrid was a place for good Princes and bad Kings."

Napoleon soon intercepted another letter from Ferdinand's wife, Maria Antonia, to the Queen of Naples, and he sent it to Carlos IV. to show what dreadful reports she gave of her father and mother-in-law, and how she not only spoke against France with the bitterness of hatred, but she offered to work with all her might to break the alliance of the Spanish Cabinet with the Emperor of the French.

The King, seeing the false position in which he was placed by the imprudence of his daughter-in-law, begged his wife to take the letter to the Princess of Asturias, and to conjure her to be more careful in the future.

The Queen seems to have been as conciliatory as possible in the interview, but Maria Antonia would not listen to her mother-in-law, and behaved in such an arrogant fashion that Ferdinand himself had to call her to reason.

The dissensions continued at Court, and Ferdinand one day asked Godoy, the Prince of the Peace, what might be the destination of the combined fleets. Fearing that the Prince's Italian wife would betray such an important State secret, Godoy purposely gave an equivocal reply, saying that the squadron at Toulon would go towards Egypt, and that the others would wait for an opportunity of falling upon Ireland.

Maria Antonia lost no time in reporting the news to her mother, and, consequently, Nelson was manœuvring in those seas whilst the Spanish and French ships set sail for America. So the Englishman lost many days waiting off Malta in his belief of the news he had received from Naples. It was thus that Godoy checkmated the plan of the Princess of Asturias to aid the English against France, which was as much the foe of Naples as it was the ally of Spain.

The fact of Ferdinand's wife manœuvring against Napoleon made her very unpopular at Court, and, although she was a model of industry and virtue, Godoy was naturally opposed to one who supported Ferdinand in his hatred of himself, whilst Escoiquiz regarded her as an invaluable tool for his designs against the French, and thus the palace was at this time a perfect hotbed of intrigue.

It was said that the two miscarriages of the Princess of Asturias were due to treatment to which she was subjected by the arrangement of the Queen or the Prince of the Peace, or by the concert of both.

The premature death of his wife was indeed an unfortunate thing for the Prince of Asturias, for, as she said a short time before her departure, she regretted she was about to leave him, as she believed that, had she lived, she would have influenced him very wisely. Report also attributed this death to the machinations of the Queen and her favourite, albeit it was known that she died from an attack of phthisis.

Some time after the Princess's death, the Prince of Asturias, who had subsequently learnt that Godoy had deceived him in his report as to the destination of the French forces on an important occasion, said to the favourite:

"But to be frank, Manuel, you were either deceived yourself or you deceived me. You told me that the French fleet at Toulon was going to Egypt."

"It is true, señor, but there was a change in affairs, and so the plan was changed."

"No," returned Ferdinand, "because the fleet went off at the first start to the ocean——"

"You will recollect," said la Paz, "it started twice, because the first time Nelson got news beforehand of it, and so it had to return to the port and take a very decided direction the second time."

"No," returned Ferdinand in a rage, "neither the expedition to Egypt nor the attack on Ireland were truly arranged. You take a pleasure in telling me a tissue of lies. It is quite evident that you regard me as a mere cipher in the palace, and you treat me worse than a porter. The heir-apparent is the representative of the Sovereign, and deserves equal respect. Would you have dared to deceive my father like that?"

"When you are King," returned Godoy, restraining his wrath with difficulty, "you will yourself justify similar conduct in your Ministers. But I have long wished to resign my office, and if Your Highness will add your request to mine in the matter it will not be difficult to succeed."

"Yes," returned Ferdinand, with a malicious smile, "you want to compromise me like that. Is it not so?" And he turned his back on the Minister and left him.

Such was the open state of enmity between Godoy and Ferdinand in the royal palace, and the Prince's hatred of the favourite was, if possible, equalled by that of the people.

The King, who was nothing but a tool in his wife's hands, joined his consort in overwhelming the man with honours, until he was finally given the post of High Admiral of Spain and the Indias, coupled with the title of Highness.

The event was celebrated by all the united bands of Madrid, and, as Ferdinand had perforce to assist at the festivities with his parents, he whispered to his brother Carlos that he considered such honours as a personal insult to himself; "for," he added, "this vassal of mine is usurping the love and enthusiasm of the people. I am nothing in the State, and he is omnipotent. My position is insufferable."

"Don't trouble yourself," returned the Infante. "The more they give, the sooner they will take it away."

The eyes of both father and son were now turned to Napoleon as the arbiter in their dissensions, and so Spain slipped gradually into the power of the great French commander.

Certainly Ferdinand's letter to the Emperor was frank, if it was not self-respecting. "I wish," he said, "to confide in you as I would in a tender father. I am full of respect and filial love for my father," he continued, "for his heart is good and generous, and, as Your Majesty knows, these very qualities are but instruments in the hands of astute and malignant people to keep him from the truth. I implore Your Majesty," added the Spanish Prince, "not only to give me a Princess of your family as a wife, but to do away with all the difficulties which will accompany the matter."

The French Ambassador, Beauharnais, husband of the future Empress of the French, checkmated the Prince's desires, for he informed Godoy of the letter addressed to his master, and the favourite prevented the matter from going any farther. However, although he knew that his hopes had been defeated, Ferdinand, schooled in the science of duplicity, caressed his mother and kissed the hand of his father, and all in such a cheerful and pleasant way that it was thought that he had overcome his naturally gloomy nature. But "still waters run deep," and Ferdinand's hatred of his mother's favourite was now a consuming fire, and at the same time that it was said that Maria Luisa was hatching a scheme for a change in the dynasty, Ferdinand was engaged in a dreadful plot against his parents. It was at this time that the Prince presented his mother with a copy of his translation from the French of Vertot's "Revoluciones Romanas," and the title was naturally very obnoxious to the Sovereigns. The very word "Revolucion" struck terror in the palace in those days, as it summoned up pictures of the execution of Louis XVI. and Marie Antoinette, so Carlos IV. remonstrated with the Prince on the direction taken by his literary tastes, and stopped the sale of the work; so the book remained at the printer's until its translator ascended the throne of Spain.

As the King was glad to see his son occupied, he told him that, if he really wished to cultivate his literary taste, he would advise him to translate Cordillac's "Étude de l'Histoire," and when Ferdinand asked his father what motto he would suggest for the book, Carlos promptly returned: "Les hommes ne sont pas grands par leurs passions, mais par leur raison."

Thus, by the time the Court returned to the Escorial for the autumn months, the royal parents congratulated themselves that Ferdinand's literary occupations had banished his misanthropic humours; and when the Queen was told one day by the Marquesa de Perijaa, who was out walking with her, that her son passed the nights in writing, she explained to the lady that the Prince was engaged in the translation recommended by his father, and the information of his absorption in writing suggested no ulterior design.

However, one day Carlos IV. found a letter placed in a room in the palace ready to meet his eye. "Urgent" was written on the cover, and the letter had no signature. Indited evidently with a trembling hand, it ran thus:

"Prince Ferdinand is plotting something in the palace, the Crown is in danger, and Queen Maria Luisa is in imminent peril of dying from poison. The prevention of the deed is implored without an instant's delay. The faithful vassal who gives this information is not in a position to fulfil his duty in any other way."

All efforts to discover the writer of this epistle failed, and proof of its authorship was never found; but the writer's object was gained, and the King determined to investigate his son's labours. So he appeared one night in the Prince's study with the excuse of asking him to compose something to celebrate the recent successes in America; and this he did in a tone of friendliness, as he did not really give any credit to the anonymous accusation which had reached him. However, Ferdinand's confusion at his father's visit was suspicious, and, following the Prince's eyes, the King saw they were turned with anxiety to some papers on the table, and his request to see them was met with insolence. So the Sovereign promptly had the Prince put under arrest, with the understanding that he was not to leave his room or speak to anybody.

As Godoy was ill in Madrid at the time, Carlos sent for Caballero, the Minister of Grace and Justice, in post-haste, and to him was read one of the documents he had found on Ferdinand's table, which the Prince had written at the dictation of Escoiquiz to present to his father. In this paper the character of Godoy was painted in the darkest colours, and the favourite was even accused of aspiring to the throne by plotting the death of the King and the rest of the Royal Family. The monarch was advised in the letter to ascertain these facts by lying in wait and listening to the tools of Godoy during a day's shoot in the Pardo or in the Casa de Campo.

The King was also counselled to hold no communication with his wife during the time of the inquiry, so as to avoid her tears and plaints, and he was told to associate his heir with him in the Government and to give him the command of the troops; and, finally, His Majesty was implored by his son to keep the letter a profound secret from his mother, as he did not wish to be exposed to her resentment and the revenge of his enemies.

In another document written to the Prince of Asturias, Escoiquiz advised quite a different course of action, for he suggested that the fall of Godoy should be accomplished by an appeal to the Queen herself. Ferdinand was counselled to implore his mother on his knees to give up the favourite, whilst supporting his appeal by an account of the amours of the Prince of the Peace with other ladies;

and the letter concluded with the advice to avoid all thought of a marriage with Godoy's sister-in-law. The King had also found in his son's room the cipher and key of the correspondence used between the Prince and the Archdeacon of Toledo, and these were the same which had been used by his late daughter-in-law with the ex-Queen of Naples.

And, lastly, among the papers there was a letter in Ferdinand's own handwriting, which was closed but not directed, and evidently meant for his adviser. In this note the Prince said he would look for a priest to put the document in his father's hands. He said, moreover, that he had taken St. Hermenegildo for his patron saint in the matter; but although he had put himself under this sacred protection, it was with no desire to accept the vocation of a martyr, and he would therefore be very careful to ascertain what success could crown the plot for Godoy's overthrow before starting on it. But if the plot succeeded, he wished the storm to fall only on the head of Sisberto (Don Manuel Godoy) and Govinda (Queen Maria Luisa, his mother), and Leovigildo (Carlos IV.) was to be brought over to his side with cheers and applause.

The perusal of the papers completed, the King turned to Caballero, saying:

"What punishment does the law impose for a son who acts like that?"

"Señor," was the reply, "royal clemency is out of court in this matter; the criminal deserves death!"

"What!" cried the Queen, "have you forgotten he is my son? By my right as his mother I will destroy these papers which would condemn him, for he has been deceived, he has been ruined!" And so saying, the unhappy mother flung herself into a chair, weeping bitterly and clutching at the incriminating letters. It was thus that they never appeared in the inquiry.

Caballero advised a frank statement of the facts to the nation, so a royal manifesto was addressed by the King to the country, explaining "that, albeit his son was familiar with all the principles of Christianity indoctrinated by his paternal affection, he had favoured a plot to dethrone him."

13

The King, moreover, wrote the following letter to Napoleon:
"San Lorenzo,
"October 20, 1807.

"My Brother,

"At the time in which I was concerting means for the destruction of our common enemy, and when I thought that the designs of the Queen of Italy had ceased with the death of her daughter , I find that the spirit of blackest intrigue is within the very palace. My eldest son, the heir-presumptive to the throne, has conceived a fearful design to dethrone me and to attempt the life of his mother. Such an atrocious crime can only be punished by the severity of the law. That (law) which calls him to succeed me must be revoked, for one of his brothers will be more worthy to take his place in my heart and on the throne.

"Now I am trying to discover his accomplices, to find the thread of the fearful misfortune, and I will not lose an instant in informing Your Imperial Majesty of the matter, begging you to aid me with your opinion and counsel.

"This I beg, etc.,

"Carlos."

That day, when Ferdinand thought his father had gone hunting, he begged his mother to come to his room or to let him go to hers. The Queen declined to comply with these requests, but she sent Caballero to the Prince, and, with the cowardly duplicity in which he was an expert, Ferdinand told the Minister that the serious steps with regard to the Queen had been suggested by his mother-in-law, the ex-Queen Caroline, and that they had filled both him and his late wife with horror. He added that, if the persistence of his evil counsellor had led him to be a little weak, it must be remembered he had resisted the seductions for four years, and that he had sought to introduce reforms into the kingdom.

When Godoy had recovered sufficiently from his indisposition to go to the Escorial, he appeared in the room of the disgraced Prince.

Ferdinand threw himself into the arms of the favourite against whom he had plotted so darkly, exclaiming through his tears:

"Oh, my Manuel, I have wanted so much to see you. I have been deceived and ruined by those rogues. You alone can get me out of this trouble."

"I have come for that purpose," returned Godoy. "You are the son of my King and Queen. Many a time I have held you in my arms, and I would give you a thousand lives if I had them. And I wept," said Godoy, who tells this story in his "Mémoires," "even more than the Prince, although his tears came from his heart."

"Yes, I am certain," continued the Prince, "that you would not come to see me like this if you did not intend to help me. You have spoken with my parents? I cannot hope that they will pardon me. I have given the names of my evil advisers. What more can I do to show my repentance? If there is anything more I can do, only tell me, tell me, for I will do anything in which to please my dear parents, and you too. I beg of you to help me, for pity's sake."

"Señor, señor," returned Godoy, "there is an immense distance between this humility to a mere slave of your family and changing your opinion of me. This I do beg of you to do; and as for the rest, I have only come for your good."

"May God reward you!" replied the Prince. "You are the only one who can speak for me without any fear of compromising himself. Will you not dictate me a letter to my parents?"

"The best words you can write," said Godoy, "are those from your own heart, and those I will take myself to your parents."

The result of this advice was two letters. The first was addressed to the King:[*]

"Señor, dear Papa,

"I have done wrong, I have sinned against you as a King and as a father; but I repent, and now I offer you the most humble obedience. I ought to have done nothing without telling Your Majesty, but I was taken by surprise. I have revealed the culprits, and I entreat Your Majesty to pardon me for having lied the other day, and that you will permit your grateful son to kiss your royal feet.

"Ferdinand."

The other missive ran thus:

* "History of Ferdinand VII.," 1843.

"Señora, dear Mamma,

"I am very sorry for the grave offence I have committed against my parents and my King and Queen; and it is with the deepest humility that I beg Your Majesty to intercede with papa for permission to kiss his royal feet.

"Ferdinand."

The Prince's plea was granted, and the King pardoned his son, whilst ordering the inquiry to be completed against those who had instigated the plot.

Ferdinand sought to prove his horror of the counsels of his late tutor by showing his parents the books he had sent him, with the passages marked which the tutor had considered most appropriate to his situation. The works were "The Life of St. Hermenegildo," the poem by Morales in honour of the same saint, that of Alfonso the Wise and those of the Prince of Viana, Louis XIII., King of France, and his mother, Marie de Medicis.

Maria Luisa's maternal affection, and Napoleon's refusal to allow the publication of any information bearing upon himself or his Ambassador Beauharnais, took all the significance from the inquiry, and, as the matter was thus gradually dropped, the country exonerated the Prince of Asturias from all blame.

Ferdinand's opposition to Godoy and his mother certainly seemed to have been founded more upon personal aversion than political policy, for when the favourite cooled towards the French on finding that his designs on Portugal were not to be realized, Ferdinand himself began to show favour to the foreigners, and this is proved by his correspondence with Napoleon, which was published in Le Moniteur in 1808.

II.

THE OVERTHROW OF GODOY
1804–1808

As Napoleon considered that Ferdinand was only fit to be a tool and reign as a vassal of France, he suggested that the Prince should marry the daughter of his brother Lucien, and this proposal was made quite regardless of the aversion with which his niece regarded the proposed bridegroom.

To the keen insight of the warrior who wielded the sceptre of France, Charles IV. and his Ministers and Prince Ferdinand and his advisers all seemed like a tree waiting for the axe. But the Prince of Asturias represented the dawn of a new era to Spaniards. He was the centre of popular enthusiasm, and to be one with his cause was to be one with the majority of the nation.

Bonaparte, naturally, did not at once reveal his designs of gaining supremacy on the Peninsula to the King, and to lull any doubts on his part he gave him a magnificent pair of horses; and although Charles IV. had written to him, after the settlement of the matter of the Escorial, that he approved of his son's union with the Imperial Family, Napoleon said he could not proceed in the arrangements for such an advantageous marriage without his son's consent.

As the confiding Charles thought that his son's demonstrations of affection after being set free were sincere, and being anxious to secure the peace of his household, he made up his mind to the great sacrifice of parting with Godoy, if by so doing he could quench the spirit of intrigue and jealousy in the palace.

With this view the King sent for the Prince of Asturias to explain to him the course which he considered necessary in face of the constant disturbances in the country and the absolute necessity of union within the realm.

To the surprise of his father, Ferdinand opposed the idea of the overthrow of the favourite. The Prince's smiling countenance filled the King's heart with joy, and it was with no doubt of his sincerity that he listened to his son's opinion that Godoy should not be asked to retire from the Court; the Prince of the Peace was himself pleased when the heir-apparent gave him his hand with friendly looks, and bade him sacrifice his own feelings to the welfare of the kingdom and remain where he was appreciated. Neither King nor courtier could foresee that, even whilst inspiring confidence by his open, friendly demeanour, Ferdinand was preparing at Aranjuez the sequel to the plot at the Escorial.

In the meanwhile the French invaded Portugal, the Spanish soldiers materially aided them in the campaign, and Godoy began to see that the way in which the forces of Napoleon took possession of San Sebastian argued more the course of a conqueror than that of an ally. Barcelona, moreover, was also occupied by the French, and Charles IV. and Maria Luisa were filled with alarm at these signs of the supremacy of the French. The Prince of the Peace tried to persuade Their Majesties to repair to Andalusia, and sought to open their eyes to the astuteness of the Corsican and the misfortunes which it augured. Carné declares that Bonaparte only wished to be the regenerator of Spain by introducing, by the aid of royalty, the required reforms which were afterwards insisted on in the name of liberty, but the tumults and scandals of the Court finally led him to fall into the temptation which was the origin of all the misfortunes of the country.

It must be remembered that the Escorial matter had idealized the Prince in the minds of the people. His innocence, his sufferings, and his virtues, were all real in the eyes of the public; whilst Godoy was only regarded as an atheist who sought to reform the friars through his brother-in-law, the Archbishop of Toledo. The French and their leader were therefore regarded as means for the assistance of the Prince of Asturias, and this idea was circulated throughout the provinces by the convents and the confessionals. The colossal power of the Church had indeed imposed itself on the throne. Its influence spread throughout all classes, and in the daring painting showing the world bound round with a San Franciscan cord, the end is held by a brother with these words, "We can do all."

Murat, the Grand Duke of Berg, with whom Maria Luisa had so much subsequent correspondence about her family affairs, now took up his abode at Burgos as the Emperor's lieutenant. Thus, poor Charles IV. was not only exposed to the treacherous designs of his son, but they were hatched under the wings of the Imperial Eagle.

The King and his wife were now in the Palace of Aranjuez, on the banks of the Tagus, and thither went the Prince of the Peace to announce the signs of disaster. The orders for the Madrid garrison to proceed to Aranjuez confirmed the suspicions of the people of the terrible crisis which was taking place in the Court, and it was thought that the desire of Their Majesties to go to Seville meant the extension of their journey to Mexico.

Then came the historic 17th of March, when the murmur of the Tagus was drowned by the voices of the people surrounding the mansion.

Between eleven and twelve o'clock a carriage was seen to leave Godoy's mansion with his "friend" Joseta Tudo closely veiled. A shot was fired by someone who sought to make the lady disclose her identity, and then the Prince of Asturias put in his window the light which was the sign for the commencement of the tumult. The trumpet sounded the call to horse, and all ran to take possession of the different roads to the palace by which it was possible Godoy might escape.

The King and Queen sent for Ferdinand, and the Queen told her son that, as his poor father was suffering acute rheumatic pains, he was unable to go himself to the window, so she begged her son to go and tranquillize the people in his father's name. This Fernando declined to do, under the pretext that the sight of him would make the firing commence.

The cries of the mob sacking Godoy's dwelling were now

audible, and the furniture and pictures were all hurled from the windows. It was curious that the people seemed to have little thought of appropriating the art treasures of the favourite. Their one desire was to find the poor man, and wreak their vengeance for his reported misdeeds; but no sign of him was to be found. At last they gave up the search, and accompanied the wife and son to the palace. To show that their hatred did not extend to these personages, as the dissensions between Godoy and his wife were public property, they took the horses out of the carriage and drew it themselves.

On the following day Charles IV. signed the decree which removed Godoy from his position as Generalissimo and Admiral, and he sent a letter to Napoleon to acquaint him with the fact, adding that his rheumatic pains prevented him doing more than dictate the letter.

But there was no peace for the poor King. The following morning (March 19) two officials of the Guard came with the utmost secrecy to acquaint His Majesty with the news that a worse tumult was brewing than that which had broken out the preceding evening, and that only the Prince of Asturias could prevent it.

Ferdinand was then sent for, and his mother entreated him to prevent the riot by sending his own people to calm the excitement of the populace, and commanding the instigator of the disturbance to return to Madrid.

But hardly were these requests complied with when fresh tumult was heard. It seemed that Manuel Godoy was preparing to go to rest on the night of March 17, when he heard the noise of the mob at his house. He caught up a cloak, filled his pockets with gold, armed himself with pistols, and strove to save himself by a secret passage which led into the house of the widowed Duchess of Osuna. But the key was evidently not there, so the wretched man lay in his hiding-place like a mouse in a trap for thirty-six hours, suffering all the pains of fatigue and hunger and thirst, and fearing every minute to be assassinated.

At last he returned into his own salon. A sentinel saw him, and he was seized by those in possession of his house. Of course he might have made use of his firearms, but, worn out with the sufferings of body and mind during the last thirty-six hours, he gave himself up to his persecutors.

Like wolves after their prey, the people hounded the wretched man, and they tried to stop the Guard acting in his defence by putting poles under the horses' bellies to prevent their advance. At last, however, the fugitive was bravely hoisted on to the saddle of the horse of one of the Guard, and he was taken off at a quick trot from the scene of his sufferings.

When the news reached Madrid of the imprisonment of the Prince de la Paz on March 19, the mob flocked to the Plazuela del Almirante, where his house adjoined that of the Dukes of Alba. There the scene of Aranjuez was repeated: the furniture and treasures were cast out of the windows, and were for the most part devoured by the flames of the fire which was lighted close to the door. Then, drunk with vengeance, the populace proceeded with burning torches to the houses of the Prince's relatives, and sacked that of his mother, his brother Don Diego, the Marquis of Branciforte, his brother-in-law, and those of the ex-Ministers Alvarez y Soler, of Don Manuel Sixto Espinosa, and Amoros.

The riding-school of the fallen favourite was converted into an altar to St. Joseph.

It is from the pen of Maria Luisa that we have the most graphic description of the events, for in a letter to her daughter she writes thus:*

"My beloved Daughter,

"Tell the Grand Duke of Berg what is the situation of the King, myself, and the poor Prince de la Paz.

"My son Ferdinand was at the head of the plot. He won the troops over to himself; he had a light put in one of his windows as a sign for its explosion. At that instant the Guards and the persons at the head of the revolution had two shots fired. They have tried to show that these shots were fired by the Guard of the Prince de la Paz, but it is not the truth; for the Gardes de Corps and the soldiers

---

* "History of Ferdinand VII.," 1843, and the correspondence of Napoleon with the Bourbon family, published in the Moniteur in 1808.

came at the people's call, and went where they liked without receiving any orders from their superior officers.

"The King and I sent for my son to tell him how trying it was for his father not to be able to appear at the window, and that he was to go himself to tranquillize the people in the name of the King; but he replied very firmly that he could not do so, because it would be the sign for the firing to begin, and that he did not wish to give.

"The next morning I begged him to put a stop to the tumult and tranquillize the rebels, and he replied he would do so. Then he sent for the second officers in command of the bodies of the royal horse, commanding many people to return to Madrid who had come to increase the revolution, and not to let any more come.

"When the King had given these orders, the Prince de la Paz was found, and the King sent word to his son that the unhappy Prince, who was the victim of his friendship for us and the French, and particularly of the Grand Duke, was to be extricated from his position. My son went and commanded them not to touch the Prince de la Paz, and to conduct him to the barracks of the Royal Guards. He did it in his own name, although it was at the instance of his father; and he said to the Prince de la Paz, as if he were the King himself, 'I grant you your life.'

"The Prince de la Paz, in spite of his great injuries, asked him if he were King; and he returned that he thought of being so. This was because the King, the Prince de la Paz, and I, intended to abdicate in favour of Fernando, when we had seen the Emperor and arranged all the matters, among which was the marriage. My son returned: 'No, so far I am not King, but I soon shall be.'

"Certainly my son commanded everything, as if he were King without being so, or knowing if he would be. The orders given by the King my husband were not obeyed.

"Then on the day of the 19th, when the abdication took place, there was another worse tumult, threatening the life of the King, my husband, and this obliged him to form the resolution of abdicating.

"From the moment of his abdication, the King was treated by Ferdinand with all the contempt that can be used to a King, and without any consideration for his parents.

"Then he sent for all the people concerned in his cause who had been disloyal to his father, and did all he could to grieve him. He bade us leave the place as soon as possible, and notified the town of Badajoz for our residence. In the meantime he had no consideration for us whatever, and he showed great pleasure at being King and that we were withdrawn.

"As to the Prince de la Paz, he did not want anybody to think of him. The Guards who had him in custody had orders not to reply to any questions that were asked, and they treated him with the greatest inhumanity.

"My son made the conspiracy to dethrone his father the King; our lives have been in great danger, and that of the Prince de la Paz is so still.

"The King, my husband, and I are hoping that the Grand Duke will do what he can in our favour, as we have always been faithful allies of the Emperor and great friends of the Grand Duke, and the same can be said of the poor Prince de la Paz. If he could speak, he could give proofs of this, and even in the state in which he now is he does nothing but call for his great friend, the Grand Duke.

"We beg the Grand Duke to save the Prince de la Paz, and that, whilst saving us, he will always allow him to be with us, so that we can pass the rest of our days quietly together in a warmer climate, without intrigues and without commands, but with honour.

"This is what the King and I want, and the Prince de la Paz equally so. He would be always ready to serve my son in everything. But my son has no character whatever, and much less that of sincerity; he never liked him, and he always declared war against him, as he has against the King, his father, and me.

"His ambition is great, and he regards his parents as if they were not so. What will he do to others? If the Grand Duke could see us, it would give great pleasure to us, and also to his friend, the Prince de la Paz, who suffers for having been always attached to the French and the Emperor. All our hope is in the Grand Duke, to whom we also commend our poor daughter Maria Luisa, who is not loved by her brother. With this hope we are about to take our journey.

"Luisa."*

A few remarks on this favourite daughter of Queen Maria Luisa may not be amiss. Maria Luisa of Bourbon, Queen of Etruria, was only fifteen years of age when the eldest son of the Duke of Parma came to Madrid and married her. The Prince had come to Spain for the purpose of marrying her sister, Maria Amalia; but, as this Princess was silent and reserved, the bridegroom-elect showed his preference for her sister, and, as Godoy favoured this change of arrangements, Prince Louis wedded Maria Luisa, although the originally destined bride had evidently been favourably inclined to him.

In 1801 Napoleon Bonaparte arranged for Tuscany, under the name of the kingdom of Etruria, to be given to the Spanish Princess and her husband, who was called Louis I. But the people never took to their new rulers, and the French did not evacuate the place.

In 1802 the King and Queen of Etruria went to Spain to be present at the marriage of Ferdinand with Maria Antonia of Naples, and that of her brother, the heir of the Two Sicilies, with the Infanta Maria Isabel; and this sister of Prince Ferdinand became subsequently the mother of his fourth wife, Queen Maria Cristina, mother of Isabella II.

On this journey to Spain the young King of Etruria died of brain disease, and the Queen became, by the will of her late husband, Regent for her little son, who was crowned Louis II. of Etruria. But Napoleon deprived the royal lady of her kingdom in virtue of the Treaty of Fontainebleau in 1807; and when the Queen came to Spain and joined her petitions to those of her mother in the correspondence to Murat and Napoleon, she never returned to her kingdom, which was taken from her with the promise of having Portugal in return.

When Napoleon heard of the revolution of Aranjuez, he said to the Duke of Rovigo: "I never thought of such a thing; matters have taken an unexpected turn. I know that the father is right in accusing the son of conspiring against the throne; this fact will unmask the son, and it will never be approved. When Charles V.

* "Memorias de Don Juan Nellerto" (Llorente), tomo 2.

24

abdicated, he was not contented with a written declaration; he confirmed it with the ceremonies customary for such occasions, he renewed it various times, and he did not abandon the reins of the government until he had given solemn assurance of his wish to do so."*

Once on the throne, Ferdinand VII. sent for the persons who had taken part in the Escorial conspiracy. Don Miguel José de Azanza, the ex-Viceroy of Mexico, was made Minister of the Interior instead of Miguel Cartegano Soler, and Pedro Ceballos, who had married Godoy's cousin, and who had worked for the ruin of the dethroned King, was retained in his position as Minister of Foreign Affairs by a special royal decree.

The celebrated littérateur Gaspar Melchor de Jovellanos also returned to Court.

But the man who was most triumphant was Ferdinand's old tutor, Don Juan Escoiquiz. His wish was fulfilled—he was a power at Court, and he was decorated with the Cross of Carlos III.

Moreover, the Duke of San Carlos, spoken of by Maria Luisa in her correspondence as the falsest of all, was made chief Mayordomo of the palace. In fact, all who had played any part in the Escorial affair were exalted, whereas those who had pleased Godoy by their capacities or virtues were proscribed and persecuted. Among these were the Duke of Almodovar, brother of the Prince de la Paz, Viguri the Intendant, Norrega the Treasurer, Marquina the Corregidor of Madrid, the littérateur Escala, and the Fiscal Viegas, who had demanded penal punishment for criminals in the Escorial matter. The property of all the above-mentioned men was confiscated, and Godoy himself was taken from Aranjuez to the Castle of Villaviciosa.

The government was practically in the hands of the Dukes of Infantado and San Carlos and the Councillor Escoiquiz. The opinions and character of the latter are well known. He was utterly disingenuous, and he was expert in the science of intrigue, which had played such a part in the antechamber of the palace. But for really ruling the affairs of a kingdom he was quite incompetent,

* "Mémoires du Duc de Rovigo," vol. iii.

and was only conspicuous for his want of knowledge and his mean spirit. Apart from his artifice in conspiracies, the character of this Archdeacon of Alcaraz was seen in the pamphlet he published in defence of the Inquisition. San Carlos shamefully maligned Maria Luisa and the Prince de la Paz, albeit he was proud of being related to the favourite. Infantado was destitute of any consistency in government except when it savoured of persecution and oppression.

The three statesmen were united in one desire, and that was the marriage of Ferdinand with one of the Bonaparte family; and they all shared the people's joy at the entrance of Murat, Grand Duke of Berg, in Madrid on March 23. The townsfolk were mad with delight, for they regarded the French as supporters of their idol Ferdinand, and sharers of their joy in the state entry of the young King into the capital.

The function was indeed a brilliant sight, and the Sovereign, crowned with the rich diadem of the two worlds, roused so much enthusiasm that it took him six hours to pass from the Gate of Atocha to the palace. The roar of the cannon, the peal of the bells, the clamour of the cheers, were indeed deafening, and the men laid down their cloaks for the King to pass over, and the women waved their pocket-handkerchiefs.

The Grand Duke of Berg unfortunately gave rein to his pride, and wounded the Spaniards in their tenderest sensibility by sending French troops to line part of the route of the royal entry, leaving his house in the Buen Retiro for that of the Prince de la Paz, and taking possession of the Casa de Campo.

Napoleon himself regretted this conduct, and we find him saying in the "Memorial of St. Helena," published in 1826:

"The plan more worthy of me, and the safest, would have been a sort of mediation, like that of Switzerland. I ought to have given a liberal constitution to the Spanish nation, and seen that Ferdinand put it in practice. If that had been done in good faith, and if Spain had prospered with our new customs, France would have gained a close ally, and a truly formidable increase to its power. If Ferdinand, on the contrary, failed in his new duties, the Spaniards themselves would soon have come to beg for another King."

Murat, with his misleading pictures of a country which he did not know, tickled the conqueror's ambition, and this resulted in Napoleon writing to his brother Louis, who was then in Holland:

"Being concerned that I shall have no solid peace with England without giving a great impulsion to the Continent, I have decided to put a French Prince on the throne of Spain."*

Murat's power was mainly due to the reports which had reached Spain of his great feats of arms, and the priests had admired Napoleon as the restorer of the churches in France; but Murat had not counted on the revulsion of feeling which ensued when the Spaniards found that the soldiers of their ally were impregnated with the doctrines of Voltaire and Rousseau, and as the imprudence of the French fanned the flame of suspicion it gradually worked up to a fire of fanaticism.

But the Emperor was quite firm in the idea of his imperial hand wielding the Spanish sceptre, so he sent for Izquierdo, and asked him if the Spaniards would not be glad to have him as their Sovereign.

"Very," returned Izquierdo, "if Your Majesty will first renounce the diadem of France."

Bonaparte did not feel flattered at the Spaniard's reply, but, anxious to set the affairs straight in the Peninsula, he left Paris for Bordeaux on April 2.

In the meanwhile Maria Luisa and her husband had been highly pleased at the arrival of Murat at the Court. The unhappy Sovereigns had been treated with the greatest disrespect by their son since his accession to the throne. They were told to go to Badajoz, in spite of their protestations of the unsuitability of the climate to their ailments. They were full of fears that the people's rage would lead any moment to the death of their idolized Godoy. Misfortune seemed imminent at any moment, and poor Charles, with his rheumatic pains, and unable even to count upon his royal income, was in a sad state of depression when the news of Murat's installation in the palatial abode of the fallen favourite inspired them with hope.

---

* "Des Documents Historiques publiés par Louis Bonaparte," Paris, 1820.

Neither the Grand Duke of Berg nor the Ambassador Beauharnais had recognized the son as King, although all the rest of the diplomatic corps had done so; so, encouraged by this fact, they wrote to Murat through the medium of their daughter, the Queen of Etruria. The perusal of this correspondence gives an idea of the humiliation of Charles IV. and his Queen, for, as the Duke of Rovigo says:

"The letters of the royal parents show their consternation and depression, and the violence must have been very great for them to be in fear of their lives, and to implore a retreat which would suit their health, and where they could spend the rest of their days in safety."*

The picture of her son drawn by the Queen is worthy of the study of the historian; for the remarks scattered through the various letters run thus:

"From Ferdinand we have nothing to expect but misery and persecution. He has formed this conspiracy to dethrone the King his father; he has no character whatever, much less that of sincerity; he is false and cruel; his ambition is limitless, and he does not treat his father and mother like parents. Nothing affects him. He is unfeeling, and not inclined to clemency; he promises, but he never fulfils his promises; he does not care for the Grand Duke or the Emperor; he only cares for despotism; he has a very bad heart; he has never professed affection either for his father or for me; his councillors are bloodthirsty, and love to do harm to everybody, not excepting the father and mother."

These remarks of the Queen-mother are supported by that of the father, who said in his letter to Napoleon that "he found himself in the necessity of choosing between life and death."

And it was in this state of affairs that Maria Luisa commenced her correspondence with the Duke of Berg by the following note, sent through her daughter, the Queen of Etruria:

"The King, my husband (who makes me write, as the pains in his hand prevent his doing so), is anxious to know if the Grand Duke of Berg will undertake to treat efficaciously with the Emperor

* "Mémoires du Duc de Rovigo."

for the preservation of the life of the Prince de la Paz, with the assistance of some of his employés or chaplains. He is anxious to know if the Grand Duke can go and release him, or at least give him some counsel, for he puts all his hope in the Grand Duke of Berg, his great friend. He hopes all from His Highness, to whom he has always been attached.

"Therefore the Grand Duke will perhaps arrange with the Emperor for sufficient supplies to be granted to the King, my husband, and me, and the Prince de la Paz, for us to live together where it suits our health, and where we have neither commands nor intrigues.

"The Emperor is generous, he is a hero, and he has always helped his faithful allies, and even those that are persecuted; and nobody is so much so as we are—and why? Because we have always been faithful to the alliance.

"Of my son we can expect nothing but misery and persecutions. He began by inventing, and he will go on by inventing all that he can to make the Prince de la Paz (the innocent and attached friend of the Emperor, the Grand Duke, and all the French) appear criminal in the eyes of the public and the Emperor. You must believe nothing. Enemies have the power and all the means of justifying as true all that is false.

"The King desires, as I do, to see and talk with the Grand Duke, and make the protest which it is in his power to make. We are both grateful to you for sending your troops, and for all the proofs you give us of your friendship. Your Highness must well know the friendship we have always had and have for yourself. We put ourselves in your hands and in those of the Emperor, and trust that he will grant our request.

"These our desires we place in the hands of such a great and generous ruler and hero."

On March 22 the Queen of Etruria also wrote to Murat in intercession for the unhappy prisoner, who, she says, "invoked incessantly the terrible moment of his death."

Charles IV. added to his daughter's letter fresh pleas to be allowed to go to a country which would suit him better, with the

Prince de la Paz, and his wife added her request to be allowed to finish her days in tranquillity in a climate favourable to the delicate state of their health.

On the 26th Maria Luisa sent her daughter the before-mentioned letter, giving the account of the affair of Aranjuez, and this the Queen of Etruria sent to Murat with this letter:

"Sir, my Brother,

"My mother sends me the enclosed letter for me to forward to you to keep. Do us the kindness, dear sir, not to abandon us. All our hopes are in you. Give me the comfort of your going to see my parents. Reply something to cheer me, and do not forget a friend who loves you from her heart.

"Maria Luisa.

"P.S.—I am ill in bed with a touch of fever, which prevents my leaving my room."

Murat then sent General Monthion, the head of the royal staff, to Aranjuez to ascertain the truth about the King's abdication, and it was then that Charles sent his letter and protest to Napoleon.

In handing the letter to the French General, the King said:

"My position is of the saddest. They have taken off the Prince de la Paz, and will, I believe, kill him."

"Sire, my Brother,

"You will doubtless have heard with regret of the events at Aranjuez and their results, and you will not view with indifference a King forced to renounce his crown and put himself in the hands of the great monarch, his ally, whilst placing himself entirely at the disposition of the only person who can afford felicity to himself, his family, and his faithful vassals.

"I have only abdicated in favour of my son by force of circumstances, when the clash of arms and the clamours of an insurrected garrison made me know what it was to choose between life and death, and my death would have been followed by that of the Queen.

"I was forced to abdicate, but I was reassured by my complete confidence in the magnanimity and genius of the great man who has always shown himself my friend. I determined to conform to whatever the same great man may demand of us—myself, the Queen, and the Prince de la Paz.

"I therefore address to Your Imperial Majesty a protest against the events of Aranjuez and against my abdication. I throw myself entirely upon the heart and friendship of Your Majesty, trusting that God will keep you in His safe and worthy keeping.

"I am, Your Imperial Majesty's

"Most affectionate Brother and Friend,

"Charles."

The Queen's daughter also wrote to Murat:

"Sir, my Brother,

"I have just seen your esteemed commander, who has given me your letter, by which I regret to find that my father and mother have not had the pleasure of seeing you, although they wish it so much, as all their hope is placed in you, who they trust will restore them tranquillity.

"The poor Prince de la Paz is covered with wounds and contusions, and is cast into prison, where he constantly invokes the terrible moment of his death. He thinks of nobody but his friend the Grand Duke of Berg, and says he is the only person to whom he looks for his salvation.

"My father, mother, and I have talked with your respected commander. He will tell you all. I trust in your friendship, and that by that you will save us all three and the poor prisoner.

"I have not time to say more, but I trust in you. My father will add two lines to this letter.

"I am, from my heart,

"Your most affectionate Sister and Friend,

"Maria Luisa."

To this letter Carlos IV. added a postscript:

"Sir and very dear Brother,

"Having talked to your worthy commander, and informed him of all that has happened, I beg you to tell the Emperor that I intreat him to set free the poor Prince de la Paz, who only suffers from having been a friend of France, and at the same time beg of him to let us go to a place which will suit us, and take with

31

us the same Prince. We are going now to Badajoz. I beg your reply before then, in case we are absolutely left without means of seeing each other, for my life is only in you and in the Emperor. In the meanwhile I am,

"Your very affectionate Brother and Friend,

"Carlos."

The General was also given a letter from the Queen to Murat, which ran thus:

"Sir, my dear Brother,

"I have no friend but Your Highness. The King, my beloved husband, writes to you imploring your friendship, for in that lies our only hope. We both beg of you to prove you are our friend by informing the Emperor of our sincere friendship, and of the affection we have always professed for him, you, and all the French.

"Poor Prince de la Paz, who is wounded and imprisoned for being our friend, is passionately attached to all France, and he is suffering now for having desired the arrival of your troops, and for having been our only permanent friend. He would have gone to see you had he been free, and now he does not cease to speak of you and express his desire to see the Emperor. Help us to end our days quietly in a place suitable to the health of the King, which, like mine, is delicate, and let it be in company with our friend, who is also that of Your Highness.

"My daughter will be my interpreter if I do not have the satisfaction of knowing Your Highness personally and talking to you. Could you make an effort to see us, if only for a minute, by night or when you like? Your worthy officer will tell you all we have said.

"I hope you will be able to manage what we want, and that you will pardon all the slips and omissions in the matter, for I do not know where I am, and you must believe that this has been from no slight to you nor lack.

"May you live many years!

"Your most affectionate

"Luisa."

The Queen became quite desperate as the days went by, bringing no definite help from the Grand Duke of Berg, and in one of her letters to her daughter she writes:

"If the Grand Duke does not see that the Emperor gives orders for the stoppage of the intrigues against his friend the Prince de la Paz, against me and my daughter, none of us will be safe. All the malevolent people get round my son, and he believes them like oracles, and on his own part he is not very inclined to magnanimity and clemency. He must expect sad results from all this. I and my husband think that, if my son sees the Emperor before he has given his orders, he and those with him will tell him so many lies that he will doubt the truth. For this reason we would beg the Grand Duke to let the Emperor know that we are absolutely in his hands, hoping he will give tranquillity to the King, my husband, me, and the Prince de la Paz, whom we desire to have with us, and end our days peacefully in a place suited to our health without giving the least trouble to anybody. We urgently beg the Grand Duke to let us have daily news of our mutual friend, the Prince de la Paz, because we know absolutely nothing."

The King added the following words in his own handwriting:

"I asked the Queen to write this, as my pains prevent my writing much."

The next letter from the Queen of Spain to her daughter for the Grand Duke of Berg is without a date:

"The King, my husband, and I do not wish to be importunate nor troublesome to the Grand Duke, who has so much to do; but we have no other friend but him and the Emperor, and in him rest the hopes of the King, those of the Prince de la Paz, the friend of the Grand Duke and our own intimate one, and those of my daughter and myself. My daughter wrote me yesterday afternoon what the Grand Duke had said, and our hearts are filled with gratitude and comfort, hoping for all that is good from the sacred and incomparable personages of the Emperor and Grand Duke. But we do not want him to be ignorant of what we know in spite of nobody telling us anything or answering our questions, important as it was for us to have a reply. However, we regard it all with indifference, and the only thing which interests us is the welfare of our only and innocent friend, the Prince de la Paz, who is also the Grand Duke's, as he exclaimed in his prison in the midst of the horrible treatment to which he was exposed; for he always called the Grand Duke his friend, as he did before the conspiracy, and he says constantly: 'If I could only have the good fortune for the Grand Duke to come here, I should have nothing to fear.'

"He wanted you to come to the Court, and he was flattered by the pleasure the Grand Duke showed in accepting his house as a dwelling. He had some presents ready to give you, and he thought of nothing but the moment when he could present himself to the Emperor and the Grand Duke with all imaginable ardour. But now we are in continual fear that he will take his life, or that he will be more closely imprisoned if his enemies know that there is a question of his being saved. Would it not be possible to take some precautionary measures before the definitive resolution? The Grand Duke could send some troops without saying why. Could they not come to the prison and disperse the guard over him, without giving it time to fire a shot or do anything against the Prince? For there is reason to fear that it would do so, as they all know his wish to die, and they would glory in killing him. So the guard could be absolutely under the command of the Grand Duke; and if not, the Grand Duke can be sure that the Prince de la Paz will die if he continue in the power of the worthless traitors and in the hands of my son. Hence we repeat the plea that he should be removed from the power of the bloodthirsty gardes de corps, my son, and his evil companions; for we are in continual fear of his life, although the Emperor and the Grand Duke wish to save him. We repeat, therefore, the entreaty that the Grand Duke should take every measure for this object, because if time be lost his life is not safe, as it would certainly be easier to protect the Prince in the midst of carnivorous lions and tigers.

"After dinner yesterday, my son was with Infantado, Escoiquiz, who is a malignant cleric, and San Carlos, who is worse than all; and this makes us tremble, as the secret conference lasted from half-past one till half-past three. The gentil hombre who is with my son Charles is a cousin of San Carlos; he has talent and some learning, but he is a malignant American and a great enemy of ours, like his cousin San Carlos, in spite of all they have received from the King, my husband, at the request of the Prince de la Paz, to whom they say they are related. All those who are with my son Charles are mixed up in the same intrigue, and inclined to do all possible harm, and what is reported as true is the greatest untruth.

"I hope the Grand Duke will pardon all my blunders and mistakes when I write French, as it is forty-two years since I came to Spain at thirteen and a half years of age, so, although I speak French, I do not speak it well.

"The Grand Duke will know what helps me, and will pardon all my faults of the language.

"Luisa."

Ferdinand, in his blind belief in Escoiquiz, disregarded the counsel of other men, and, as Escoiquiz only thought of conciliating the Corsican so as to advance his plan of Ferdinand's union with a member of the House of Bonaparte, the power of the French increased daily.

It was believed that all the intrigues of Beauharnais were only to keep the sceptre in the hand which held it, and the silly credulity on the part of Escoiquiz was the chief cause of the consequent misfortunes.

To a genius like Napoleon the situation of Spain was an easy prey to his ambition, and its state of submission to the French was seen in the fact of Caballero conforming to Murat's desire to become the possessor of the sword which was surrendered to Charles V. by Francis I. of France after the Battle of Pavia.

The function in which Spain lost this heirloom is described in the Gaceta de Madrid of April 5, 1808. The sword was borne in state to the Grand Duke's house. It was placed on a silver tray covered with a puce-coloured silk cloth trimmed with a wide bright fringe, and Don Carlos Montarges, the honorary Chief Armourer, and his attendant, Don Manuel Trotier, went in the gala carriage with the trophy. The carriage was drawn by mules in gala attire, and three royal lackeys in full livery walked by the side of each. In the other carriage, also drawn by four mules and accompanied by lackeys, came the Duke del Parque. The sword was borne into Murat's presence by the two armourers, and, after giving him the King's letter, they solemnly presented him with the historic weapon, which was received with many expressions of thanks.

Murat now set no bounds to his ambitious aims, especially as he knew that his brother-in-law had decided on the dethronement of the Bourbons in Spain. So, dazzled by the brilliance of his position, he precipitated matters by his intrigues. He suggested the advisability of the Infante Don Carlos going to meet Napoleon as far as Burgos, so this journey of the Spanish Prince was arranged, Pedro Macanáz and Don Pascual Vallejo being in attendance.

As Napoleon did not trust entirely to the perceptions of Murat, he sent the astute Savary to reconnoitre the state of affairs in Madrid. The clever Frenchman was as successful in Spain as he had been in Russia, and it was soon arranged for Ferdinand to take the undignified course of going to meet Bonaparte at Burgos, for Escoiquiz thought that it would gain the favour of the great Frenchman.

Before starting, Ferdinand wrote to his father begging for a letter in which he would assure Napoleon that he (Ferdinand) professed the same sentiments of friendship with the French as his father. The reply to this request came from the Queen, and she said that the pains in the King's hand prevented his writing himself, but she had written to the Grand Duke of Berg saying that the desired letter had not been sent because they knew that Ferdinand had no love for France.

III.

HOW NAPOLEON I. CHECKMATED
THE SPANISH ROYAL FAMILY
1808–1814

As Napoleon was not quite satisfied with Murat's reports, he determined to go himself to Spain, and Ferdinand was advised by Escoiquiz to go to Bayonne to meet the Emperor. After holding a council on the subject at Vittoria in the bedroom of Escoiquiz, who was ill, Ferdinand wrote a humble letter to the Emperor, promising to go and meet him, in spite of Savary's objections to the want of dignity in the suggested proceeding. In his letter to Napoleon, Ferdinand declared that he had been raised to the throne by the free and spontaneous abdication of his father, and to this epistle the Emperor replied:*

"In Bayonne,

"April 16, 1808.

"My Brother,

"I have received the letter of Your Royal Highness. You will have seen by your father's papers what an interest I have always shown in him, so you will allow me now to speak to you with frankness and loyalty.

"I had hoped to come to Madrid and persuade my august friend to make certain necessary reforms in his dominions which would give public satisfaction. The separation of His Majesty from the Prince of the Peace seemed to me absolutely necessary for his happiness and that of his vassals. Events in the North retarded my journey, and the occurrences of Aranjuez have intervened.

* Published in the Moniteur in 1808.

37

"I do not constitute myself a judge of what happened, or of the conduct of the Prince of the Peace; but I know very well that it is very dangerous to Kings for the people to become accustomed to shedding blood in their own attempts to obtain justice. God grant that Your Highness may not find it so yourself! It would not be for the interest of Spain to persecute a Prince who has married a Princess of the Royal Family, and who has so long governed the kingdom. He has no friends already, and Your Highness will have none, either, if you come to be disgraced one day, for people like to avenge themselves for the respect they have had to show us.

"Moreover, how could a Cause be framed against the Prince of the Peace without framing it also against the King and Queen, your parents? This Cause would foment hate and seditious passions, and the result would be fatal to the crown. To this crown Your Royal Highness has no rights beyond those transmitted by your mother. If the Cause soils her honour, Your Highness destroys your own rights. Do not listen to weak, perfidious counsels. Your Highness has no right to judge the Prince of the Peace; the sins which are imputed to him disappear in the rights of the throne.

"I have often expressed my wish for the Prince of the Peace to be removed from affairs. If I have not been more insistent, it has been because my friendship for King Charles overlooked the weakness of his affection. Oh, miserable humanity! Weakness and error are our lot. But all this can be made right if the Prince of the Peace is exiled from Spain, and I offer him an asylum in France.

"As the abdication of Charles IV. took place at the moment when my armies were occupying Spain, it will seem in the eyes of all Europe and of posterity that I sent these troops with the sole object of dethroning my ally and friend. As a Sovereign and a neighbour, I must therefore hear all about the event before recognizing the abdication.

"I tell Your Royal Highness that if the abdication of Charles was spontaneous, and he was not forced to it by the insurrection and consequent meeting in Aranjuez, I have no objection to admitting it, and acknowledging Your Royal Highness as King of Spain. I therefore desire to confer with Your Royal Highness on this matter.

"The circumspection I have observed for the past month in the matter ought to convince Your Highness that you will always have my support if factions of any kind disturb you on the throne.

"When King Charles told me of the recent events in October, I flattered myself that I had contributed by my entreaties to the peaceful conclusion of the Escorial matter.

"Your Highness is not free from faults; the letter you have written me is sufficient to show that, and I have always wished to forget it. Being a King, you know how sacred are the rights of the throne; any step of an hereditary Prince towards a foreign Sovereign is criminal. I consider the marriage of a French Princess with Your Royal Highness would be conformable to the interests of my people, and, above all, as a circumstance which will unite me by fresh bonds to a house which I have had every wish to honour ever since I ascended the throne.

"Your Royal Highness ought to beware of the consequences of popular insurrections; you might be able to make an assault on my scattered soldiers, but it would only lead to the ruin of Spain.

"I have seen with regret some letters from the Captain-General of Catalonia which tried to rouse the people.

"Your Royal Highness knows all the depth of my heart; you will observe that I am full of many ideas which require consideration; but you can be sure that in any case I shall behave to you as I have to the King your father.

"Your Royal Highness must be assured of my desire to conciliate matters, and to find occasions of giving you proofs of my affection and perfect esteem.

"May God have you in His holy and worthy keeping!

"Napoleon."*

The King, oblivious of the veiled insult of the Emperor, that he had no right to the throne beyond that transmitted by his mother, still cringed to the Frenchman, and wrote:

"Vittoria,

"April 18, 1808.

---

* From the "Memorias" of Nellerto and the "Manifestation" of Don Pedro Ceballos.

"Señor, my Brother,

"I have received with great satisfaction your letter of the 16th, sent by General Savary. The confidence with which Your Majesty inspires me, and my desire to show you that my father's abdication was the consequence of his own impulse, have decided me to go immediately to Bayonne. I hope therefore to leave to-morrow for Irun, proceeding thence to the country-seat of Marrae, where Your Majesty is.

"I am, my good Brother, with the highest esteem and sincerest affection,

"Ferdinand."

When Ferdinand arrived at Bayonne, the Emperor went to see him at once, and Ferdinand went down to the door to meet him. The interview was short, but the Spanish King was invited to dinner that night. It was noticeable that, although Napoleon was very friendly, he never addressed his guest as "Majesty"; and hardly was Ferdinand back in his rooms, when a message was conveyed to him by Savary to the effect that the Emperor had determined that the Bourbons should not return to the throne of Spain, and that, as he had determined to put a French Prince upon the throne, he required the son of Charles IV. to renounce the diadem of both worlds in his own name and in that of all his family.

Pedro Ceballos was loud in his indignation at such usurpation, when Napoleon, who had heard his remarks from the next room, entered the apartment, upbraided him for his treachery to Charles, and declined to enter further into the matter until Ferdinand's father was there to speak for himself.

After Charles had sent Napoleon a protest against his abdication, he concentrated all his efforts on gaining the liberty of the Prince of the Peace. Indeed, the old man seemed more upset at the risks run by his ex-Minister than he was at the treatment he had himself received.

Pursuant to Murat's advice, Charles and his wife repaired to the Escorial, and there, in this imposing but gloomy abode, they brooded over the turn in their affairs until despair filled their hearts.

Murat, faithful to the promise made to Charles in the presence of the Queen of Etruria on the eve of his departure for the Escorial, did his best for the dethroned Sovereigns, and persuaded the Union to depute him to accompany them to Bayonne to take part in the conference with Napoleon. The fact of Godoy being in Bayonne was another reason for the royal couple to wish to go there, as they had not seen him since his release from captivity. The following letter, which the King wrote to Napoleon announcing his departure for Bayonne, shows the esteem in which they held Bonaparte:

"Aranda,

"April 25, 1808.

"Sir and Brother,

"A prey to rheumatic pains in my hands and knees, I should be completely miserable were not my troubles alleviated by the hope of seeing you in a few days. I cannot hold a pen, so I beg of Your Majesty to pardon my not writing with my own hand to express the great pleasure I have in going to enjoy your generous kindness, for I am obliged to use a secretary.

"The Queen also writes to Your Imperial Majesty, and we beg you to accept our united sentiments of love and confidence.

"Your protection is balm to the wounds of my heart, and I feel that the moment in which I shall find myself in your arms will be one of the happiest of my life, and the first, after all that has happened, on which I shall feel sure of my existence.

"May my wishes be fulfilled!

"My sir and Brother,

"I am, Your Imperial Majesty's faithful Ally and Friend,

"Charles."*

The Queen's letter to Napoleon ran thus:

"Sir and Brother,

"I should have written before to Your Imperial Majesty if the trying situation in which we undertook the journey had not presented so many obstacles. We have now just arrived at Aranda of Duero. The King is in a terrible state. He is troubled with rheumatic pains in his hands and knees, but, in spite of all, we

* Published in the Moniteur, 1810.

41

are longing for the happy moment of throwing ourselves into the arms of Your Imperial Majesty, whose great generosity is beyond all expressions of our gratitude.

"We ought to have arrived at Bayonne before now, but, unfortunately, circumstances do not correspond with our ardent desires, because my son's journey has left us without horses, money, and all other necessaries. Heaven grant that the moment of our interview will be as interesting to Your Imperial Majesty as it will be to us, your faithful, worthy friends! We are quite sure of the protection of Your Majesty, and nothing in the world can compare with the complete and sweet confidence which leads us to place our fate under the most powerful protection of Your Majesty, whose immutable equity is so great, as the critic of the situation of his faithful friend and ally, since the unhappy epoch of the unheard-of events at Aranjuez.

"If Your Majesty's troops had arrived then, they would have protected our legitimate rights as their great captain deigns to do, but Heaven sent us calamities which came like thunderbolts because we had no help, nor had we anyone to support us.

"I do not know what day we shall arrive at Bayonne, because, if the King's indisposition permit it, we hope to take double journeys every day. Your Imperial Majesty may be sure that we shall fly to your arms, so great is our desire to strengthen the sweet ties of alliance and friendship.

"May God have you in His safe keeping!

"Sir and Brother,

"I am, Your Imperial Majesty's most affectionate Sister,

"Luisa."

The affectionate tone of these royal letters shows that the royal couple thought that Napoleon was about to restore to them the sceptre which had been torn from their hands.

When the King and Queen arrived at Villareal, they asked what reports were circulated about affairs, and the Duke of Mahon replied: "It is said that the Emperor of the French is calling the Royal Family of Spain together at Bayonne in order to deprive them of the throne."

The Queen looked surprised, but she thought for a moment, and then said:

"Napoleon has always been a great enemy of our family. Nevertheless, he has made Charles repeated promises to protect him, and I cannot believe he is now acting with such scandalous perfidy."

The royal arrival at Bayonne was announced by a salute of 101 guns, the garrison lined the streets, and Charles, on dismounting from his carriage, showed his pleasure at the reception vouchsafed to him by talking even to those he did not know.

A shadow came over the King's genial countenance when he saw Ferdinand standing with his brother at the foot of the staircase, and it was only the younger Prince who was given a cordial "Good-day" by the King, and who was embraced fondly by his mother. Although Ferdinand saw that he was ignored, he made a step forward to greet his parents. But Charles stopped, made a movement of indignation, and began mounting the stairs with a severe face. The Queen, however, who was behind, could not forget that she was a mother, and folded her treacherous son to her bosom.

Then the Princes repaired to their apartments, and their parents hastened to greet the exile Godoy with tears of joy.

The Emperor of the French lost no time in paying his respects to the royal travellers, but he did not ask them to dinner until the following day.

As Charles's rheumatism gave him some difficulty in mounting the stairs of the imperial abode, he gladly accepted Napoleon's arm, saying: "I have not the strength that I had. It has been all knocked out of me."

"We will soon see about that," returned the Emperor. "Lean on me, and I will find strength for both."

Thereupon the King stopped, and said emphatically: "So I believe, and I base all my hopes upon you."

On taking their seats at the table, Charles noticed the absence of Godoy, and he exclaimed with tender concern: "And Manuel? Where is Manuel?"

So Napoleon, anxious to please his ally, sent for the Prince of the Peace, and the party was complete.

At the meeting at which it was hoped Napoleon would bring the Royal Family to a satisfactory understanding there were very violent scenes. It was natural that the sight of their renegade son should revive all the bitterness of the King and Queen's recent trials, but it was a pity that they did not restrain the passions which made them lose their royal dignity.

The Emperor announced that Ferdinand would restore on the morrow to His Majesty the crown he had snatched from his father's brow. This Ferdinand stoutly declared he would not do, and Maria Luisa, who had destroyed the proofs of her son's guilt in the conspiracy of the Escorial, was now so mad with rage that, according to the report of Caballero, she cried to the Emperor to punish the crimes of her son by committing him to prison.

Ferdinand was silent during the interview, but a few hours later he wrote to his father, maintaining that the abdication had been a fait accompli and declaring that he would only give up the crown at the request of the Cortes and all the tribunals.

To this letter the King replied:

"My Son,

"The perfidious counsels of the people about you have brought Spain into a very critical condition, and only the Emperor can save it.... You have been too easily led away by the hatred which your late wife had for France, and you have thoughtlessly shared her unjust feelings against my Ministers, your mother, and myself.

"I was obliged, in support of my rights as a King and a father, to have you arrested, for your papers contained proof of your crime. But as I am approaching the end of my life, and I was miserable at the idea of my son dying in a dungeon, I let myself be softened by your mother's tears. And yet my subjects have been upset by the deceitful courses of the faction you formed, and from that time I have had no peace in my life....

"You introduced disorder into my palace, you summoned the Royal Guard against my own person. Your father has been your prisoner; my Prime Minister, whom I created and received into

44

my family, was covered with blood, and taken from one prison to another.... I am King by the right of my fathers. My abdication was due to force and violence. I have nothing to accept from you, nor can I consent to any meeting or to any new and base suggestion on the part of the people about you."

However, Ferdinand was obstinate, and there seemed no chance of a peaceful settlement of the disgraceful family feud.

The above letter was dated May 2, 1808, and it was on that day that the historic blow was struck in Madrid for Spain's emancipation from the French. It was the sight of the young Infante Francisco's tears at leaving the Palace of Madrid at the call of Napoleon which acted like a match to gunpowder. The valiant Velarde, Daoiz, and Ruiz were martyrs on this occasion, and the dramatic way in which the Spaniards always keep this anniversary shows that those who struck that blow are not forgotten in the land.

When Charles IV. heard the news of the riot, he at once thought that it had been instigated by his sons.

"Manuel, send for Charles and Ferdinand," he said, in a firm tone.

Napoleon remained in the room restless and gloomy; Charles and Maria Luisa looked worried and anxious. They were all seated when Ferdinand appeared and silently stood alone before them, for his brother was ill in bed.

The King then asked his son if he had heard the news from the capital. When Ferdinand replied in the negative, Charles returned vehemently, "Very well, I will tell you," and rapidly related what had happened. "Judge, then," he added, "if it be possible to persuade me that you had no part in this? And did you hasten your miserable associates to dethrone me in order to massacre my subjects? Who advised you to this carnage? Do you only aspire to the glory of a tyrant?"

The Duke of Rovigo, who gives us this scene in his "Mémoires," says that he and the other people who were listening in the adjoining salon could not catch Ferdinand's reply, but they heard the Queen exclaim: "Didn't I always presage your perdition? See into what abysses you throw yourself and us! Ah, you would have killed us if we had not left Spain! What! you have made up your mind not to answer? You do not forget your old ways. You never know anything when you do something bad."

During this dialogue Charles IV. angrily moved about the cane which he used when walking, and he so far forgot his dignity as to raise it in a threatening way to his son, in his anger at his impenetrable countenance. When Maria Luisa finished her diatribe, she lifted her hand as if to strike the Prince, but she checked herself in time.

The final touch to Ferdinand's humiliating position was given when the Emperor said in cold, clear, chilling tones:

"Prince, I had formed my resolution from the events which brought you to France, and now the blood spilt in Madrid confirms my decision. This carnage can only be the work of the band which calls you chief, and I will never recognize as King of Spain one who breaks the old alliance of two nations and orders the assassination of the French soldiers, whilst asking me to sanction the impious act of dethroning your father. Such is the result of bad counsels. You are brought to the precipice. It is to your father alone that I am in any way bound, and if he wish it I will restore him to his throne and accompany him to his capital."

But Charles IV. exclaimed vehemently: "But I don't wish it. What could I do in a country where they have worked up such passions against me? And I, who have always rejoiced at seeing my country peaceful in the midst of the upset of Europe—I should dishonour my old age if I made war in the provinces and condemned my subjects to prison. No, no; I don't wish it. My son will undertake it with more pleasure than I." Then, looking at Ferdinand with majesty mingled with pity, he said: "Do you think it costs nothing to reign? You have followed these perfidious counsels. I neither aspire to command nor can I do anything. Now you must avoid the precipice as best you can."

As Napoleon told Ferdinand that resistance about his resignation was useless, and would only make his fate worse, it was agreed that the crown should be handed over to France.

So the Treaty of Bayonne was formally signed on May 6 by the Prince of the Peace for Charles IV., and by Marshal Duroc for Napoleon, and this step, disastrous to the nation, can thus be distinctly traced to the family feuds induced by the Queen's unbridled passion for the Prince of the Peace.

Charles had passed the twenty years of his reign in a self-indulgent, simple life, and although he did nothing to show great devotion to his kingdom, he certainly of his own accord would have done nothing to disturb its peace. The Count of Toreno repeats the account which Charles gave of his daily routine to the Emperor:

"Every day, winter and summer, I hunt till twelve o'clock, when I dine. Directly afterwards I hunt again till evening. Manuel tells me how things are going on, and I go to bed, to begin the same life next day, unless there is some important ceremony."

With a Sovereign so inert, Godoy did not demur on signing the deed of renunciation of the throne, and as Escoiquiz sanctioned the deed, it shows that he also felt that Ferdinand was but a broken reed.

After the humiliating events of Bayonne, the poor Queen of Etruria sought to return to Etruria, but was detained at Nice. Miserable at having been obliged to leave her young son ill at Compiègne, she tried to escape to England, but, the plot being discovered, one of her two agents was shot, the other died in prison, and she herself was condemned to confinement in a convent at Rome; so she did not recover her liberty nor see her child again until the fall of Napoleon. The Queen's claims on Etruria were subsequently nullified by the Congress of Vienna, and she had to be contented with the nomination of her sons to the dukedom of Lucca.

Although after the Treaty of Bayonne the city of Madrid was in the hands of Napoleon Bonaparte, the palace could not count the Emperor as one of the residents in the palace, for during his stay in the Spanish capital he was installed in the mansion of the Duque del Infantado at Chamartin, and it was from this house that he made his entry into Madrid. "Je la tiens en fin cette Espagne si désirée," said the French conqueror as he passed up the magnificent staircase of the royal palace, and placed his hand upon one of the lions on the balustrade; then, as his eyes travelled up the matchless marbles and fine panels and pictures of the staircase, he turned to his brother Joseph and said: "Mon frère, vous serez mieux logé que moi."

When passing through the magnificent apartments, he stopped before a portrait of Philip II., and after gazing at it for some minutes in silence turned away. Who knows what recollections may have passed through the conqueror's mind, of stories of this Sovereign read in boyhood, and how little he had then thought that the throne of this King would ever be at his disposal!

Thus ended the rapid and only visit of Napoleon to the Spanish capital, for he went back to Chamartin, and from thence set out for Galicia.

King Joseph soon found he had a difficult part to play at the royal palace as ruler of a foreign nation, but, although the Spaniards could not be supposed to be fond of him, tribute was paid to the kindness of his heart. After a meeting held at the palace to concert steps for dealing with the fearful famine which was devastating Madrid, the father of Mesoneros Romanos said to his son: "Joseph has certainly not lost his head at his elevation, neither is he unduly set up by his rank. He seemed profoundly moved at the misery of the people, and proclaimed his intention to do all in his power to assist them. Certainly," concluded the speaker, "the man is good. It is only a pity he is called Bonaparte!"

The preference entertained by Joseph Bonaparte for a beautiful lady, the Countess Jaruco, widow of the Governor of Havana, is well known. The lady died, and on the night of her burial her body was exhumed (one can imagine by whose orders), and was interred under a shady tree in her own garden. Joseph subsequently married the Countess's daughter by General Merlin. The hatred of the people got on the poor Frenchman's nerves, and for the last four years of his enforced reign in Madrid he kept quite in retirement, spending a good deal of time in the Casa del Campo, to which he passed by a tunnel entrance.

But it was not very long, as we know, before the day came for Joseph to leave Spain.

"The excitement in our house," writes Mesoneros Romanos, "at the news of the evacuation of the royal palace by the French was extreme, and it was the same in every Spanish home. The hatred of the foreigners who had taken possession of us was very deep-rooted, and those who had joined the Gallic banner were not safe from actual persecution.

"The shades of a dreadful nightmare were passed, and men talked excitedly, and women and children laughed for joy. The Virgins del Carmen and of the Paloma were promised new robes, and the children ran to light up the altar, backed with a valuable picture of the Immaculate Conception—a relic of the sacking of Godoy's house; and after a Paternoster and a Salve my father said: 'Now we must go to bed, for we must be up early to-morrow to see the entry of our friends.'

"By this was meant the Anglo-Spanish army, with its chief, Lord Wellington, and the Generals Alava, España, and Conde de Amarante. It was indeed a fine sight; the streets were decorated, and after a repast served in the Town Hall the English Commander-in-Chief appeared at the windows in response to the vociferous cheers of the crowds, and his speech, which was as cordial as was compatible with the stiff English manner, was received with the enthusiasm of our Southern nature."

Then Wellington repaired to the royal palace, which the municipality had put at his disposal. The English General's official proclamation, placed at the corners of the streets, struck cold on the hearts of the Spaniards, for it savoured more of a fierce Murat than of the General of a liberating force. The following copy is taken from the only remaining one in the archives of the city:

"The inhabitants of Madrid must remember that their primary duty is to maintain order, and to render the Allied Armies every assistance in their power to continue their operations.

"The Constitution established by the Cortes in the name of H.M. Ferdinand VII. will be proclaimed to-morrow, after which will follow the immediate formation of the Government of the City according to the form it prescribes.

"In the meanwhile the existing Authorities will continue in the exercise of their functions.

"Lord Wellington,

"Duke of Ciudad Rodrigo."

It was soon seen that Wellington did not intend to rest upon his laurels, for he scoured the rural park of the Retiro, where a French detachment still lingered, and took 2,000 prisoners and 200 pieces of artillery. This act completely confirmed the confidence of the Spaniards in the English commander, and the heads of families eagerly repaired to the churches to take the oath of the Constitution, which, however, conveyed little to them beyond their emancipation from the French and the approaching return of King Ferdinand VII.

It cannot be said that Wellington made himself very popular whilst he was at the royal palace. He received the attentions showered upon him in his cold and stiffly courteous way, and took little pains to be cordial with the people of importance who called upon him.

Wellington's fancy to have his portrait painted by Goya nearly led to the future hero of Waterloo losing his life.

For, be it known, the illustrious Spanish painter was irascible to a degree, the more so that he was completely deaf. So when the great General made his appearance in the studio on the banks of the river Manzanares, the painter's son interpreted the Englishman's wishes in deaf and dumb language to his father.

The sittings took place, and the artist worked assiduously; and when he thought the portrait was far enough advanced to be seen by the General, he placed it before him. But, unfortunately, the picture did not please the commander, who shrugged his shoulders contemptuously, and said in English to his friend that he would not accept such a caricature as a gift. General Alava declined to translate this depreciatory remark; but the artist had noticed the scornful gestures of the Englishman, and the son in alarm saw his father turn his eyes to the loaded pistols which always lay ready to hand on the table. The young man's fear was increased when Wellington rose from his seat in a discourteous way, and put on his hat preparatory to departure. Then Goya, enraged at the officer's contemptuous manner, seized the pistols, and the General clapped his hand to his sword.

The scene would have ended in a tragedy had not Lord Alava assured the irate General that the artist was suffering from sudden mental aberration, and young Goya restrained his father by force from using the deadly weapons.

Wellington gave a great ball at the Town Hall the night before he left Madrid, and with this return for the bull-fights, serenades, and fêtes, which had been given in his honour, he took his departure from the Spanish capital.

The English camp in the Retiro was raised a month later by General Hill, and it is a matter of regret that the step was accompanied by the blowing up of the royal manufactory of porcelain, for the fabrication is now extinct. The magnificent walls and ceilings of one of the salons of the royal palace, decorated with cherubs, fruit, and flowers, in this beautiful ware, show that Spain boasted an industry which rivalled that of Sèvres, Dresden, or Worcestershire.

The reason given for this act of vandalism was that the French might have used the building as a barrack; but it did not satisfy the Spanish, who could not contain their indignation at the deed, which was made worse by the English withdrawing to Portugal and leaving the capital.

Ferdinand, with his usual duplicity, wrote to Berthémy from Valençay, where he was practically a prisoner. In this letter he pleaded in a cringing way for the protection of Napoleon, who had robbed him of his crown.

"My greatest desire," he writes, "is to be the adopted son of His Majesty the Emperor, our Sovereign. I believe I am worthy of this adoption, which would make the happiness of my life, by reason of my love and affection to the sacred person of His Majesty, and by my submission and entire obedience to his intentions and desires.

"Moreover, I am anxious to leave Valençay, for this place is in every way disagreeable to us and in no way suits us.

"I am glad to trust in the magnanimity of conduct and the generous beneficence which always distinguish Your Imperial Majesty, and to hope that my ardent desire will be soon fulfilled.

"Receive, etc.,

"Ferdinand."

When Napoleon decided to publish this correspondence with Ferdinand, he wrote and asked him to send a letter to show that he had his authorization for doing so.

So, before the appearance of the letters in Le Moniteur, Ferdinand, in obedience to the imperial request, wrote to Napoleon:

"Valençay,

"May 3, 1810.

"Señor,

"The letters now published in Le Moniteur show the whole world the sentiments of perfect love which I entertain for Your Imperial Majesty, and the deep desire I cherish of becoming your adopted son. The publicity which Your Imperial Majesty has deigned to give my letters makes me hope that you do not disapprove of my sentiments nor of the desire I have formed, and this hope fills me with joy.

"Permit me, sire, to confide to you the thoughts of a heart which I do not hesitate to say is worthy of your adoption. If Your Imperial Majesty would unite me to a French Princess, you would fulfil my most ardent wish. By this union, apart from my personal happiness, all Europe would be convinced of my unalterable respect for the will of Your Majesty, and it would see that you deign to make some return for such sincere feelings.

"I will venture to add that this union and the sight of my happiness will exercise a beneficial effect on the destiny of all Spain, and will rob a blind and furious people of the pretext of covering a country with blood in the name of a Prince, the eldest son of an ancient dynasty, who has, by a solemn treaty by his own choice and by the most glorious of all adoptions, made himself a French Prince and a son of Your Imperial Majesty.

"I venture to hope that such ardent wishes, and an affection so absolute, will touch the magnanimous heart of Your Majesty, and that you will deign to make me share the fate of the many Your Majesty has made happy.

"Señor, I am, etc.,

"(Signed) Ferdinand."

Charles Leopold, Baron de Colly, an astute and intriguing youth, proposed to the Duke of Kent a plan for releasing Ferdinand from his ignoble position at Valençay by taking him on board an English man-of-war to a port of Spain.

The Duke of Kent referred the matter to his father, who sent Ferdinand two letters by the Baron. Provided with a set of passports and all papers necessary for the undertaking, besides supplies, in the form of diamonds and an open draft on the house of Maensoff and Clanoy, and a ship loaded with provisions for five months, Colly commenced operations. He reached Paris in safety, sold part of the diamonds, and began his preparations; but the police got wind of the plot through Colly's secretary Albert, and he was promptly shut up in the Castle of Vincennes.

Fouché tried to persuade Colly to continue his work, so that Ferdinand might be caught in the act of escaping; but the Englishman preferred his prison to such treachery, and in this prison he remained until the fall of Napoleon.

In the meanwhile Fouché sent to Ferdinand a man called Richard, personating Colly. But the Prince was not caught in the trap, for, in his rooted desire to conciliate the Emperor of the French, he sent at once for Berthémy, the Governor, and said to him:

"The English have done great harm to the Spanish nation by using my name, and they are now the cause of the blood which is being spilt. The English Ministry, in their mistaken idea that I am kept here by force, have sent an emissary to me who, under the pretext of selling me curios, has given me a letter from His Majesty the King of England."

The letter from George III. to Ferdinand, which was subsequently published in Le Moniteur, ran thus:

"Sir, my Brother,

"I have for a long time wished for an opportunity to send Your Majesty a letter signed by my hand, to express the deep interest and the profound feeling which I have entertained for you since you were taken from your kingdom and your faithful subjects. Whatever the violence and cruelty with which the usurper of the throne of Spain oppresses that nation, it ought to be of great consolation to Your Majesty to know that your people retains its loyalty and love for its legitimate Sovereign, and Spain makes continual efforts to maintain the rights of Your Majesty and to re-establish those of the monarchy. The resources of my kingdom, my squadrons, and my armies, will be employed in aiding the vassals of Your Majesty in this great cause, and my ally the Prince Regent of Portugal has also contributed with all the zeal and perseverance of his faithful friend.

"The only thing which is wanting to your faithful subjects and your allies is the presence of Your Majesty in Spain, where it would give fresh energy. Therefore I ask Your Majesty, with all the frankness of alliance and friendship which bind me to your interests, to think of the most prudent and efficacious way of escaping from the indignities which you suffer, and to present yourself in the midst of a people unanimous in its desire for the glory and happiness of Your Majesty.

"I beg Your Majesty to be sure of my sincere friendship, and of the true affection with which I am—in the palace of the Queen, Monday, January 31, 1810—sir, my Brother,

"Your worthy Brother,

"George R."

"By command of the King,

"Wellesley."*

But Ferdinand's cross-grained nature was unable to follow any straightforward advice or adopt any clear course. However, we all know how the people's desire to have a Spaniard on the throne, aided by the troops of England, was finally successful, and Ferdinand the Desired entered his capital on May 13, amid cries of delight from his people, who were wild with joy.

---

* "Monitor de Paris, traducido por Don Juan Maria Blanco en el 'Español' publicado en Londres."

IV.

KING FERDINAND VII. AND HIS HOME LIFE
1814–1829

So Spaniards once more had a King of their own blood. The pity of the matter was that the man himself was so unworthy of the people's trust. Brought up in a Court honeycombed with intrigue, truth and sincerity seemed unknown to Ferdinand, and although he constantly said, "I hate and abhor despotism," there never was a Sovereign more despotic than this son of Charles IV.

Being untrustworthy himself, he thought everybody was unreliable, and so he set spies on his entourage, and stooped to listen to stories from his servants.

Thus, no Minister or officer was safe from being sent off to prison, and with the duplicity which had been perfected by constant practice in his youth sentence of condemnation would be given by Ferdinand with an air of friendliness, with a wave of his cigar or the offer of his caramels, followed by thrumming on the table, or the pulling of his ear, or the slapping of his forehead, with which his courtiers were familiar as signs of bad temper.

The Duke of Alagon was the King's most constant attendant in any gallant adventure, and, indeed, his departures in that respect were those of a man who seemed to atone for his want of personal attractions by a surplus of gallantry to the fair sex. It was whilst pursuing one of these intrigues with a charming widow at the royal resort of San Lorenzo that General Trinidad Balboa, in his anxiety to show his zeal for the King in his position as commander of the police at Aranjuez, wrote to headquarters saying:

"There is nothing fresh to report beyond the anxiety felt by the

King's faithful servants at His Majesty so constantly risking his precious health by being out in the cold night air of the gardens."

But the official's zeal was untimed, and he was politely informed that any further reports of this nature would end in a visit to Ceuta, which is the severest Spanish prison.

As there was but one Government in the reign of Ferdinand VII. and but one army, and that was the Government and the army of the King, the effect of the influence of the women who surrounded the monarch was immense, and this was especially seen in the royal country resorts, where the King's Court numbered many coquettish sirens who courted him for favours of all descriptions.

The greed and corruption of men in authority at Court became an open secret.[*] Don Pedro Macanáz, the Minister of Grace and Justice, sold offices at high prices, and large sums of money thus passed into the hands of a certain Luisa Robinet, who had followed the diplomat from France. This fact came to the ears of the King, and he determined to stop the matter in his own way; so on November 8, 1814, Ferdinand rose early and sallied quietly forth from the palace, only accompanied by his confidential friend, the Duke of Alagon.

When they had gone some way, they were joined by a company of the Guard, and with this escort they arrived at the house of the suspected Minister. The unhappy man was in bed, but the King mounted to his room, demanded his keys, and went to his desk, and there he found a letter in which a certain person offered him 12,000 reals for a post which he solicited. Armed with this and many other incriminating papers, Ferdinand returned home to his courtiers, who applauded his action, and Macanáz was condemned to imprisonment for an indefinite time in the Castle of San Antonio in Corunna.

The corruption of the Ministers and the despotism of the King naturally led to secret societies in Spain.

Alagon was the King's constant companion, and at night the King used to sally forth with him in search of adventure. Don Ramon de Mesoneros Romanos relates that one night a small boy

* "History of Ferdinand VII.," 1843.

met two imposing-looking figures dressed as ordinary citizens with wide-collared cloaks, and, as there was not room on the sidewalk for him to pass them without going into the road, he made as if he would push by them, with the discourtesy of youth. But, as the man on the inside of the pathway removed his handkerchief from his face, the boy gazed at him with such open-mouthed astonishment that the imposing-looking gentleman quietly put forth his hand, and the boy found himself removed to the middle of the road. The next day the boy's schoolfellows were regaled with an account of his encounter with the Sovereign.

"Yes," said the boy, with glee, "it was King Ferdinand VII. himself—his very self."

During the public audiences at Court, Alagon used to stand by the King with his hand in the breast of his coat, and by a secret language he acquainted the King with the political opinions of the persons who were soliciting his favour, and it was by the same dumb language that the monarch learnt particulars about any beauties who appeared at the Alcazar.

It was soon found that to pander to the King's love of the table was a sure way to favour, so not only would an impecunious noble give him a magnificent banquet in return for exemption from paying his debts, but the religious houses, the barracks, and the prisons, regaled the royal monarch with great feasts, which were always followed by a request for his patronage on behalf of some relation or connection of those in authority at the institution.

On February 3, 1815, Ferdinand suddenly appeared with the Captain of his Guard in the Council of the Supreme Inquisition. He told the assembly to resume their seats and to continue their work, and this work of persecuting humanity appeared so attractive to the royal visitor that he decorated the Inquisitor-General with the Grand Cross of Charles III. The superior officer a few days afterwards gave a magnificent lunch to the monarch on the understanding that he would favour the work of condemning heretics; so on March 17 we find Ferdinand creating an Order of Knighthood for the Ministers of the Holy Office.

Ferdinand's marriage, when he was thirty-two years of age, to

Isabel de Braganza, opened a new era for Spain. As we know, Isabel's sister, Doña Maria Francisca de Asis, had married the King's brother, Don Carlos, the future claimant to the throne.

The King's bride was soon beloved by all her subjects for her sweetness and intelligence. Indeed, so true was her judgment in matters of policy that, when her husband occasionally consulted with her about affairs, he never regretted accepting her opinion.

The young Queen was, moreover, very artistic, and it was her love of the fine arts and her skill in painting that led to the foundation of the Academy of San Fernando, intended especially for the exhibition of foreign pictures.

But, clever as the young Queen was, she was woman enough to wish to win her husband's admiration, and in this aim she resorted to all sorts of girlish artifices.

Once, when the King was passing through the royal apartments with his pompous step, he was accosted by a charming maiden in Andalusian attire. With her fine features shaded by a rich white mantilla, her beautiful blue eyes bubbling over with fun, and her lovely hands holding up the castanets, she gracefully took a few steps of a Sevillian dance before curtseying to His Majesty. When the King saw that the charming girl was the Queen, he was surprised into admiration for his beautiful wife, and every time that she astonished him by such successful artifice she increased his love for her.

But, unfortunately for Isabel's happiness, Ferdinand was constantly on his guard against falling, like his father, too much under the influence of his wife, and, as a weak nature like his was bound to be under some domination, it was subjugated by such men as the dissolute Duke of Alagon and his servitor Chamorro, and the Queen's influence was shunned.

However, the bright, buoyant, loving way in which Isabel sought to gain her rightful place in Ferdinand's affections would have succeeded in any Court less corrupt than that of Madrid. But the stream of a sweet, pure influence was checked by the stagnating effect of flattery and lies, and the King shut himself out of the joys of a happy home life by the barricades of self-interested friendship, and he strove to satisfy his young wife by showering such public marks of favour upon her as having the Buen Retiro made into a perfect garden of Paradise for her use. But, even as the beautiful Queen trod the lovely glades and gazed at the gorgeous flowers, she sighed for more frequent signs of her husband's love and confidence, which would have filled her heart with a joy unobtainable by any outward pomp and prettiness.

Alagon and Chamorro indeed formed an insurmountable barrier between the royal couple, and all Isabel's efforts seemed powerless to break it down.

The King's charming compliments to his wife sometimes soothed her chafed spirits, and consoled her with the hope that, if not supreme in his confidence, she had at least no rival in his heart. But this consolation was not long left her, for the day came when she found that the man who had been treacherous to his father and his mother, his family, and his friends, was also false to his wife.

The Queen was sitting one evening in the royal palace. If her pretty forehead puckered sometimes in thought, it was probably because she was planning some fresh fantastic surprise for the husband who was enthroned in her heart, or perhaps she was forming some plan for an exhibition in the Art Institution she had founded, when her brother-in-law, Don Carlos, came into the room and informed her that the King had gone out into the city in his mysterious way with his confidants Alagon and Chamorro, and expeditions conducted in this secret form signified to the Prince an affaire de cœur. Isabel at first declined to believe the Infante's statement, as Ferdinand had told her that he was only going on business to the Mayordomo's office. So the Prince accompanied his sister-in-law to the office in question, and when the King was not to be found there, and his companions also proved to be missing, the Queen determined to wait for her husband in a room near the door by which he would re-enter the palace. The hours of waiting were long, and when Ferdinand finally returned it was to find the gentle Queen too overwrought to be able to restrain her rage.

"You have deceived me!" she cried. "You come from the house of your dear one! I congratulate you!"

The King replied in terms which showed how great was his anger with the tale-bearer, and the dialogue between the royal brothers might have led to fatal results had not Doña Francisca intervened; and, as the influence which the Princess exerted over her brother-in-law was always of great weight, the painful scene ended with the wound to poor Isabel's heart which never was healed.

Deceived in her husband, the young Queen devoted herself assiduously to her baby daughter, and was never so happy as when she was doing everything herself for it; and when the little Infanta succumbed to an illness, Isabel's grief was intense, and the King also was much affected at the death of his baby daughter.

It was about this time that the serious discontent in the realm led to a plot which was to compass the assassination of the King. Don Vicente Richard was the chief conspirator, and as each participator in the plot knew of only two others concerned in it, and the triangular sections were all quite separate from each other, the names were never disclosed. When it was time to put the match to the train, some thought that it would be well to surprise the King in the house of a certain beautiful Andalusian lady called Pepa, so that the whole country should know that the perfidy of the King extended to his domestic life as well as to matters of public concern.

But Richard's two co-operators betrayed the plot to the palace, and although the conspirators met the fate which such actions invite, and the King spared neither time nor money in trying to find out their co-operators, no further information was discoverable.

The Freemasons were at this time a great object of persecution on the part of the Inquisition. In a curious old book called "Narration of Don Juan Van Halem, Field-Marshal of the National Troops," we have an account of a secret audience he had with Ferdinand for the purpose of making certain revelations to His Majesty on the subject.

According to the account written by Halem himself, a certain Don Ramirez Arellano came into his cell at seven o'clock in the evening, when he was suffering imprisonment at the hand of the Inquisition, and told him that the King was graciously pleased to receive him, but warned him solemnly against any indiscretion. Halem wished to put on his uniform, with the stripes and decorations accorded to those who had followed Ferdinand to Valençay. But Arellano forbade it. "Nothing in the way of uniform," he said—"nothing, nothing that may attract attention;" and he made him don his plain cap and jacket, and, accompanied by the alcalde and another man, they repaired to the palace.

"We reached the gallery," writes Van Halem, "by unfrequented stairways, and, opening a coloured window, which was a secret door, came to the King's private room, commonly called the camarilla.

"There Ramirez Arellano left us for a while, and I found that the other incognito was Villar Frontin, the King's secretary. At the end of half an hour a fine-figured lady passed through the room, followed by Arellano. He nervously made a sign to the secretary and me to follow him, whilst the alcalde was to remain behind. When we all three arrived at the door of the salon, Arellano called out in a loud tone:

"'Señor.'

"'What is it?' cried a voice from within.

"'Here is Van Halem.'

"'Enter.'

"So we entered, leaving Villar Frontin near the door outside.

"The King was quite alone; he was seated in the only chair in the room, but as we advanced he rose to his feet. The King's dress is so familiar to his people, down to the cut of his trousers and the stud of his shirt-front, that there is no need to describe it.

"At a little distance from the chair was a large table, at which the King despatched business with his Ministers, and upon which were several papers, an inkstand, a writing-case, and a box of cigars.

"By the side of the table was a case, which was doubtless the same in which Irriberry said the King kept the papers sent from Murcia for him.

"The King rested one hand on the table, whilst I bowed to his feet according to Spanish etiquette, and giving me the other to kiss, he raised me, saying: 'And what do you want? Why do you wish to see me?'

"'Because I am perfectly sure that, if Your Majesty will listen to me quietly, all the suspicions with which Your Majesty has been inspired, and which have led to my treatment, will be allayed!'

"'But you are taking part in a conspiracy, and you ought to divulge it to me. I know all. Don't be frightened. Who are your accomplices?'

"'The desire for good is not conspiracy. If Your Majesty knows all, there will be nothing new in what I can say, and any explanation you may deign to authorize me to make will disarm your anger, and show you that the only reason anybody hides from your august personage is to escape from the scourge with which people seek to make your illustrious name odious.'

"'Who are those who have seduced you with these errors? Tell me who they are. Do not hesitate.'

"'Señor, if Your Majesty knows all, you know—you must know—that nobody has seduced me, and that I speak from an impulse of conviction from within; and that the order of things and the distrust nowadays is such that I cannot say I know anybody personally.'

"'You must know the means of discovering them; you are bound in honour to obey me. Choose, then, between grace and disgrace.'

"'Put yourself, Your Majesty, at the head of the society, and you will know all....'

"Then Ramirez Arellano advanced like a fury towards the King, and cried to me in a loud voice, most unfitting for the presence of a King: 'Here, here, we want no more preambles and sophisms! On this table are pens and paper, and here you must put down the names of all the conspirators. No circumlocution or subterfuges. The King is at the head of his kingdoms, and nothing under the sun ought to be hidden from him. I have read Barruel, Señor; I have been in France, and I know what these Freemasonry secrets are. Where, where are the solemn oaths made to your religion and your King?'

"During all this storm I kept my eyes on the monarch's face, which seemed turned to stone from the moment Arellano joined in the conversation. Disregarding the miserable man as much as I could, I turned to the King, and said:

"'Señor, I know nobody.'

"Then Ramirez said: 'Señor, the tribunal, the tribunal will make him vomit.'

"Then the King, turning away from Ramirez, said in a tone of vexation:

"'It is impossible that you know nothing about it; your silence is criminal.'

"'Señor,' I returned, 'if I were hiding a crime I should shun your royal presence, and if I had committed a sin I should profit by the opportunity of being in the royal presence, to ask pardon.'

"The King stood looking at me thoughtfully for some time, and then said:

"'Put down in writing all that you have to tell me.'

"After a slight pause he took one of the cigars from the table, lighted it, and began smoking.

"'Do you smoke?' he said.

"And when my answer was in the affirmative, he said to Arellano: 'Give him some cigars.'

"This act was followed by a sign for me to leave, and when I kissed His Majesty's hand he pressed mine with a certain touch of feeling, but, on turning to make my bow at the door, I heard him say to Arellano: 'What a pity—such young man!'"

Thus, the attempt to give the King some idea of the matter did not succeed, as the Freemason was not allowed to make any verbal explanation, and to have followed the royal suggestion of putting in writing any information about the society would have been to put one's neck into the noose.

According to Van Halem's own story, he subsequently escaped from prison through the help of a maid-servant.

It was on the evening of December 26, 1818, that sweet Isabel died, and Ferdinand again found himself a widower.

The news was a great shock to the whole country. Mesoneros Romanos relates that he was at a large municipal evening party, when the Mayor entered in his official garb, and said in a solemn voice: "Señores, this festivity must cease. The Queen our lady" (and he reverently doffed his hat) "has just expired after being delivered of an infant, which has also died." Dismay filled the assembly, and it was with sad hearts that the company repaired to their homes, for not only had they lost their lovable young Queen, but the death of her infant had also destroyed their hopes of an heir to the throne.*

It is said that Ferdinand showed more grief at this bereavement than ever he had before, and, robbed of the one person whose advice was always good and disinterested, he was soon utterly ruled by his favourites of the camarilla, who wove intrigues to the ruin of the country.

Obedient to the wishes of the State, that there should be a direct heir to the crown, the King soon wedded Maria Josefa Amalia, Princess of Saxony, a young girl of sixteen, just out of the convent where she was educated; and it was soon seen that she had little or no influence on the character and actions of her husband, for, although the verses from her pen show that she was very intelligent, she was never known, during the eight years of her married life, to express any opinion on public affairs, and she occupied herself entirely in making garments for the poor. With the extreme piety of her disposition, which had been fostered in the convent, Maria Amalia never frequented balls or theatres, and her drive in the Pardo was the only pleasure she allowed herself. Studious by nature, the Queen soon mastered the language of her new country, but study was not the accomplishment by which she could gain ascendancy over a man like Ferdinand.

The change from the society of the eager, intelligent Isabel to that of the cold, formal Maria Amalia was great, and, as the phlegmatic Queen never sought her husband's confidence, it was now entirely monopolized by his self-interested camarilla, who flattered and fawned upon the King, and encouraged him in courses which gradually robbed him of all the respect of his subjects. The King's promises to support the Constitution were

* "Memorias de un Setenton, Mesoneros Romanos."

64

recklessly broken, and despair at the decay of all hopes of a good monarchical government led, in 1820, to such a systematic proclamation of the Constitution in Corunna, Vigo, and many garrisons of Spain, that the country became in a state of revolt. Then the courtiers became alarmed, and the King himself could not hide his anxiety at seeing the affection of his subjects slipping from him. The day came when the palace was surrounded by a discontented mob. The Queen sat silently in a corner of her room engaged in prayer, whilst Chamorro tried to drown his master's fears in ribald laughter.

Ferdinand paced the apartment deep in thought, and the silence which met his companion's ill-placed mirth showed it was unwelcome to the monarch. At last the King's good genius conquered, and, putting aside the courtiers who sought to stifle every good impulse, he sent for better councillors, and by their advice he strove to avert the threatened blow by signing a document in which he promised to act in conformity with his brother Don Carlos and the Junta, of which he was President.

But the expressions in this manifesto were vague and obscure instead of being open and frank, and Ferdinand found that the realm which had been outraged by six years of autocratic tyranny was as difficult to get back to subjection as an unbridled horse left to its own course.

Discontented with the lack of any binding promise in the King's manifesto that he would protect their constitutional rights, the people returned in crowds to the palace, and the air echoed with their loud cries for justice. The Royal Guard itself was lax in checking this public ebullition of feeling, and the people began to press up the royal staircase, when the King sent his emissaries to check their progress and calm the sedition with promises to give attention to their petitions. But these promises did not satisfy the people, and the Marquis of Miraflores returned to the King to say that the citizens demanded His Majesty to take his solemn oath of the Constitution of the country in presence of the Corporation and the Commissioners of the people.

Despotic as he was when in safety, Ferdinand was weak and

cowardly in danger, so he concealed his annoyance at the demand of the Commission, and, with well-assumed benignity, took the desired oath in the Ambassadors' Salon at the palace. But afterwards, when alone with his favourites, Ferdinand gave vent to the rage which he felt at having been thus forced to do what was contrary to his love of despotism.

Indeed, this despotism was inherent in Ferdinand both by instinct and education, and Queen Amalia's sphere of usefulness was limited to her never-ending self-imposed task of making garments for the poor. Spain saw the sad hearts of those whose parents, husbands, sons, or friends, were condemned to exile or poverty for no better cause than for having been friendly with the French, whom their King himself had flattered with every expression of obedience and service.

The promises for the restitution of the property which had been thus confiscated came too late to check the surging insurrectionary state of the people, and on the night of July 8, 1820, the insurrection in the barracks of the King's own Guard, in favour of those who were proclaiming Liberty throughout the country, struck terror into the pusillanimous heart of the King, and it was only the death of the standard-bearer which prevented the revolution becoming very serious.

Moreover, the palace itself was the seat of a plot headed by Baso, the King's secretary, and Erroz, his private chaplain.

The object of this plot was to get possession of the King's person on the road from Burgos, and to proclaim a republic.

But Baso, who was attached to the Infante Don Francisco, warned him so that he could repair to Old Castile, and the matter thus got wind, and reached the ears of Echevarri, the Chief of the Police. This official promptly ordered the bells to be set ringing in every place on the King's route, and the crowds of people thus brought to the road from Burgos prevented the King being taken captive.

It was on the day following the frustration of the plot that Ferdinand opened the Senate in state. The King went with stately step to the royal apartments of Queen Amalia, and, accompanied by the Infantas, grandees, gentlemen-in-waiting, and all the pomp of the occasion, Their Majesties proceeded to the Senate in the magnificent state coach drawn by sixteen cream horses with nodding plumes. Seated on the throne, with the Ministers, Deputies, and Bishops, on the benches, and a brilliant assembly of courtiers and ladies in the boxes, the King read his opening speech; and, as he promised to maintain the rights of the people, it seemed as if King and State were once more in union.

But the seeds of discontent were not so easily uprooted, and a Commission of the Patriotic Society of the Café of Lorencini went at twelve o'clock one night to the palace to request the removal of the Marquis of las Amarillas, the Secretary of War. This request angered the monarch, the bad feeling between Ferdinand and his Ministers increased daily, and in the meetings the King did not hesitate to exhibit his bad temper in spiteful and satirical allusions accompanied by a malignant smile.

It was at this time that Riego was made Captain-General of Galicia. He was a pleasant, valorous young fellow who suddenly became a favourite of the populace through the bold way in which he stood up for the constitutional rights of the nation. But after his triumphal entry into Madrid he quite lost his head, and, instead of being the Rienzi the people had hoped for, he had not sufficient eloquence with which to harangue the people when they shouted for him to come and speak for them, and the populace had to be contented with the sight of his face in the light of their torches. Riego was indeed wanting in the intellectual force required to lead a nation, and, though he had thought to be its idol, he soon found he was only its plaything, but his vanity spurred him on in the campaign for the assertion of its rights.

Ferdinand, meanwhile, had been told by one of his secret agents of the weak side of the leader of the insurgents; and having sent for Riego, he flattered him by showing him how advantageous it would be to schemes of constitutional liberty if he were to join the Ministry.

Riego then boldly declared his hope that the Ministry would be changed, and Ferdinand, who was at that moment anxious to get rid of his Cabinet, entered into the plan of replacing the Ministers by friends of Riego.

It was on September 3 that Riego's party proceeded to the theatre after a great banquet, and there broke into a couplet composed in Cadiz—the "Trágala" ("Swallow It," meaning the Constitution).

Ferdinand strove to counteract this public anti-monarchical exhibition by secret agents following him with cries of "Viva el Rey" as he passed to and from the palace.

Fresh friction arose between the monarch and the Ministry when the law which had been approved by the Cortes for the reform of the convents was brought to the King for his sanction. For, supported by the wish of the Pope, conveyed by the Nuncio, Ferdinand determined to take no step to check the fanaticism which he himself so strongly favoured.

The people were furious at this blow to their hopes for progress, and when all was prepared for the departure of the King and Queen to the Escorial on October 25, his secretaries told him that a plan was laid by his enemies to prevent his departure till he had passed the decree to check the power of the friars and prevent their inquisitorial courses. The King was enraged at this announcement, and he hastily decided to leave Madrid that very minute. So he left with the Queen and the Infantas at eleven o'clock in the morning, and brilliant illuminations and rejoicings marked the evening of Their Majesties' return to the Palace of San Lorenzo. Shut up in the Escorial, Ferdinand devoured his rage in secret, and when the day came for closing the Congress, he excused himself from attendance on the plea of a severe cold.

It was on November 21 that the Court returned to Madrid. But at some distance from the capital crowds of people met Their Majesties singing the "Trágala"; and when Ferdinand, as usual, went to the window of the palace to see the march past of the regiments in the city, he was met by a storm of frantic cries and threatening gesticulations from the crowds of people assembled in the Plaza del Oriente. The King was about to turn away with an imprecation from such a scene, when he caught sight of a child being held up above the sea of angry faces, and a look of horror came over his face as the populace pointed to the little boy, crying, "Lacy! Lacy!" For by this name he knew that the child was that of the unhappy General Lacy, the leader of the victory over the French in the Mancha, but he had met a secret and violent death at Majorca after the failure of his pronunciamento in favour of the Constitution had led to his plot in Catalonia in 1817.

The King stood horror-struck when the cries of "Viva Lacy's son!" and "Viva his father's avenger!" filled the air, but he kept his place till the defile of the regiment was over. Then the King turned back into the salon with a face which showed that he realized the portentous nature of the movement he had witnessed.

The Queen was sitting weeping bitterly at these signs of discord, and the Infantas looked distressed at the dangers which were threatening the dynasty through their brother's want of keeping faith with his subjects.

The sense of danger became more pronounced when it was found that within the very precincts of the palace a plot was brewing.

It was the honorary chaplain, Don Matios Vinuesa, and a gentle-man-in-waiting, who formed the idea of sending for the city author-ities one night and making them prisoners of the King in the royal domain, whilst the Infante Don Carlos was to take command of the troops of the garrison in virtue of the Absolutist party. This plot was discovered by the betrayal of the secret printing of the proclama-tions, and Vinuesa was hurried off to prison on January 21, 1821.

On May 4, Vinuesa, the Canon of Tarazona, was sentenced to ten years' imprisonment in Africa. But this punishment did not satisfy the fury of the people at the discovery of the plot favoured by the King. A meeting was held in the Puerta del Sol, and from thence the outraged people proceeded to the prison, to which their admission was only opposed by one locked door. All the rest were open, and, penetrating the cell of the unhappy cleric, they gave him two blows on the head with an iron hammer. The murdered man had tried to avert his death by falling on his knees and begging for mercy; but it was useless, and the bloodthirsty mob followed the mortal blows dealt on the head with several more with other weapons.

An assassination which had been connived at by those in power filled the King with fear, for he felt that a people who could thus take justice into their own hands might resort to the same course any day with him.

In this state of alarm, he ordered the Guard to assemble in the wide colonnaded square of the palace. The Guard was composed of soldiers who had fought bravely in the Battles of Bailen, Talavera, and Albuera, and the King did wisely to appeal to the chivalrous feeling of such men.

"Soldiers!" he cried, with a voice which became penetrating in the speaker's desire to make it ring in the hearts of his hearers—"Soldiers!" he cried, "the deed committed this afternoon against the person of the priest may to-morrow be committed against me or against yourselves. Soldiers! I trust in you, and I come before your ranks now to ask if you are disposed to defend your constitutional King."

To this appeal the Guard cried: "Viva the absolute King!" and, satisfied with this demonstration, Ferdinand returned to the royal apartments, somewhat reassured after the fright he had suffered.

After this episode the King seemed to avoid Madrid, with its discontented Ministers and the insulting cries of the "Trágala" revolutionary song, which so often fell upon his ears by the Manzanares, and, after going with the Queen to take the baths at Sacedon, he spent some time in the Palace of San Ildefonso at Aranjuez. There the unstable King could be oblivious of his duties as a constitutional monarch; and in frivolous games and boating-parties, picnics and dances, he passed the hours away. With the gallantry with which Ferdinand sought to compensate for his want of personal good looks, he made himself conspicuous with many of the frivolous, pretentious ladies who sought for his favours.

However, the King's health began to fail visibly, and he became a martyr to gout, which finally shortened his life.

Ferdinand's constant struggle of his ambition against the natural weakness of his character, and his propensity for the pleasures of the table and gallantry, undermined his constitution, and at an age when many men are in their prime he was broken with suffering.

When the revolution at last broke out under the Generals Alava, Copons, and Riego, the King was in a great state of mind, and horses were saddled and kept ready for flight at a minute's notice.

When Ballesteros, who had been victorious with the militia in the Puerta del Sol, arrived at the gates of the palace, the Royal Family was horror-struck. The two battalions of the Guard were idle at the royal domain, because the King would not let them go to the assistance of the four battalions fighting in the town, and he had passed the night endorsing the lists of proscription which his alarmed councillors had presented to him. The King had, moreover, signed the warrant for the committal to prison of Riego, Ballesteros, Palarea, etc., who captained the militia, and the sentence was to have been executed that very night.

But for such a task a strong Guard was needed, as despots can only condemn citizens to death when protected by a strong line of bayonets. The cannon thundered in the Puerta del Sol, and the militia with Ballesteros having appeared right at the gates of the palace, a bullet entered one of the windows.

Then the King forgot all his plans for revenge, and the dignity of the Castilian crown was dragged in the dust, for he sent a messenger to Ballesteros beseeching him to desist from firing, as his life would be in imminent danger.

The General replied: "Tell the King to command the attendants about him to lay down their arms immediately, or, if not, the bayonets of free men will penetrate to his royal chamber."

However, Ballesteros did order a truce to the hostilities, and sent back the messenger to Morillo with his own Aide-de-Camp.

The permanent deputation of the Cortes, which, in virtue of Article 187, was entitled to form a regency in the case of the physical or moral deficiency of the King, thought it was time to do so, and it assembled in the house called the Panaderia.

Word was sent to the militia that His Majesty desired the cessation of bloodshed, and it did not seem befitting the splendour of the sceptre for the King's Guard to be obliged to lay down their arms. After an animated discussion it was decided that the four battalions which had attacked the town should lay down their arms, and that the other two should go out armed and take up their positions in Vicalvaro and Leganes.

But late in the afternoon, when this arrangement was going to take place, the four aggressive battalions, having made another attack on the militia, fled away by the stone steps which lead from the square of the royal palace to the Campo de Moro. Morillo brought more artillery into play, and Ballesteros, after attacking with his cavalry the groups of peasants who were proclaiming absolutism, also started in pursuit of the Guards. It spoke well for the democrats that, when the palace was momentarily left without any guard, until the Count of Carthagena arrived with the regiment of the Infante Don Carlos, it was perfectly respected, and no attempt was made to invade it.

But when Morillo arrived with his troops at the royal gates, Ferdinand rushed to the window and incited his General to attack the people, crying out: "After them! after them!" Such cowardice and treachery seemed incredible.

Instigated by his love of double-dealing and intrigue, Ferdinand sent again for Riego, the revolutionary leader, and deceived him by his conciliatory assertions that he only wished his welfare and that of all Spaniards, and that he did not believe his heart was capable of nourishing the counsels of perfidious men.

Riego, unacquainted with the dissimulation of the Court, was quite enthusiastic at the sudden conversion of the King, and in this spirit he would not have the "Trágala" sung any more, and declared he would have those who did so arrested.

The astuteness and deception of the King gave rise to inextricable confusion in affairs. On one side he promised the French Minister that he would establish the two Chambers, and on the other side he was telling Mataflorida to take the reins of a Regency and proclaim Absolutism. When the three Generals met the King as he crossed the bridge at Cadiz connecting the island with the mainland, and represented to him that it would be well for him to place the Regency in their hands, he exclaimed, "Hola! But I am not mad! That is good!" and continued his way to Cadiz.

As this is not a political book, we need not enter more fully into the long struggle of Ferdinand's Absolutism against the Constitutional party, and how he was obliged to leave Madrid.

The country again saw the French called to interfere in the affairs of the nation, and it was indeed, as we know, only due to Angoulême that Ferdinand, after his time of humiliation in Andalusia, returned to the capital.

Once more the people went mad with delight at the sight of the King. Riego the revolutionist was dragged in a basket at an ass's tail, to be hanged and quartered as a felon, and the people who hailed the return of the absolute monarch were indeed bidding welcome to the return of the chains which had shackled them.

V.

MARIA CRISTINA, FERDINAND'S FOURTH WIFE
—INTRIGUES AT COURT
1829–1832

On May 17, 1829, Queen Maria Amalia passed away. She was a most virtuous and conscientious lady, and had she realized that the duties of a Queen were not synonymous with those of an Abbess, the King and the country would have been more benefited by her irreproachable life. The atmosphere of the convent hung always about her, and when not engaged in working for the poor she was occupied with her devotions.

When the King wished to walk with the Queen, he generally had to wait till some sewing for the poor was completed; and in all the dissensions between the King and his subjects his wife would sit silently weeping or praying, but never try to understand anything about the struggle between despotism and constitutionalism, which was tearing the realm asunder. Moreover, Maria Amalia left the field free for the presumptuous, frivolous women of the Court, when she decided never to go to any theatre nor to allow any balls or parties at the palace.

A drive in the Retiro or the Prado was the only relaxation the royal lady permitted herself, and it was there that the Portuguese Princess, Maria Francisca de Braganza, the wife of Don Carlos, also took her daily airing in a beautiful carriage drawn by six mules. The Princess of Naples, Princess Luisa Carlota, wife of the Infante Don Francisco, had long felt herself slighted by this haughty Princess, and by her sister, the Princess de Beira, widow of the Infante Don Pedro, and after the death of Queen Maria

Amalia she determined to mature a plan by which her position at Court would be improved. For, knowing the susceptible nature of Ferdinand, and that his obstinate nature was weak and yielding where the fair sex was concerned, his sister-in-law determined that this susceptibility should be turned to account in the person of her sister, Maria Cristina. The position of Luisa Carlota had, moreover, always been somewhat ambiguous, from the open secret of the relation of her husband with Godoy; and as this Prince and Princess always thus felt themselves somewhat alien from the rest of the Royal Family, they were strongly in favour of the Liberal party, which was in direct opposition to Don Carlos, his wife, and the widowed Portuguese Princess.

Thus, intrigue and enmity reigned between the two parties, and Luisa Carlota could hardly conceal her triumphant feeling when, on showing the King the portrait of her beautiful sister, she saw that his face expressed admiration for the bonny girl, who was daughter of Francis I. of Naples, the brother of his first wife, and therefore his niece by marriage; and on December 11, 1829, the beautiful young Princess made her formal entry into Madrid as the bride of the King.

When the Princess arrived at Aranjuez with her parents, she was received by the Infantes Francisco de Paula and Don Carlos, and so the first formal words of welcome in the name of the King were addressed to the bride by him who afterwards became her most bitter enemy and rival.

The impression made upon the Spanish people by the Italian Princess during her journey from Barcelona to the capital was favourable. Her beauty and youth appealed strongly to the susceptible Spaniards, and her kindness of heart was seen in her suggestion that the soldiers should put their cloaks on in the inclement weather; and on the day of her triumphal entry into Madrid as their Queen, with the King at the right side of her carriage and the Infantas on the left, the people went wild with joy at what they considered as the dawn of a new era for the realm. It was soon evident that the young Queen had great influence over her husband. Unlike her predecessor on the throne, Maria Cristina loved to take an active part in the affairs of the realm; and Don Carlos, who had always had ascendancy over Ferdinand, found that his position in the confidence of his brother was gradually on the wane.

The beautiful Princess tempered Ferdinand's fury against those who had revolted against him, and her gentle words and calm counsel were a beneficent antidote to the advice of Calomarde and the Bishop of Leon.

As the influence of Maria Cristina increased, the power of the Portuguese Princesses was lessened, and the enmity of the parties became more and more marked.

When it was evident that an heir to the throne might be expected, Don Carlos and his wife placed all their hopes on the chance of it being a girl, for in that case he laid claim to be heir to the throne by virtue of the Salic Law of Philip IV. Although Charles IV. had privately abrogated this law, Don Carlos still considered that his right was valid, as he was born in 1788, a year before its abrogation.

The power of the Queen over the King was still more marked after the birth of their little daughter on October 10, 1830. As heiress to the throne, Ferdinand commanded the same honours to be accorded the infant Princess as were customary to be given to a Prince of Asturias. With fresh hopes for the future of his family, the King turned his thoughts to more liberal forms of Government than he had ever before entertained. By an autograph letter he decreed the establishment of a Liberal Ministry. But Calomarde and the Bishop played on the King's natural vacillation and cowardice to persuade him that the Liberals would abuse the power against the throne.

Gout meanwhile made great inroads in the health of the King. One attack followed another, until it became evident that the King's life would not be a long one. In view of her unsettled position, Queen Cristina determined to ingratiate herself with the army, and to this end she celebrated the completion of Isabel's first year by bestowing on different companies of the soldiers banners worked by her own hands.

The ceremony took place in the historic Hall of Columns in the Palace of Madrid, and as the Queen graciously handed her beautiful work to the Generals, she said: "On a day so dear to my heart I wished to give you a proof of my affection by placing these banners in your hands, which I trust they will never leave. And I am quite persuaded that you will always know how to defend them with the valour which is proper to the Spanish character, sustaining the rights of your King, Ferdinand VII., my very dear husband, and of his descendants." A public proclamation to the army expressed the same sentiments, and the bestowal of the gifts received wide appreciation.

However, the intrigues in the palace grew apace, and one of the most constant companions of the Queen was Teresita, a dressmaker, who was raised to such a high position of favour that even Ministers asked her intervention with Her Majesty for the introduction of people of such high degree as grandees of Spain, etc. As Maria Cristina's influence increased, she managed to get rid of the Portuguese Princess de Beira, under the pretext that her brother required her in her native land.

After the birth of a second little Princess, the King was with his wife at La Granja, when he fell dangerously ill. The Infante Don Francisco and his wife were in Andalusia, and Don Carlos with the Princess of Beira; Don Sebastian and Doña Amalia were at the palace with the King.

The attack of illness, which commenced on September 13, became so serious that his life was despaired of. It was then that Cristina showed her true wifely affection. Dressed in the costume of Señora del Carmen, the royal lady was a constant and indefatigable attendant on the patient. It was from her hands alone that he received his medicines, and it was she who administered all the means of alleviating his sufferings. Ferdinand seemed to cling to his wife during this terrible time, and to her he confided his distress at the thought of leaving her a widow with the orphaned Princesses.

Indeed, distress of mind added so much to his physical sufferings that Cristina sent for Calomarde to see what he could do to calm his master. Calomarde gladly profited by the permission to enter the royal apartment, for the Infantas were refused admittance.

When the King, between the fits of exhaustion that followed the attacks of pain, explained to his Minister with great difficulty the ground of his anxiety, Calomarde perfidiously expressed his opinion that, in the event of his Majesty's demise, the kingdom would declare in favour of Don Carlos, and that the only means of saving the crown for his daughter would be to associate his brother in the Government. It was, indeed, suggested that the Queen was to be authorized to despatch business during his illness, but it was to be with the help and advice of the Prince.

The Bishop of Leon was then called into the King's chamber to give his opinion, and he echoed the advice of the Minister.

In the meanwhile the apartments of Don Carlos were a hotbed of intrigue. "Now or never" was the feeling of the Pretender to the throne, and self-interested people came and went in constant consultation with the Prince, and to bring news of the condition of the King. The Portuguese Princesses were keen and intent on all that went on, whilst their faces betrayed their anxiety. When the Count of Alcudia appeared with the King's decree, Don Carlos definitively declined to share any duties of government with the Queen, and on the departure of the messenger the Infante again reverted to his silent and thoughtful attitude.

The Count soon reappeared with a new decree, to the effect that Don Carlos, in company with Cristina, should be appointed guardian of the Infanta Isabel. To this Don Carlos also gave a haughty refusal, saying that he could not thus resign the legitimate rights which God gave him at his birth; and with these words he closed the door to all negotiations for recognition of the little Princess's right to the throne. So the King was again a prey to anxiety, and the Bishop of Leon and Calomarde so worked on Cristina's nerves in their accounts of the horrors that would beset the country under the civil war, which was imminent with little Isabel as Queen, that, at her wits' end to know what to do, the poor lady finally exclaimed: "Only let Spain be happy and tranquil with the benefits of peace and order!" And in this overwrought state she herself besought the King to revoke the Salic Law. So the deed was done, and the King commanded a codicil to be drawn up, declaring that he had made this supreme sacrifice for the tranquillity and peace of the kingdom, but the fact was to be kept secret until after his death.

This moment seemed to follow very quickly on the portentous deed; for Ferdinand fell into a lethargy which was believed to be death, for he lay without any signs of life, and all efforts of the doctors to revive him were useless.

Poor Cristina put her hand to her husband's heart, and even as she failed to detect any movement, and thought she was a dethroned widow, she saw Calomarde, the Bishop of Leon, and all the other councillors, leave the room without a word of sympathy or an offer of help. That moment taught the Queen more of the worthlessness of friends of the camarilla type than she could have believed possible. The sight of those men leaving her in that callous way, alone with her supposed-to-be-dead husband, showed her that Madrid would be no place for her and her little children were Don Carlos on the throne.

So, with tears pouring down her face, Cristina at once began to collect her jewels and make ready for her departure, whilst her brother-in-law was already addressed as "His Majesty" in the antechamber, and the Portuguese Princesses embraced each other with joy at the success of their plans.

But two unexpected events happened which put a check to the triumph of the Carlist party—the King showed signs of life, and the Infantas Don Francisco and Doña Luisa Carlota suddenly arrived from Andalusia. A few minutes' conversation with her sister put Luisa Carlota in possession of the whole story.

After reproaching Cristina for the weakness which had led her to sacrifice her daughter's throne to the intrigues of the Infantas, the Princess sent for Calomarde, and a terrible scene took place. She upbraided the Minister for the treacherous way he had played into the hands of the Queen's enemy, and had abandoned her in time of need; and when he sought to justify himself, she gave way to such fury that she struck him on the face.

For a moment the Princess seemed shocked at her own loss of temper, but Calomarde's courtier-like remark, that "white hands offend not," showed that no further resentment on his part would be shown. In the meanwhile, as the King was supposed to be dead, the secret societies noised abroad the news of the Revocation of the Pragmatic Sanction, and Don José O'Donnell sent a secret circular to the authorities and persons of the places in favour of Don Carlos.

In fact, albeit after September 28 immediate anxiety about the King's life was past, Maria Cristina felt that she was on the brink of a revolution.

It was due to the magnanimity and kind-hearted nature of the Queen that the King at this time finally signed the decree which buried the hatchet of the revolution in Seville, and allowed all people to return to their native land; and it was by this deed that the beautiful young Queen gained a surer hold on the hearts of her subjects.

Cristina was, moreover, relieved from the presence of Calomarde on the recovery of the King, for, as he could no longer expect the favour or confidence of his Sovereigns, he left Spain for France, and there remained until the day of his death.

It was on October 19 that Ferdinand and Cristina returned to the capital after all the events which had so surely sifted true friends from false flatterers. The atmosphere seemed clearer; the King saw that it was necessary to make Cristina Regent during his daughter's minority, and with this triumph of her authority Cristina wore the bright and joyous look of a tender wife, a loving mother, a heroic Queen, and the liberator of Spain.

Ferdinand was certainly a wreck after his severe illness. As Don Carlos said, "he was more a corpse than a man"; but he was alive, and, after that terrible moment when Cristina had thought she was alone and unprotected with the dead body of her husband, the fact of his being by her side gave her a sense of protection.

The entry of the Sovereigns into Madrid was followed by a manifesto from the Queen, in which she set forth her love to Spain, and a declaration was published by the King, in which he annulled the codicil which would have abrogated the Pragmatic Sanction. After stating the facts of the Pragmatic Sanction, the King said:

"Perfidy completed the horrible plot which sedition commenced.... Being conversant now with the falsity with which the loyalty of my beloved Spaniards was calumniated, as they are always faithful to the descendants of their Kings; and being quite persuaded that it is not in my power, nor in my desires, to break with the immemorial custom of the succession established for centuries past, sanctioned by the law, and followed by the illustrious heroines who have preceded me on the throne; and solicited by the unanimous votes of the kingdoms, and free now from the influence and coercion of those fatal circumstances—I declare solemnly of my own free will that the decree signed at the time of my illness was torn from me by surprise, and that it was the effect of the false terrors which upset me, and that it is now null and void, being contrary to the fundamental laws of the monarchy and the obligations which I owe my august descendants, as father and as King.

"In my Palace of Madrid,

"December 31, 1832."

Ferdinand's feeling for his wife was shown in the public letter of gratitude which was published soon after his return to Madrid. It ran thus:

"The King to my very dear and beloved Wife, the Queen.

"During the very grave and painful illness with which the Divine Providence saw fit to afflict me, the constant care and inseparable companionship of Your Majesty have been my consolation and delight. I never opened my eyes without seeing you by my side, and finding palliatives for my pain in your face and words; I never received food which did not come from your hand. It is to you I owe consolation in my afflictions and the assuagement of my pain. Weakened by so much suffering, and condemned to a long and tedious convalescence, I then gave you the reins of government, so that the despatch of business should not be delayed; and it is with joy that I have seen the singular wisdom and diligence with which you have directed them, and have abundantly justified my

81

confidence. All the decrees that you have expedited have been to advance public education, to dry the tears of the unhappy, or to increase the general prosperity and the receipts of my Exchequer. In fine, all your determinations have, without exception, pleased me much as the wisest and the best for the happiness of the people.

"Recovered from my illness, I once more take over the affairs, and I give Your Majesty the most heartfelt thanks for your zeal in my assistance, and for your efficiency in the government.

"The gratitude for such signal offices, which will always live in my heart, will be a fresh stimulus and justification for the love with which your talents and virtues have inspired me from the beginning.

"I am proud, and congratulate myself that you have not only been the delight of the Spanish people since your advent to the throne, but you have given me joy and peace, and are now an example of wifely solicitude to wives and a model of administration to Queens.

"In the Palace, etc."

In another decree the King commanded a medal to be struck in commemoration of the actions with which the Queen had immortalized his name.

It was indeed an affecting sight to see the way in which the King clung to his domestic happiness at the decline of his life. Seated in his large gilded chair, he smiled with pleasure at his children, and he followed every movement of his wife with eyes in which love and gratitude were evident. In the light of this love the cruel and self-interested influence of the camarilla was weakened. His nervous nature found repose in the firm counsels of Cristina, and, with the confidence with which she inspired him, he had no need to resort to the duplicity which is so often born of distrust.

But a secret power was at work in the provinces, where the Bishop of Leon sought to work the people up in favour of the Carlists, whilst pretending devotion to the King. "What name can be so sweet to me as the monarch's?" he said—"a monarch to whom I owe all, and from whom I have received confidences in matters of grave importance which I cannot reveal, and therefore I know how much he desires the order and tranquillity of his people."

When the time drew near for the administration of the oath to Isabel as heir to the throne, Ferdinand sent a letter to Don Carlos to ask if it was his intention to attend the ceremony or not. To this question the Infante replied that his conscience and his honour would not permit him to be present at the function, as he could not resign his legitimate rights to the throne in the event of his brother dying without a male heir. God had given him these rights at his birth, and he hoped his brother would explain the reason of his absence to the other Sovereigns at the ceremony.

To this communication Ferdinand replied:

"My very dear Brother of my Life, the Charles of my Heart,—I have received your letter of the 29th ult., and I am glad to see that you and your wife and your children are well. We are the same, thank God. I have always known how much you have loved me, and I believe you know the affection which I have for you. But I am father and King, and I have to consider my rights and those of my children, as well as those of my crown. I do not wish to thwart the dictates of your conscience, nor can I hope to dissuade you from your pretended rights; as, being founded on a determination of men, God alone can change them. But my love as a brother impels me to avoid the disagreeables which would attend you in a country where your supposed rights are not recognized, and the duties of a King oblige me to remove the presence of an Infante whose pretensions might serve as a pretext to malcontents. So, as you cannot, for high political reasons, and by the laws of the kingdom, and for the sake of the tranquillity of the country, return to Spain, I give you permission to travel henceforward with your family in the Pontifical States, acquainting me with your destination and the place of your residence.

"One of my men-of-war will arrive shortly at Lisbon to take you. Spain is independent of all action and foreign influence in what concerns internal arrangements, and I should be acting against the free and complete sovereignty of my throne, and against the principle of non-intervention adopted by the Cabinets of Europe, were I to make the communication you ask me to make in your letter.

"Good-bye, my dear Charles; believe me that you have been loved, you are loved, and you will be always loved, by your most affectionate and unchangeable brother,

"Ferdinand."

It was thus that Don Carlos made himself an exile, and the two brothers, who had always been together in the many vicissitudes of their lives, were now parted for ever.

To the King in his declining days it was doubtless a grief to be so separated from one with whom he had always shared his thoughts, and on whom he had so much depended. The companionship of Don Carlos during his years of enforced residence at Valençay had saved him being forlorn. However, the bright and cheerful society of Cristina during these days, when the letters of Don Carlos showed how irreparable was the breach between the brothers, was a great solace to the King.

The Queen was always energetic, bright, and busy. The painting of "Cupid and Psyche" by her own hand, given to the Academy of San Fernando, showed her talent for art; and her interest in literature was seen in her asking Ferdinand to have a bust of Cervantes placed on the front of the house of the great author. Moreover, the School of Music owed its foundation to the same royal patroness.

The ceremony of the administration of the oath to Isabel, as heir to the throne, finally took place with all the pomp and ceremony for which the Court of Spain is so famous. The King and Queen stayed the night preceding the function at the house called San Juan, in the Buen Retiro, and from thence they proceeded in state to the same Church of San Geronimo where Ferdinand himself received the oath of allegiance in 1833, and where our Princess Ena became the bride of Alfonso XIII. Gentiles hombres, grandees, and generals, made a brilliant procession. Then came the Infantes Don Francisco and Don Sebastian, followed by Their Majesties, walking on either side of the heir-apparent, Princess Isabel, who was carried in the arms of a lady-in-waiting. The procession concluded with the Ambassadors and Chamberlains, and the Royal Guard playing the national air.

The Patriarch of the Indias was seated in front of the high-altar to receive the oath, which was read aloud by a Camarista de Castilla.

The Infantes came in turn to the altar, where they knelt and repeated the words of allegiance. Then they each kissed the hand of His Majesty, who threw his arms round their necks; and they then kissed the hands of the Queen and the Princess, and returned to their seats. The same order of procedure was then followed by the other Infantes, Cardinals, Archbishops and Bishops, grandees and dignitaries; and, the ceremony over, the city was gay with fêtes.

A long correspondence then took place between the royal brothers, when Don Carlos declined to leave the Peninsula.

As Don Carlos was favoured by the Jesuits of Spain, the plots of the party were incessant; and in the palace itself the intrigues of the party were seen in the Royal Guard.

It was on July 29 that Ferdinand died. He had been left alone with the Queen to rest, when he was seized with a sudden attack of apoplexy. As the death was so sudden, the Queen, remembering the recent occasion when the alarm was false, said she would not have the body touched for forty-eight hours.

At last the poor King was laid in state in the Salon of the Ambassadors, and the funeral took place at the Escorial.

"Señor! Señor! Señor!" cried the Duke of Alagon, the Captain of the Guards of the Royal Person; and as the solemn silence following these cries was unbroken, the Captain said, "As you do not reply, señor, you are really dead," and then broke his wand of office and placed it at the foot of the table on which lay the remains of his royal master.

VI.

MARIA CRISTINA AS REGENT AND AS WIFE OF MUÑOZ
1833

The testimony of Ferdinand to Maria Cristina's fidelity and devotion was indeed true, and, as the Queen said afterwards to her daughter Isabel, when pleading with her not to sacrifice duty to inclination, she herself had never wavered an instant in her loyalty to the King, in spite of the difference of their ages, and the tax upon her time and temper from his bad health and exacting ways. Even a Court bristling with intrigue could find no word of complaint against the Queen in her matrimonial relations with the King; and her grief was very genuine when she found herself a widow, with her two little girls. When General Cordova came to pay his respects to the Queen, he found her weeping bitterly, and the sight of the poor woman's tears did more to win him over to her side than any arguments of policy, so he roundly declared that as he had been loyal to the father, so he would be faithful to the daughters.

When General Prim was invested as a grandee, on his return to Spain after his glorious campaign, he declared it was his first duty to do homage to his Queen and her Ministers for having raised him to such rank that he could consort with the noblest in the land. "It is the duty of a general," he added, "as that of every soldier, to serve his Queen and country with all possible loyalty, and therefore I will defend your rights to the throne to the last drop of my blood and the last breath of my body."

But Maria Cristina was not always surrounded by loyal subjects, for the clerical partisans of Don Carlos made her position very precarious. Men who had declared themselves Liberals became lax in their allegiance, and her only hope of saving the crown for her child was to bend to the widespread desire for the Constitution of 1812.

The Marquis of Miraflores, who was Ambassador of Spain in England at the time of the coronation of Queen Victoria, writes:

"Hardly was the corpse of the monarch cold when the Queen-Regent did me the honour of seeing me; and it was at this critical moment that I heard her say, amid her tears and sobs: 'Nobody desires more than I do the welfare of the Spaniards, and for that I will do all that I can; and where I do not, it will be because I cannot.'"

And Miraflores also says, in his "Contemporaneous History," that he had himself heard the King, referring to the codicil to his will by which the throne would have gone to Don Carlos, say that, both as a King and a father, he would have done wrong had this act not been abrogated.

The outbreak of cholera in the city soon after the King's death cast additional gloom on the capital. Cristina's partisans declared that the clerical party had poisoned the water, and a young man who was said to have been seen throwing powder into the fountain which was then in the Puerta del Sol was assassinated on the spot. Such animosity was stirred up against the clerics that the monasteries were invaded, and the friars killed at the very altars; and these deeds were not limited to the capital. Indignation against these attacks on the clerics added force to the Carlists in the north.

Martinez Rosa's position as Prime Minister was fraught with difficulty. It was characteristic of the courage of the Queen-Regent that in such a time of danger and dissension she calmly repaired from the Pardo to Madrid to fulfil her duty of opening the Parliament.

It was very soon after this act that Don Carlos, in defiance of all political obligations, appeared in Madrid to join his troops; and Miraflores advised the Queen putting herself at the head of her army.

The immense power of the secret societies in Spain was now

seen in La Granja. The Government flattered itself that the Royal Guard, at least, was proof against the power of these unions which permeated the country, and the Queen-Regent was considered safe with her little daughters in the Palace of San Ildefonso, with its barracks flanking the fine promenade in front of the royal domain. But the secret societies had gauged the force of money, and 12,000 crowns, distributed among those who were bound in honour to defend their Sovereign, were found sufficient to cause an insurrection of six or seven hundred soldiers within the precincts of the royal palace itself.

A hundred and fifty grenadiers on horseback sought to quell the émeute, but their superior officers seemed powerless to still the ever-increasing cries of "Hurrah for the Constitution!" "Death to Quesada and San Roman!" "Hurrah for England!" Maria Cristina was terrified at this unexpected uproar at her own gates, especially when she found herself obliged to receive a deputation of sergeants and soldiers, who pressed for an audience within the palace. In this historic scene the Queen was attended by Barrio Ayuso, the Minister of Grace and Justice; the Duke of Alagon, the Captain of the Guards, who had been such a favourite of the late King; the Count of San Roman; the Marquis of Cerralbo; and the commanding officers of the regiments.

The deputation was plain and curt in its demand that the Queen-mother should at once sign the Constitution of Cadiz of 1812. Maria Cristina sought to temporize by promising that the Cortes, which was about to open, would take the matter into consideration. But the insurgents insisted on their demand, so she sent them into the antechamber whilst she consulted with her advisers in the salon.

It was two o'clock in the morning when the deputation again appeared in the presence of the Queen, and in this audience the insolent and threatening tones of the leaders were emphasized by the accompanying cries and constant gunshots of the rebels without.

In this state of things, Barrio Ayuso resigned his portfolio, and the Mayor of the place also offered his resignation; and Izaga there and then drew up and presented to the Queen for signature the following decree:

"As Queen-Regent of Spain, I order and command that the political Constitution of 1812 be published; and in the meantime the nation will express its will in the Cortes on another Constitution in conformity with the necessities of the same."

Maria Cristina read the paper, and in despair put her name to it.

The rebels were not, however, contented with Maria Cristina signing this document. They insisted on the chiefs of the palace also swearing allegiance to it in front of the banners; and then, contented with their work, the rebels finally left the palace at four o'clock in the morning.

This was one of the most bitter experiences in the life of the Queen-Regent; and Barrio Ayuso's laconic message to Madrid— "Send help at once, or I don't know what will befall Their Majesties"—showed that in his opinion the Royal Family was in real danger.

By permission of a hurriedly summoned Council of Ministers, General Roman summoned the troops, but enthusiastic cries for the Constitution and Liberty were mingled with "Vivas" for the Queen and the Queen-mother; and when the soldiers filed past the palace, its shuttered windows were eloquent of the terror which reigned within.

It must have been with a heavy heart that Maria Cristina waited in La Granja till the time came for her to go to Madrid, for there were divisions amid the revels as to what she was to be permitted to do. Those hundred hours of deep humiliation and disillusion as to her influence in the land left their mark upon her face. The winged figures and mythological groups of statuary in the beautiful Italian gardens of the palace must have mocked her, with their air of jubilation, as she walked to and fro on the terrace and thought over her position; and the fountain, topped with the figure of the flying Pegasus draining the goblet of joy, was symbolical of the draughts of popularity which she had quaffed, until now there was nothing but the dregs of dismay.

At last, after much discussion with the rebels, the Queen-Regent set out for Madrid, after both Villiers, the English Ambassador, and the French Minister, had frankly explained to her the danger of withstanding the evident will of the nation with regard to the Constitution.

It was at this time that the gallant Espartero appeared upon the scene. The danger threatening Madrid brought him by forced marches to the city, where he led eleven battalions and several squadrons in review before the palace.

The severe rebuke administered in the Congress by General Sevanes to the commanding officers whose sergeants had rebelled at La Granja against all royal authority led to a duel between the speaker and Captain Fernando Fernandez de Cordova, in which the General was wounded.

Madrid was soon threatened by another revolution, for Don Carlos appeared before the city, with a large number of followers, but, annoyed at the threat, 20,000 citizens armed themselves in defence of their Queens. This remarkable body of loyal subjects was reviewed in the morning on which they assembled by the Infante Don Francisco; and when the Queen-mother, accompanied by Isabel, who was then seven years old, and her little sister, drove down the lines of Royalists in the afternoon, the enthusiasm of the assembly was intense.

When Espartero arrived at Madrid, Don Carlos withdrew from the capital, and from that time the General became the most influential man in the kingdom, though he had a powerful rival in Don Ramon Maria Narvaez.

It was certain that a Government which had witnessed twice in one year peril at the hand of rebels could hardly be called successful, and Espartero thought to put it on a more secure basis by instituting military rule. He seems to have wished to act the part of a Roman military consul, and the fact of Narvaez leading eleven battalions past the Palace of Madrid aroused his jealousy to a great degree.

Don Carlos, whose wife had died in England in 1834, now, in 1838, married the Princess of Beira, and when this lady came to Madrid she boldly proclaimed herself the Queen of Spain, and the eldest son of Don Carlos the Prince of Asturias. The effect of two Courts in the country was most disastrous, and, in this fresh struggle with the Portuguese Princess, Maria Cristina did not have the support of her sister Luisa Carlota, as in the early days of her arrival in Spain, when the same lady had, with her sister, been so jealous of her popularity in Spain; for Luisa Carlota, who had, indeed, been instrumental in the marriage of Maria Cristina to King Ferdinand, and who had always been the ally of her sister, was no longer on friendly terms with her.

The main reason for this quarrel with the Queen-Regent was evidently her secret marriage with Don Fernando Muñoz, whose rapid rise in the royal favour savoured very much of that of Godoy with Queen Maria Luisa.

The story of this passion of Ferdinand's widow is graphically told in an unpublished manuscript by a Don Fermin Caballero, who was a contemporary of the episode.

Born in 1806, in Naples, Maria Cristina had had a very poor education, as her father, Francisco I. of the Two Sicilies, and her mother, Maria Isabel, Infanta of Spain, thought that much intellectual work was unnecessary for a girl, and the rollicking, jovial maiden herself preferred the pleasures of horsemanship and hunting to any kind of brain-work.

Gossip was busy with the name of the handsome Princess in connection with that of Luchessi Bailen before her marriage with Ferdinand, but from the time she came to Spain as the wife of Ferdinand VII. until three months after his death there was not a word to be said against her, as she was a model wife and mother. Her buxom form, clad in the brown garb of a Sister of the Carmelite Order, was never absent from the bedside of her husband, and for two months after his death she duly mourned his loss.

But the reaction came. The simple, somewhat ignorant, but affectionate nature of Maria Cristina was captivated by Muñoz, who certainly could not be said to belong to the upper classes, as his parents kept a tobacco-shop; and it was as the friend of the fiancé of the dressmaker Teresita, who exercised so much power over the Queen, that the young man was found a place at

Court. The Queen's new friend was bald, common, and of poor education, but the influence of his royal patroness soon raised him to be an officer of the bodyguard.*

It was about five months after Ferdinand's death that Maria Cristina impetuously took the reins of her destiny into her own hands, and on December 17, 1833, she gave voice to her intention to go to La Granja, under the escort of the Adjutant-General, Don Francisco Arteaga y Palafox, General of the Guards, the gentil hombre Carbonell, and the honoured Muñoz. By chance or by arrangement, the favourite had the place in front of the Queen, and the party proceeded on the way. But the snow was so heavy that the road from the height of Navacerrada was quite impassable, and they had to turn back, though not before the royal carriage had collided with a bullock-cart, loaded with wood, and the broken glass of one of the windows had cut the hand of the Queen.

The three gentlemen were all loud in their sympathy, but it was the handkerchief of Muñoz which Cristina accepted, and she also distinguished him by allowing him to bandage her hand. Undaunted by the return to the capital rendered necessary by reason of the weather, the Queen commanded the same party to be in attendance for the same expedition on the following day.

As Arteaga and Carbonell watched their royal mistress and Muñoz on the long drive to Segovia, they saw that this expedition, undertaken without the attendance of any lady, signified a very serious predilection on the part of the Queen for the parvenu.

The carriage finally turned from the interminable road across the plain, which separates Segovia from La Granja, into the estate of Quitapesares, whose gates open on to the Spanish chestnut-lined avenue.

When the party took a walk in the gardens in the afternoon, the Queen soon suggested some commission to Carbonell, and Arteaga was also dismissed on the plea of an umbrella being wanted from the palace.

Thus designedly left alone with Muñoz, the Queen soon made known to him her royal favour.

* "Estafeta del Palacio Real," by Bermejo.

92

"Who is a greater prisoner than a Princess?" the Queen may have exclaimed, says Don Fermin Caballero, "for she can never descend to the honest level of an ordinary woman to show her feelings and her inclinations with the honourable liberty dictated by the noble sentiment of her heart? Why should the glitter of a crown oblige me to stifle the purest and most disinterested feelings, which must necessarily bring upon me the disdain of those of my rank and the murmurs of the multitude? Do not let my words surprise and shock you, Fernando. My young heart requires a solace for the onerous weight of my affairs. It longs for the contact of a living soul to assuage the continual pain caused by the ambition of men and their party interests. It can never be said that in search of this consolation I turned my eyes to the brilliant position of a royal personage, or to the support of any of the great captains who defend my daughter's throne, or to the influence of any of those occupied with the cares of the State. No, modest in my aspirations, and only obedient to the impulses of my heart, I have fixed upon a modest soldier in whose sympathy I believe I can trust. Yes, Ferdinand Muñoz, nothing need restrain you from accepting the hand of the Queen-Regent of Spain, who is disposed to grant it you."

"Your hand as a wife?" asked Muñoz in astonishment. And Cristina replied: "What else do you think? Have I, like other unhappy Princesses, prostituted the throne by the caprice of a disordered appetite? Did you imagine, at the commencement of my discourse, that for the satisfaction of a voluptuous feeling I pursued gallantry to the injury of honesty? Did you think that I did not foresee from the first that religion must sanctify the bond which I desire? Is she, who was chaste and severe as the wife of Ferdinand, to be wanting in morality as his widow? My heart is only vexed that State reasons prevent my making public my modest inclinations."

The soldier knelt in gratitude and adoration before the Queen who had distinguished him in such an unmerited fashion.

So when Cristina was satisfied with the result of her declaration, she took one or two others into her confidence, and on December

28, 1833, the morganatic marriage of the widowed Queen with the gentil hombre Don Fernando Muñoz took place at ten o'clock in the morning, the witnesses being Herrera y Acebedo and the cleric Gonzalez, who left a bed of sickness to perform the ceremony. Teresa Valcarcel and a lady in retreat called Antonia were the other witnesses of the rite.

The fact of this event, if not actually known by all the Court, was surmised, for Muñoz was seen wearing the cravat pins of the late Ferdinand; he had a room in the palace, a magnificent carriage; he dined with the Queen, and he was seen driving with her as an equal; moreover, he was created Duke of Rianzares, decorated with the Order of the Golden Fleece, and raised to the rank of grandee of the first order.

It was certainly a marriage which, if wanting in class distinction, was not failing in morality. The Queen-mother was now so taken up with "Fernando VIII.," as he was called, that she preferred the more private life of the royal country-seats to that of the palace of the capital. So on March 15, 1834, we find her at Aranjuez, at Carabanchel on June 11, and then at La Granja, whose beautiful gardens formed a fitting scene for the happiness she had found with Muñoz. It was at Pardo that her child was born, and to an affectionate nature like Cristina's the obedience to the law of circumstances, which took the baby from the mother's arms, cost her many a tearful and sleepless night. The little daughter was confided to the care of the widow of the administrator Villarel, who had settled at Segovia, and for this reason La Granja was the favourite resort of the Queen-Regent, as she could have her child brought to her to Quitapesares, the beautiful estate on the road to the palace, where she had wooed its father.

Doña Teresa Valcarcel, the daughter of the Court dressmaker, was, as we have said, the great confidante of Queen Maria Cristina, and it was as her friend that she first met Muñoz, who soon exercised such a fascination over her.

When Teresa accompanied the Queen to Bayonne, she sent letters to her mother with the official correspondence, and the well-known leader of a gang of thieves, Luis Candelas, having discovered this fact, determined, with the complicity of a man in the employment of the dressmaker, to turn the fact to his advantage. Calling one day in the uniform of an official, the servant introduced him as an agent of the French post. The dressmaker was rather astonished at the visit, but she admitted him. Hardly had he entered the room than he was followed by others, and Candelas declared he had come to inspect the place. This act the dressmaker declared was illegal except in presence of the Mayor. Then, casting off all disguise, the robber and his gang proceeded to pillage the place, pocketing all the jewels and money they could find. Two ladies who called at this time were bound and gagged like the modiste and her workers.

The robbery proved considerable, and the fact of its having taken place in the house of the Queen's dressmaker led to strong steps being taken for the capture of this Spanish Robin Hood. For be it known, that although the adventurer openly took all he could lay hands on, he never shed blood or injured anybody if he could help it.

The efforts of justice were successful, and the fact of the robbery being connected with the correspondence of the Queen-Regent led to the removal of the scourge from the capital, for hitherto the police of Madrid paid little heed to these open attacks against the safety and the property of the citizens.

Candelas was publicly hanged on December 6, 1837, but his partner in his burglarious campaigns escaped.

Of course, the luxurious carriage in which the child visited its mother, and the care which attended the drive from Segovia, opened the eyes of the people to the relation between Cristina and her little visitor, and the coach would be followed by cries of "There goes the Queen's daughter!"

In the revolution of the sergeants in August, 1836, Muñoz was in the Palace of La Granja, but he did not make his appearance on the scene, as he was not supposed to be there. The apartments in which he spent his time with his wife were commonly termed "Muñoz's cage," and on the night of the insurrection he escaped from the royal domain by the channels and conduits of the fountains.

But the time spent thus with Muñoz in the royal retreats was not of unmixed joy; for whilst the Queen sought to please her husband and his relation by playing lottery with them, or battledore and shuttlecock with the chaplain, Muñoz soon showed that he preferred going out after pretty girls with the Duke of San Carlos. Naturally this conduct fired the heart of the Queen-Regent with jealousy, and, woman-like, she gave vent to her pique by allowing a play called "Making Love to a Wig" to be acted in the Conservatoire of Fine Arts, for the play made humorous allusions to the baldness of Muñoz.

The disaffection of her sister, the Infanta Luisa Carlota, was a fresh trouble to Maria Cristina, who was experiencing so many disillusions both in her private and public life. Naturally the sister, who had been so proud of the position to which she had been instrumental in bringing the Queen, was much aggrieved at the wild fancy shown for Fernando Muñoz. She called Cristina the "Muñonista," and, in virtue of what she termed the nullity of Cristina's position to be guardian to her daughter, she proposed herself and her husband as those fitted for the office. This fact outraged the poor Queen-Regent both as a wife and as a mother, and her anger was shown by her declining to authorize the appointment of her brother-in-law, Don Francisco de Paula, as a senator.

Thus war between the sisters was declared, and Luisa Carlota sought by every means to enlist the support of the powerful Espartero in her favour.

At this time there was some talk of the marriage of Isabel with a Prince of the House of Coburg. The report was without foundation; but the Infante Don Francisco sent for the Spanish Ambassador in Paris, and made a solemn declaration of his disfavour to any project of the Princess marrying with any but a Spaniard. The Ambassador was accompanied in the interview by his secretary, and he sent the Infante's message to Madrid, adding his own opinion in its favour, and this was echoed by the Queen and the Government.

In the meantime Don Carlos was obliged by the foreign

diplomats and Vergara to retire to the frontier of Spain, so the country once more settled down under the Queen.

But Espartero was the ruling power. The soldier who, but six short years before, had arrived in Madrid to take his orders as a brigadier officer was now Captain-General of the Army, Count of Luchana, Duke of Victoria and Morella, held decorations of the highest order, including that of the Golden Fleece, and was a grandee of Spain.

The enthusiasm for Espartero was unbounded, for not only was the country grateful for the way he had led the royal troops to the rout of the Carlist companies in the North, and thus put an end to the long Seven Years' Civil War, but he represented the Progressive party, which was favoured by England.

Queen Maria Cristina wished to share the popularity of the hero, and so she arranged to meet him at Lerida, on her way to Barcelona, under the pretext that sea-baths were required for her daughter Isabella. In the interview with the General, the Queen suggested that he should take the post of Prime Minister; but this honour the soldier declined, unless the Congress were closed and the Bill for the election of the Mayors of the Corporations by royal order abandoned, as it was contrary to the Constitution of 1837. These conditions the Queen declined, and she did not see Espartero again until he entered the Catalonian capital in triumph, after giving the final blow to Carlism by the rout of Cabrera at Berga. The ovation given to the General was tremendous. "Viva Espartero! Viva la Constitution! Down with the Law of the Corporations! Down with the Government!" came the cries from the people.

The Queen-Regent was alarmed, and it is said on good authority that she sent for the Count of Lucena, the bizarre Don Leopold O'Donnell, and told him of the difficulty.

"Well, you have only to send for a company of grenadiers to shoot Espartero," said the leader of the Moderate party; to which Maria Cristina returned: "Be silent! You frighten me."

At last the military hero arrived at the palace, which then stood where there are now some little houses, opposite the old Custom-house.

The interview seems to have been somewhat stormy. Maria Cristina is reported to have said: "I have made you a Count, and I have made you a Duke, but I cannot make you a gentleman."*

At last the Queen-Regent had to submit, and she had to agree to the conditions under which Espartero was willing to accept the post of Prime Minister.

On August 21 there was a meeting in Barcelona for the purpose of manifesting loyalty to Maria Cristina, and when the Queen-Regent appeared in her carriage, with her little daughters, the leaders of the meeting exclaimed: "This is the true expression, lady, of the opinions of Barcelona!" It was commonly known as the "frock-coat meeting," as it consisted of those of a superior class; but the confusion caused by the "blouse" people led to a cessation of the cries of "Viva la Reina!" The matter would have blown over if Francisco Balmes, a lawyer partisan of the Queen-Regent, and Manuel Bosch de Torres, had not been shot in a street fray on the following day.

Then, unfortunately for Maria Cristina, she acted under the advice of the French Ambassador, M. de Redotte, who came to pay her his respects in the Palace of Barcelona, and declined to dissolve the Cortes or to withdraw the project for the Corporation elections by royal decree.

Maria Cristina was evidently now very unpopular, and the press was full of calumnious attacks about her secret marriage with Muñoz.

When, moreover, the Ministry suggested that the Queen's post as Regent should be shared with Espartero, the Prime Minister, she proudly declared that, as she had decided to go abroad, it could be given to whom they thought fit.

The scene was worthy of Maria Cristina as Queen and mother. Fate had been against her. She had failed where success had seemed so easy, and the most dignified thing was to leave the field to him who, she declared, whilst pretending to maintain her influence, had never ceased to undermine it. So on August 28 the

---

* Series of biographies of Spanish generals published in La Vanguardia during 1907.

Queen-Regent left Barcelona for Valencia, without even bidding farewell to the Corporation.

The parting between the Queen-mother and her little girls was very sad, and, while going in the carriage of Espartero's wife down to the port, she was eloquent in her injunctions to the General to protect her fatherless children; and when the ship left the port, it was to leave Espartero practically master of the situation.

The triumph of Espartero was accentuated by the banquet given in his honour on August 30, when he was given a crown of gold laurel-leaves.

From Valencia Maria Cristina strove to form a new Ministry, but, though she would not accept the Progressists' programme, she was finally obliged to put the reins of power in Espartero's hands, who was proclaimed in Madrid sole Regent of Spain; whilst Maria Cristina left her land for France. The well-known General O'Donnell accompanied his royal mistress into exile, and remained with her till Espartero's overthrow in 1843.

So it was on October 12, 1840, that the royal children returned to Madrid for the opening of Parliament under the new condition of affairs, in which Espartero was Regent. It was said that he had the same solicitous affection for the little Queen and her sister as he had for his own children. He certainly did well in appointing Don Manuel José Quintana, the illustrious poet, as preceptor to the Queen his charge, Agustin Argüelles as tutor-guardian, and Martin de los Heros as steward of the royal household.

When Espartero had the Regency in his hands, he was practically ruler of the whole country, and this supremacy of an officer whose ideas of military rule left little room for constitutional liberty was bitterly resented by some of the other generals. La Concha, Leon, and O'Donnell, formed the bold idea of getting possession of the persons of the young Princesses, so as to use them as a lever for a less autocratic form of government. Espartero was also opposed by the Carlists, and before many months had gone the bold design was formed, by the disaffected chief, of getting hold of the royal children, and putting them in the hands of the Moderate party, under Maria Cristina, who was under the protection of the French.

VII.

QUEEN ISABELLA'S GIRLHOOD,
AND THE DANGERS WHICH BESET IT
1840–1846

The little Princesses now lived in the imposing Palace of Madrid, with all the retinue befitting their position, but far from the mother who, with all her faults, loved her little girls, and had only left them to save them from the greater losses with which they were threatened. Espartero, who was now a sort of Dictator of Spain, took up his residence in the Palace of Buena Vista, in the Alcalá in Madrid, which is now the Ministry of War.

The secret influence which was working in Madrid in favour of Luisa Carlota and her husband led to their being suggested as guardians to the royal children, in a little book called "The Maternal Guardianship of H.M. Isabel II. and Her Royal Highness's Sister, Maria Luisa Fernanda."

But Government declared against the appointment of personages who were known to nourish such hatred to the mother, who sent an indignant protest from Paris against the project. So Argüelles was appointed guardian, and in his choice of coadjutors certainly did his best to improve the environment of the little Princesses. Of course the appointment caused much discontent on some sides. The uncle and aunt declared that it was made in the desire to separate the Princesses from their relatives, and that it was wrong to put them under a man who had been an enemy of their father.

Argüelles had indeed suffered at the hand of Ferdinand VII., who gave him seven years at Ceuta when he returned to Spain as

King; but this had only been for his political opinions. Indeed, the Minister was so eloquent that he was called "the divine Argüelles."

As the army reigned supreme, in the person of Espartero as Regent, the counter-influence of Argüelles in the palace was very beneficial.

The Royal Guard, both outside and inside the palace, was now formed of the famous halberdiers, and it was on the night of October 7, 1841, that the valour of this body of soldiers was put to an unexpected test.

General Don Manuel de la Concha and General Leon plotted with Queen Maria Cristina to get possession of the persons of the young Princesses, carry them off to France, and hand them over to Don Evaristo Perez de Castro and a Canon, a partisan of the ex-Regent, by whom they would be escorted to their mother in Paris; and for this bold proceeding they had only a small number of soldiers. General Concha was to get possession of the person of the Regent, whilst General Leon was to carry off the Princesses from the palace. General Dulce was the guardian angel of the little girls that night. He was standing on the landing of the grand staircase, when he saw a company of armed soldiers coming up the steps, under the command of a young lieutenant called Boria.

"Where are you going?" asked Dulce.

"Where my duty takes me," was the curt reply.

"Then, you ought to stop your men in this shameful course; you are young, and to-morrow you will repent your conduct."

As he did not reply, Dulce checked his progress by putting his sword to his breast; but the young man stepped aside, and cried with a loud voice: "Lads, fire!"

But here General Concha interceded by exclaiming: "Stop, Manolito, stop the firing! For God's sake remember we are in Her Majesty's palace!"

So the firing was stopped, and the little girls, alarmed at the noise, fell into each other's arms, and cried with fright, whilst the Countess of Mina strove to still their fears. The noise of firing was heard down the corridors and the staircases known by the names of those of the Lions and the Ladies. General Dulce was not content with quelling the invasion of the palace by firing down the chief staircase to prevent the ascent of any interloper, but, leaving Barrientos in command of half the Guard at that spot, he went with the other half into the Salon of the Ambassadors, and there fired on the insurgents from the windows, until the whole Plaza de la Armeria was swept free from any more possible invaders of the royal abode.

In the meanwhile Boria, Don Diego Leon, and others, were caught in the Campo del Moro, the gardens of the palace. No mercy was shown to the would-be perpetrators of such a deed as the kidnapping of the royal children, and Diego de Leon, who had been covered with laurels for his brilliant services in the civil war, was shot with his accomplices without demur.

In the meanwhile General Espartero, in his Palace of la Buena Vista, was ignorant of the tragic scenes enacted at the palace until they were over. Brought thither by the sound of firearms, he arrived just as the insurrectionary force had been driven from the palace, and hastening up the staircase stained with blood, he found the royal children in their room weeping bitterly and much terrified, albeit at the time of the alarming scene they had shown more courage than could have been expected at such an early age. The Regent led the little girls to a window of the palace to still the fears of the people, who had hastened from all quarters at the noise of the firing, and the halberdiers who had defended their young Queen and her sister so bravely were all publicly applauded, promoted, and subsequently given the Cross of San Fernando. The fact of gunshot penetrating the royal apartment was unprecedented in history, and although the halberdiers pressed into the room to protect the royal children, they abstained from firing there on the invaders without, for fear of hurting those in their charge. When the Cortes opened, Espartero escorted the Princesses to the ceremony, and they were received with enthusiastic demonstrations of loyalty.

A short time afterwards Argüelles had to insist on the Order of the Palace, by which the French Ambassador was not allowed entry to the palace without official permission from the Regent.

When the Infante Don Francisco and Luisa Carlota decided to go to Spain to see what personal influence could do in obtaining power over their nieces, the King of France did all he could to prevent the fulfilment of the plan. Difficulties were put in the way of the illustrious travellers having horses for the journey, but Luisa Carlota exclaimed: "This new obstacle will not stop us, as, if we can't get horses, we will go on foot."

The exiled Queen-mother did all she could to influence her children against their aunt, and she placed within the leaves of a book of fashions, which she sent them from Paris, a paper which ran thus: "Do not trust that woman! She causes nothing but disgrace and ruin. Her words are all lies; her protestations of friendship are deceptions; her presence is a peril. Beware, my child. Your aunt wants to get rule over your mind and your heart to deceive you, and to claim an affection of which she is unworthy."

It was in 1842 that, eluding the vigilance of the Countess of Mina, the lady-in-chief of the royal children, Luisa Carlota managed to see a good deal of her young niece Isabel. The Infanta constantly joined the young Queen in her walks, and, not content with talking to the young girl about her cousin Don Francisco, so as to make her think of him as an eligible parti, she one day gave her niece a portrait of her son in his uniform as Captain of the Hussars. This portrait Isabella was seen to show to her little sister, and so annoyed was the Marchioness of Belgida, the chief Lady-in-Waiting, at what she considered the breach of confidence on the part of the Infanta, that she resigned her post. Argüelles had striven to warn Luisa Carlota against the imprudence of her course, for the question of the young Queen's marriage was one in which the dignity of the Government, the honour of the Queen, and the good name of the Regent, had all to be considered. Therefore any attempt to compromise the Queen by forcing any opinion from her which could not be based on experience was detrimental to all concerned. In the Cortes he said: "I do not believe in absolute isolation for a young Queen, but I think she ought to be surrounded by those who will give her a good example of prudence and self-reflection." On the day that the Marchioness of Belgida's resignation was accepted the widowed Countess of Mina was raised to be a grandee of Spain of the first order, and she was appointed to the post vacated by the Countess. Then, in pursuance of the opinion of the Ministers, Espartero had the Princesses taken to Zaragossa so as to prevent further intrigues about the Queen's marriage.

In the "Estafeta del Palacio Real," Antonio Bermejo compares Olozaga with Argüelles. "He was," he says, "austere like Argüelles, who might be a little brusque, but never had a word or a single phrase left the lips of this old man which could sully the purity of a Princess. Moreover, the new guardian of the Queen was so dense that he let a book be circulated in the royal apartment, called 'Theresa, the Philosopher,' which was said to be at the root of much of the light behaviour of our girls. Who allowed this book in the palace? Whence came this vile work, calculated to pollute the throne of San Ferdinand? Narvaez and Gonzalez Brabo saw the book lying on a chimney-piece in the palace, and they indignantly cast it into the fire. It was thus that people sought to shake the foundation of the throne; it was thus that the seed of corruption was sown which resulted in so much weakness and failure!"

VIII.

MINISTERIAL DIFFICULTIES IN THE PALACE
1843

There is doubtless truth in the opinion that the wish of the Government for the majority of the Queen to be declared at the age of thirteen instead of fourteen proceeded from the desire of self-interested personages to rid the country of the Regent, and hasten the time when the power would be fully in the hands of the young Sovereign, when it could be turned to the designs of the Moderates.

This project soon took form by the Ministry presenting a petition to Isabella, saying:

"The nation wishes and desires to be governed by Your Majesty yourself. Your Majesty will have heard the result of the vote taken in the Cortes which is about to assemble, and there the oath required by the Constitution from a constitutional monarch will be received by the same Cortes."

So on November 8, 1843, the proposal was carried by a majority of 157 over 16, and Queen Isabel was endowed with full power as Queen of the realm—a Queen of only thirteen years of age, whose education had been grossly neglected, and who was inclined to follow the dictates of an undisciplined sensual nature.

Don Salustiano de Olozaga was then appointed President of the Ministry which had supported the deed, whilst Francisco Serrano, who was subsequently to play such an important part in the history of Spain, remained Minister of War, and Frias Minister of the Marine.

But on November 29 the nation was astounded by the publication in the Gazette of the decree for the dissolution of the Government which had put the full power in the young Queen's hand.

The reason for this course was not far to seek. Olozaga was not only anxious to free himself from a Parliament with a majority of Moderates (Tories), but he wished to be freed from the influence of Narvaez, who represented the influence of the Queen-mother in the palace. It was the fact of this influence which had decided both Cortina and Madoz to refuse office.

The fact of the Provisional Government having appointed Olozaga guardian of the young Queen showed that he was known to have great influence over her, and whilst holding that appointment he had been flattered by the grant of the decoration of the Golden Fleece. This distinction was declared by some to have been the outcome of his own astuteness, and it certainly made him unpopular.

The decree for the dissolution of the Parliament was promptly followed by incriminating whispers against the President of the Council.

Mysterious allusions were made to Olozaga having been so wanting in respect to his Queen that he insisted with undue force on the dissolution of the Parliament, and when she objected and wished to quit the apartment, he locked the door, and forcibly drew her back to the table, where he made her sign the document.

"There are," says Don Juan Rico y Amat, "those who say that this report was got up by the Moderates on the exaggerated story of the young Queen, as they wished to get him out of power; but this theory is opposed by the difficulty of believing that a story which tended to lessen the dignity of the Crown could have arisen only through Isabella herself, and those acquainted with the Minister knew the story was in accordance with his imperious, impetuous nature, well known in the palace. It had, moreover, often been noticed that the Prime Minister had entered the royal apartments with a freedom unbefitting the respect due to royalty."

Olozaga wrote to General Serrano, saying that the fact of the Queen sending him a letter saying she would be glad to have the decree, granted at the instance of Olozaga, returned to her, for the rectification of the first lines, saying, "For grave reason of my own I have just dissolved," etc., showed the absurdity of the invention that it had been obtained from her by force. "But if anybody," continued Olozaga, "still insists on such an idea, I will have the honour of suggesting a means whereby the truth will be declared in my presence."

None of the Moderates surrounding the Queen had the courage to seize the reins of government at this time of confusion, and Narvaez himself, whose power in the palace was well known, and whose position as Captain-General of Madrid would have assured him of a large number of followers, hesitated to take the rudder of the deserted ship.

Whilst all was hesitation in the audience chamber, a young man suddenly made his appearance, and passed with fearless step and bold bearing through the assembly of timorous people, right up to within two steps to the throne in the Salon of Ambassadors, and there assumed the leadership which was shunned by those who could have claimed it, by exclaiming in a loud, commanding tone: "The Queen before all! A revolution or I...." And thus by this splendid coup the premiership was taken by Gonzalez Brabo, a man almost unknown in Madrid, except for his talent as a journalist.

His paper, El Guirigay, had been prohibited for its gross attacks on the Queen-mother, and his Liberal ideas were well known. The splendid coolness and courage with which this young man thus contravened the storm of revolution in the very palace itself was calculated to arouse the hatred of the populace, who had looked to a revolution as a reform in all the conditions which make life burdensome.

Thus three days later, when Gonzalez Brabo crossed the Plaza de Oriente for his audience with the Queen at the palace, his coach was stopped by a mob, and the threatening attitude of the people would have checked anyone less cool and determined in his course.

The day of the reopening of the Congress after its suspension for the formation of the new Cabinet was a very anxious one, for it was clearly seen that the Queen had either been treated with flagrant disrespect or her report of the Minister's conduct had been untrue.

The mace-bearers, with their plumed hats and their breasts bearing the embroidered arms of the city, were standing in statuesque immobility on their elevated places directly under the canopy at the head of the chamber. Every seat was filled; the boxes had their full complement of ladies, and outsiders and representatives of the press crowded the gangways. The President of the Congress sat at the official table, flanked by his officials, and all was expectation when the slight, dapper figure of Brabo, dressed in black and bearing the scarlet portfolio of office under his arm, walked with determined step to the seat of honour on the black* bench of the Ministers, and from thence returned the astonished glances of the deputies with a scornful smile and a contemptuous look. After waiting for the storm of dissentient remarks to subside, the Minister rose to his feet, and in clear, concise tones declared that he had been summoned by the Queen to the palace at 11.30 on November 3, and, being admitted to the royal presence, he found that the audience included all the staff of the gentiles hombres, including General Domingo Dulce, who had distinguished himself so bravely on the night of the attempted kidnapping of the little Princesses; Don Maurice Carlos de Onis, President of the Senate; the Duke of Rivas; the Count of Ezpeleta; the Marquis of Peñaflorida, and the Marquis of San Felices, Secretary of the Senate, with Don Pedro José Pidal, President of the Congress of Deputies, the President of the Academy of Languages, etc. The gathering also included the Patriarch of the Indias and the Notary of the King. And it was in the presence of this august assembly that Her Majesty had made the following declaration: "On the evening of the 28th of last month, Olozaga proposed my signing a decree for the dissolution of the Cortes, and I replied that I did not wish to sign it, having, among other reasons, the fact that this Cortes had declared me to be of age. Olozaga insisted; I again objected, rising from my seat and proceeding to the door at the left-hand side of the table. Olozaga intercepted my passage and locked the door. Upon this I turned to the other door, but he then stepped to that

* The Ministerial seats are now upholstered in blue.

one, which he also locked. Then, catching me by the dress, he made me sit down, and seized me by the hand and forced me to sign the document. Before leaving me he told me to say nothing of the occurrence to anybody, but this I declined to promise."

"Then," continued Brabo, "at Her Majesty's request, we all signed the royal declaration, for its transmittance to the archives."

It was with great dignity and cleverness that Olozaga followed the statement of Brabo by refuting the points, holding his own as to his innocence, and yet not incriminating the Queen of untruth. When the unfortunate man had entered the Cortes with his brothers, cries of "Death to him!" came from a box filled with officers of the regiment of San Fernando, whilst shouts of "Viva!" came from other directions.

"Happen what may," said Olozaga, "I deserve the confidence of the Queen, which I won as a Minister;" and it was in a voice trembling with emotion that he continued: "The life I have led justifies me—the person of my heart, my daughter, my friends. My colleagues have all found me always an upright man, incapable of failing in my duties, and this opinion I cannot sacrifice to the Queen, nor to God, nor to the Universe. Being a man of integrity, I must show myself as such before the world, even if it were on the steps of the scaffold itself."

It is difficult to get an impartial opinion upon this episode, so fraught with importance and so conclusive of the short-sighted policy of putting the kingdom into the hands of a young girl of thirteen, who was utterly inexperienced in the art of government, as the Regent had lived away from the palace, and fate had sundered her from mother, aunts, uncles, and relatives, who, in any other station of life, might have aided her with their counsels. In the excitement of the moment the Minister had doubtless treated the Queen as he would his own daughter, and, keenly anxious to gain the decree which would empower him to rid himself of the majority of Moderates in the House, Olozaga had not stopped to consider how an exaggerated report might colour his action to the tone of that of a man guilty of gross lèse-majesté. The Queen was but a child in his eyes, and when she demurred at the seeming cruelty and ingratitude of dissolving a Cabinet which had been so favourable to the anticipation of her majority, it is probably true that the Minister patted her familiarly on the wrist, and said, with a smile of satisfaction and superiority: "I will accustom My Lady to such cruelties!"

The return of the Queen-mother was now solemnly demanded by a deputation of grandees, senators, and deputies. The necessity of the young Queen having a person of experience at her side was eloquently set forth; and those who were envious of the power of Gonzalez Brabo eagerly advised a course which would curtail his influence and lead to the supremacy of the Moderates. So Maria Cristina returned to Spain on February 28, 1844, arriving at Barcelona on March 4, and at Madrid on March 21.

However, Gonzalez Brabo managed to retain power under the new state of affairs, albeit at the price of being termed a traitor by his own party.

In spite of being accused of acting as a panderer to the Moderates, Olozaga's advice to the Queen to legalize the marriage of her mother with Don Fernando Muñoz was a step of good policy. The ceremony in the chapel of the royal palace was celebrated by the Patriarch of the Indias.

The husband was endowed with the decorations and dignities of his position, and the Queen published the following decree:

"With due regard to the weighty reasons set forth by my august mother, Doña Maria Cristina de Bourbon, I have authorized her, after listening to the counsel of my Ministry, to contract a marriage with Don Fernando Muñoz, Duke of Rianzares, and I declare that the fact of her contracting this marriage of conscience, albeit with a person of unequal rank, in no way lessens my favour and love; and she is to retain all the honours and prerogatives and distinctions due to her as Queen-mother. But her husband is only to enjoy the honours, prerogatives, and distinctions, due to his class and title; and the children of this marriage are to remain subject to Article 12, of Law 9, Title 11, Book 10, of the Novisima Recopilacion, being able to inherit the free property of their parents according to the laws.

"Signed by the Royal Hand
and the Minister of Grace and Justice,
"Luis Mayans.
"Given in the Palace,
"October 11, 1844."

Wherever the young Queen appeared with her sister in the country, their simple, unsophisticated ways filled the people with love and admiration. One day, being only accompanied by two Ladies-in-Waiting, they went to a village fête not very far from San Sebastian.

"Do you come from San Sebastian?" asked the peasants, with the freedom characteristic of the country-folk in Spain.

"Yes, we do," replied the Queen.

"And do you belong to the military?"

"No," said the Queen, repressing a smile, "we are not military people."

"But at least you are Castilians?"

"Yes," returned the Queen promptly; "we are girls from Madrid."

"And do you like this part?" queried the interlocutor.

"Very much," replied the Queen. "It is very cheerful."

"Well," continued the peasant, with frank familiarity, "sit down a bit and see the lads dance."

"Thank you very much," replied the Queen, "but we must be going."

"You will have noticed," rejoined the peasant, "that the roads are very bad, and you will get very tired. These mountains are only fit for strong feet, and not little delicate ones like yours."

"Never mind," returned Isabel; "we like to accustom ourselves to everything. You don't know, then, who we are?"

"It is not easy to guess," was the answer; "but you are certainly daughters of people of position and money."

Then Isabel said: "I am the Queen."

"The Queen! the Queen!" cried the people with delight; and cider, fruits, and cakes, were pressed upon the royal party.

The Queen and her sister received constant signs of affection in the neighbourhood of Guipuzcoa. They went to Pampeluna to receive the Duke and Duchess of Nemours and the Duke of Aumale, the arrival of the distinguished French guests was celebrated in the city by a magnificent banquet and bull-fight, and the distinguished Frenchmen stayed with the Count of Ezpeleta.

The fall of Miraflores, the able Prime Minister, was heralded by the evident desire of both the Queens for a change of Ministry, and those who wished to compass the fall of the Prime Minister were listened to by the royal ladies.

Miraflores found Queen Isabella alone one day in the palace, and Her Majesty said to the Minister:

"I have heard that the scandal this afternoon in the Congress has been so great that the President of the Congress put on his hat in his want of consideration for the Court."

Miraflores explained that this act proceeded from no want of respect for the Cortes.

"Nevertheless it must be dissolved to-morrow," was the reply.

Narvaez became Minister of War as well as President of the Congress. The part played at the palace in the change of Ministries is seen in the scene between Pacheco and the Queen-mother.

Maria Cristina remarked to the Minister that the Government would not last long. Upon this Pacheco placed two ounces of gold upon the mantelpiece, saying:

"I bet you that money that the Cabinet will not fall to-morrow as you say."

Whereupon the Queen took another two ounces from her purse, and placing them beside those of the diplomat, she said:

"The bet is made: if the Ministry does not fall to-morrow, the money is yours; if it does, it is mine." And the Ministry did fall.

This insidious influence of the camarilla was daily becoming more dangerous. Presumptuous and illegal, it held its sway over all that was prudent and constitutional, and thus the intrigues of the palace came between the Cortes and the throne, and the country and the Queen, exercising power to the detriment of the national representation, the throne, the nation, and the Sovereign. "The royal palace," says Don Antonio Bermejo, "was a gilded cage where men were slaves to envy and idleness."

IX

ROYAL MATRIMONIAL SCHEMES—HOW ISABELLA'S SISTER FLED FROM PARIS IN 1848
1843–1848

Isabella's marriage was now a burning subject of discussion and intrigue. The objection offered to her marriage with one of the sons of the Infanta Luisa Carlota was the hatred reigning between the mother of the proposed bridegroom and Queen Maria Cristina.

Louis Philippe of France had also his own designs in these marriage prospects, and would fain have united the Dauphin to the young Queen. But, as we know, England put her veto upon this alliance, as it would have upset the balance of European power; so the French King had to be contented with the marriage of his younger son, the Duke of Montpensier, with Isabel's sister Luisa Fernanda.

There was a strong party in favour of the Queen's marriage with the Count of Montemolin, son of Don Carlos, as this union would have put an end to the rivalry reigning between these two branches of the Royal Family.

But finally attention was turned to the sons of Don Francisco de Paula as the most suitable candidates for the hand of the Queen. Miraflores explains that it was natural for the Duke of Cadiz, the eldest son of the Infante, to be preferred by the existing Cabinet in Spain and the Queen-mother, as he was a quiet, judicious Prince, who had accepted and fulfilled with honour the post of Colonel of a cavalry regiment; whilst Don Henry was of a turbulent disposition, whose conduct left much to be desired at the Court of the Queen-mother, to whom he had written from Bayonne very disrespectfully, and in Brussels he had distinguished himself by publishing ideas which bordered on being revolutionary.

Whilst the royal party was at Pampeluna a mysterious document in French fell into the hands of the Minister of Foreign Affairs, signed "Legitimista." The document ran thus:

"To the Minister of Foreign Affairs.

"Before the Duc de Nemours and the Duc d'Aumale left Paris as the emissaries of His Majesty the great 'Père de famille,' French legitimists knew that the meeting at Pampeluna was merely a matter of form. The Duc d'Aumale cannot be the husband of Doña Isabel; his father knows it; M. Guizot and M. Bresson know it; and the Queen, wife of the Citizen-King, knows it, and she is the most strongly opposed to the union.

"The Duc de Montpensier will be the husband of the Infanta; this is what is arranged, and what will take place. The Citizen Louis has made a plan by which he thinks that in time Montpensier will occupy the throne of Spain by the side of the immediate heiress, Luisa Fernanda, because experienced doctors in medicine have declared to Bresson that the Queen is very ill with an hereditary disease which will take her to the grave. Why has not the Princess got it? That is a mystery which time will reveal. Who will give his hand in marriage to Queen Isabel? We hear that the candidature of Prince Henry is in favour. But this illustrious youth cannot be the husband of the Queen, neither can his brother, Don Francisco de Asis.

"The Minister whom I have the honour of addressing is ignorant of the reason, and I can give it to him.

"The Minister must know that when Princess Luisa Carlota was on her death-bed she did not, even in this sad moment, forget the troubles of her sister; and impelled by conscientious scruples, she sent for her illustrious sons, and, taking them each by the right hand, she said these solemn words to them, in a sad tone and with a tenderness which was truly Christian: 'My sons, I wish to reach heaven, I wish to quit you and the world without remorse, and therefore I declare I repent having contributed through imprudent affection to thwarting the legitimate succession of the Crown of

114

Spain, and this I swear on my salvation. So I command you as a mother, as a Princess, and as a repentant sinner, to swear that neither of you will aspire to the hand of Isabella.'"

Narvaez showed that this document was a fraud, as, at the death of the Infanta, Don Henry was at some distance from Madrid, and Francisco was at Pampeluna.

Isabella's own feelings about her marriage were hardly taken into consideration at all. As a matter of fact, she had been more inclined to Prince Henry, the younger son of Doña Luisa Carlota, than to Francisco, and it will be remembered that even as a child she had admired the portrait of the Prince, which had been secretly sent by the mother to the young Queen; but inclination had no part in the negotiations, which were regulated entirely by self-interest and policy, so the tide of influence was soon seen to be in favour of the eldest son of Prince Francisco de Paula.

Don Henry was furious when he found he was left out in the cold in the negotiation for the marriages of Isabella and her sister.

In a letter to Bulwer Lytton he writes:

"The old man at the Tuileries is very delighted and pleased. He has written three letters full of hypocritical words, telling the great Mama that she has drawn the first prize, and that she is very fortunate to be marrying her daughters to Paquito (Francisco) and Montpensier. A French fellow has arrived at the palace. You will recollect that I told you before last night that, judging from the appearance of things, you and I were going to have our noses put out of joint.

"Istarez is very pleased. Cristina is delighted, and from what I hear the weddings will take place very soon. When I see you I will give you more particulars, which I cannot trust to the pen."

The Queen-mother had been inclined to the idea of the Count of Trapani, her brother, who had been educated in a Jesuit college at Naples, as her son-in-law; but, as this idea had not been welcome to the Government, attention had again been turned to one of the sons of the Infante Don Francisco de Paula. Don Francisco, Duke of Cadiz, the eldest, was favoured by France, whilst England gave preference to Don Henry, Duke of Seville. As Miraflores says, it was natural for the Queen-mother to prefer the eldest son of Don Francisco, as he was a quiet Prince and one who had fulfilled his duties with credit as Colonel of a cavalry regiment; whilst Don Henry was of a more turbulent nature, and his antagonistic conduct to the Queen-mother had excited some disturbance in the palace. In the letters he sent from Brussels to Madrid he had manifested a revolutionary spirit, which filled the Moderates with alarm. However, poor Isabel preferred this hot-headed Prince to his more peaceful-minded brother, and long were the arguments the young Queen held with her mother against the project of her union with the elder brother. Fortunately, however, the young Queen seemed somewhat pleased with the appearance of Don Francisco, and at the fêtes given in honour of the engagement she seemed very cheerful.

In an interview with Queen Maria Cristina, Bulwer Lytton said: "I can understand your joy as a mother at seeing your eldest daughter destined for a Prince who will make for the happiness of the royal domestic hearth; but as to the marriage of the Infanta——"

Here Cristina interrupted him, saying: "It is decided that her union with Montpensier will take place on the same day as that of the Queen."

The Duke of Rianzares had evidently favoured the alliance of the Princess Luisa Fernanda with the Duke of Montpensier, for when the matter was fully arranged Louis Philippe wrote to Queen Maria Cristina:

"Please give my kind regards to the Duke of Rianzares, and thank him for the part he has taken in the matter I have so much at heart."

So France and her supporters in Spain gained the day, and the double wedding of the young sisters was fixed for October 10, 1846. It was with all the magnificent state for which the Court of Spain is famed that the reception by Isabel and Fernanda took place at the palace (for the publication of the marriage contracts) in the Salon of the Ambassadors. Alexandre Dumas was among the distinguished Frenchmen accompanying the bridegroom of the Infanta Fernanda, and the great author attended a bull-fight with the noblemen as toreadors, and the fêtes all the week were of surpassing splendour.

The religious ceremony itself was held in the Church of Atocha with all imaginable pomp and splendour. The Patriarch of the Indias received the brides at the door of the church, and noticeable among the French guests was Alexandre Dumas, author of "The Three Musketeers." All the Diplomatic Corps were there with the exception of the English.

In the ceremony the Patriarch placed upon the open palms of the Queen's bridegroom the thirteen pieces of money pledged as his dowry, which was then passed by the bridegroom to the hands of his bride, saying, "This ring and this money I give you as a sign of marriage," and the Queen replied, "I accept them."

The same ceremony was used with the Infanta and her bridegroom, and then the prelate, with his mitre and crook, escorted the royal couples to the altar, and there read the Mass. During the Epistle the Patriarch presented the candles, veils, and conjugal yoke, and at the conclusion of the Gospel the Patriarch turned to the Queen and her bridegroom, and said to the latter: "I give Your Majesty a companion, and not a servant; Your Majesty must love her as Christ loves His Church." And then the same words were said to the other couple. The periodical which published this account of the wedding remarked that the Queen and her husband looked smiling and pleased, but the Infanta looked sad.

The attempt on the life of the Queen soon after her marriage caused great excitement, and the trial of Angel de la Riva, a native of Santiago, in Galicia, and editor of a paper called El Clamor Publico, who was caught just after firing the shot, was followed with the deepest interest.

The testimony of Don Manuel Matheu, officer of the Royal Guard of Halberdiers, a man of thirty-five years of age, gives some idea of the etiquette of the time.

He declared that on May 4, 1847, he was on duty, so when the Queen returned from her drive he went as usual to receive her at the foot of the staircase with his little company of six halberdiers, and a Captain with a lamp, and two other attendants with their

117

axes. On descending from the carriage, Her Majesty said to him: "Do you know that on passing through the Calle de Alcalá two shots were fired at me."

The officer returned: "Two shots at Your Majesty?"

"Yes," was the reply; "you cannot doubt it; I saw them get down from a carriage or cab."

The Colonel was not aware if Her Majesty said an open carriage or a shut one.

"I felt something," she added, "pass over my forehead which hurt me."

"And as this was evident," continued the officer, "I could but give credit to Her Majesty's words. Moreover, Her Highness the Infanta Doña Maria Josefa added: 'There is no doubt of the fact, for I myself saw the men.'"

Then Her Majesty told the witness he was to inform the Ministers of what had happened. This he did, leaving a message at the door of the Secretary of State, and sending a halberdier to inform the Minister of War.

It is not necessary to give further particulars of the long trial of the accused. He was, as we know, first condemned to be beaten to death, and being saved from this dreadful fate by the able defence of Perez Hernandez, he was in November, 1847, condemned to twenty years' imprisonment. But on July 23, 1849, the Queen showed her generous spirit by commuting the sentence to four years' exile from Madrid and all the royal resorts, as Her Majesty nobly gave full benefit to the representation of the murderous lawyer's madness, or the influence exercised by others.

In the rapid and unexpected flight of the French Royal Family from the Palace of the Tuileries, Princess Clementina, wife of the Duke of Saxony, and the Duchess of Montpensier, were separated from the King and Queen. When the Duke of Montpensier accompanied his father to the carriages waiting for them in the Place de la Concorde, he thought he would have no difficulty in returning to fetch his wife, who had been confined for some days in her apartments on account of her interesting condition of health. But the crowds which had collected meanwhile in the gardens made it impossible for the Prince to return to the palace. He had fortunately left the Princess in the care of some of his suite and Monsieur Julio de Lasteyrie, who was distinguished for his loyalty and popularity. So the Duke mounted his horse and followed his father.

Directly Monsieur Lasteyrie saw that the palace was invaded, he gave his arm to the Duchess of Montpensier, and in the confusion of the moment they passed unnoticed from the gates and mingled with the crowd. Monsieur de Lasteyrie hoped to arrive in time to put the Princesses into the royal carriages, which, however, started off at a gallop just as they arrived within sight of them.

So Lasteyrie escorted the royal ladies to the house of his mother. In a few minutes Princess Clementina left the timely refuge, and continued her way to the Trianon, where she met her father; whilst the Duchess of Montpensier remained for the night under the protection of Madame de Lasteyrie.

There she heard from her husband at Dreux that she was to join him at the Castle of Eu, whither the King was going.

But the monarch found it impossible to get to this haven, so when the young Princess arrived there the following day she found the place deserted. Hearing an alarming rumour that a party of workmen were coming to pillage the Palace of Eu, as they had ransacked the one at Neuilly, the Duchess quietly left the place, and repaired to the house of Monsieur Estancelin, a diplomat of the Bavarian Embassy. Under the escort of this gentleman and that of General Thierry she started off for Brussels. On passing through Abbeville, the sight of the carriage attracted attention, and the people cried: "There are royal fugitives in that coach!" Monsieur Estancelin put his head out of the window, and, as his name was known in the district, he declared that the lady was his wife, and he was going abroad with her. To put the people off the scent, he then gave orders to the postilion to drive to the house of a friend of his, well known for his republican opinions. Arrived at the house, Estancelin whispered in the ear of his friend the name and rank of the lady under his escort.

But the man, in fear of the consequences of the discovery of the secret, declined to give his aid in the matter, in spite of all arguments of both gentlemen in charge of the Princess, setting forth the dreadful consequences of her being frightened or subjected to imprisonment in her delicate condition.

It was all in vain; the republican declined to receive the Princess, and they had to turn away from the door in despair, for several people had gathered in front of the house, curious to see who could be seeking shelter at such a late hour.

So Monsieur Estancelin bade General Thierry conduct the lady out of the town by a particular gate leading to the bank of the river, whilst he went in search of other friends, who might aid him to get fresh horses and a carriage with which he would meet them.

So the poor Princess started forth with her military ally. Unfortunately, the gate of the town led through a narrow exit only meant for pedestrians. So they wandered along in the cold rain, picking their way over the stones and rubbish of this out-of-the-way road. The General, alarmed at the drenched condition of the Princess and her evident exhaustion and fatigue, decided that he had better let her sit on a stone to rest, whilst he went in search of a guide or a refuge.

The officer hastened along the road, fearing to call the attention of the enemy to the lady in his care, and yet anxious to get a guide to the rendezvous appointed by Estancelin. Finally, to his delight, he was accosted by a friend of Estancelin, who had sent him in search of the couple, and, quickly returning to the Princess, they escorted her to the carriage which was waiting on the highroad to Brussels.

"What dreadful adventures this awful night!" exclaimed General Thierry, as the Duchess of Montpensier sought to recover one of her shoes which had slipped off her weary wet feet in the mud.

"Never mind," returned the brave Princess; "I prefer these adventures to the monotony of the round table of work in the sumptuous salons of the Tuileries."

The relief with which the letter announcing the safety of her sister was received by Queen Isabella can well be imagined, as in those days the limited communication by telegraph was stopped on account of the fog.

The fall of Louis Philippe relieved England of the fear of the upset of the balance of European power from the astuteness with which he had arranged the marriages of the Spanish Queen and her sister.

There was no doubt of the intentions which had led to the Duke of Montpensier being the brother-in-law of the Queen, and the unsuspicious girl was a prey to the reports which were spread by the ambitious Orleanists.

X.

A ROYAL QUARREL AND THE RECONCILIATION

It was soon seen that General Serrano's influence with the Queen surpassed the ordinary grade, and the Moderates were alarmed.

There were two parties in the royal palace—one on the side of the Queen, and the other on that of the King; and the leaders of these parties fostered the difference between the royal couple.

Francisco Pacheco, the King's partisan, declared that a President of the Congress was wanted who would give more independence to the Crown, and who would receive the counsels of an intelligent husband of the Sovereign; for the King-Consort should not be in a position so secondary to that of the illustrious mother-in-law that she can boast of having more power than he has.

When Isabella saw that Queen Maria Cristina's influence in the State was much resented by the Ministers, she advised her to go on a visit to her daughter, the Duchess of Montpensier, and this counsel was followed.

However, the want of union between the King and Queen was soon evident to the world, and when it was announced that Isabella was going to spend the rest of the summer at Aranjuez alone, whilst the King remained in Madrid, it was seen that the Serrano influence had become serious enough to cause a separation between the royal couple. Isabella's naturally good heart seemed softened when she was leaving the palace, and it was evidently remorse which prompted her to look anxiously back from the carriage, in search of a glimpse of the husband at one of the windows of the royal pile. But the coach rattled on, and the Queen's search was in vain; whilst her sad face, with its traces of tears, showed that things might have been better had not the differences of the royal couple been fostered, for their own ends, by intriguers of the camarilla.

Forsaken by his wife, Francisco followed the advice of his friends, to enjoy himself in his own way; so he repaired to the Palace of the Pardo, where banquets, hunting-parties, and other festivities deadened his sense of injury at his wife's conduct.

Those interested in the welfare of the land were disappointed when the birthday of the Queen was celebrated by her holding a reception alone at Aranjuez, whilst the King had a hunting expedition at the Pardo. The Ministers came to the reception at Aranjuez, and then promptly returned to the capital, leaving the Queen with her trinity of Bulwer, Serrano, and Salamanca. General Salamanca was at last sent by the King to Aranjuez to advise Isabella to return, but she would not accept the condition of a change in the Serrano position.

This refusal made the King decline to assist at the reception of the Pope's Nuncio at Aranjuez, and he was forbidden to return to the royal Palace of Madrid.

Benavides, a courtier, anxious to heal this unhappy division in the Royal Family, came to Francisco, and said:[*]

"This separation cannot go on; it is not good for the Queen or for Your Majesty."

"That I can understand," returned the King; "but she has chosen to outrage my dignity as husband, and this when my demands are not exaggerated. I know that Isabelita does not love me, and I excuse her, because I know that our union was only for State reasons, and not from inclination; and I am the more tolerant as I, too, was unable to give her any affection myself. I have not objected to the course of dissimulation, and I have always shown myself willing to keep up appearances to avoid this disgraceful break; but Isabelita, either from being more ingenuous or more vehement than I am, could not fulfil this hypocritical duty—this sacrifice for the good of the nation. I married because I had to marry, because the position of King is flattering. I took the part, with its advantages. I have no right to throw away the good fortune

* "Estafeta del Palacio Real," Bermejo, vol. ii.

which I gained from the arrangement. So I made up my mind to be tolerant, if they were equally so with me, and I was never upset at the presence of a favourite."

Here the King was interrupted by Benavides saying:

"Allow me, Sire, to observe one thing. That which you now say with regard to tolerance of a favourite is not in accordance with your present line of conduct, for do you not demand the withdrawal of General Serrano before agreeing to the reconciliation we are asking?"

Then, with a singular calmness, the King returned:

"I do not deny that this Serrano is the main drawback to an agreement with Isabelita, for the dismissal of the favourite would be immediately followed by the reconciliation desired by my wife; but I would have tolerated him, I would have exacted nothing, if he had not hurt me personally by insulting me with unworthy names, failing in respect to me, and not giving me proper consideration—and therefore I hate him. He is a little Godoy, who has not known how to behave; for he at least got over Charles IV. before rising to the favour of my grandmother."

The Minister of the Government listened with astonishment to the King's words. Don Francisco saw it, and continued:

"The welfare of fifteen million people demands this and other sacrifices. I was not born for Isabelita, nor Isabelita for me, but the country must think the contrary. I will be tolerant, but the influence of Serrano must cease, or I will not make it up."

Benavides replied that the Ministry deplored this unhappy "influence," which was getting burdensome to the Queen herself; but Serrano had such a fatal ascendancy everywhere, and had won over to his side the opposing elements, that any sudden step to put an end to the evil would result in deplorable consequences for the nation. "However, the Ministry has decided to get rid of this pernicious influence," continued Benavides. "It is seeking a way to do so without a collision and its consequences; and one of the things which would help to this course of the Cabinet would be the immediate reconciliation of Your Majesties, as the preliminary to the other steps which will lead to Serrano's overthrow."

The King refused. He said that his dignity demanded the withdrawal of the "influence." Fresh evident proofs had been given that this hateful man was the cause of the Queen's separation from him, and therefore he was not inclined to go back from his word about him.

So Pacheco and all the other Ministers, excepting Salamanca, determined to resign if Serrano did not retire from the Court.

Benavides and Pacheco were among the deputation who petitioned the favourite to agree to this step, but it was in vain. The Ministers went backwards and forwards to La Granja without gaining their purpose. Finally, in pursuance of the Pope's advice, the Queen decided to return to Madrid; and Salamanca, as Prime Minister, went to the Escorial to report the fact to Bulwer.

It must be noted that Salamanca's name was not in the list of Ministers suggested by Narvaez. The Queen wished it to be added, but Narvaez declined to follow suit, as he knew that this statesman was supported by Bulwer, whose dislike of the King was well known; and the way he had spoken of Francisco before his wedding naturally made the King averse to seeing him.

Bulwer worked with Bermejo against Isabella during the premiership of Salamanca, and the publication in The Times of a demand for the royal divorce was due to him.

At last Francisco and Isabella were reconciled. It was on October 13 that the King returned to the capital. He entered the gate of the palace in a carriage drawn by six horses, with a mounted escort of the Guardia Civil. He was dressed quietly in black, and Brunelli, the Pope's Legate, was seated on his left. Narvaez, Count Alcoy, Count Vistahermosa, rode by the coach, and two carriages followed with the high dignitaries of the palace.

The King looked pleased. General Serrano, whom he hated so cordially, had left Madrid, and the Queen was waiting for him at the window. Brunelli was about to follow the royal couple as they walked away after their first meeting, but Narvaez said: "Whither away, Your Eminence? Let them be alone with their tears and kisses. These things are done better without witnesses."

The Queen arrived that day at her dwelling in the Calle de las

125

Rejas. There was a family dinner-party in the evening at the palace, and, in a private interview with her daughter, Maria Cristina begged her to be more discreet in future; and she reminded her that although she had, as a widow, allowed herself to be captivated by a commoner, whilst she was the wife of the King she had never allowed her thoughts to wander beyond the circle of her rank and her duty.

The reckless extravagance of the Queen excited much remark. Courtiers are still living who recollect seeing Isabella give her bracelets to the beggars who sometimes infest the courtyard of the palace.

When Miraflores, who was considered the soul of truth, received a reckless order from the Queen to dispense a certain amount of money on some petitioner, he had the sum put in pieces on a table, and it was only the sight of the large sum which was thus laid before the Queen which showed her the extravagance of her command.

A great influence was soon found to be at work in the palace in the person of Sister Patrocinio, whose brother, Quiroga, was one of the gentlemen-in-waiting.

XI

ATTEMPT ON THE LIFE OF QUEEN ISABELLA —THE OVERTHROW OF THE QUEEN-MOTHER, MARIA CRISTINA 1850–1854

There was much variety of feeling when it was known that an heir to the throne was expected. On the day of the birth, July 12, 1850, the clerics, Ministers, diplomats, officers, and other important personages of the realm, assembled at the palace to pay their respects to the expected infant. But the bells and cannon had hardly announced to the nation the birth of the girl-child when it expired. So the dead form of the infant, which had only drawn breath in this world for five minutes, was brought into the assembly of dignitaries, and after this sad display the gathering dispersed in silence. The kind-heartedness of the Queen was shown in her thoughtful generosity to the nurses who were disappointed of their charge.

"Poor nurses, they must have felt it very much!" she exclaimed. "But tell them not to mind, for they shall be paid the same as if they had had my child."

In February, 1852, an heir to the throne was once more expected, and the birth of the Infanta Isabella was celebrated by the usual solemn presentation. When the King showed the infant to his Ministers, he said to the Generals Castaños and Castroterreño:

"You have served four Kings, and now you have a Princess who may one day be your Sovereign."

It was on February 2, 1852, that the dastardly attempt was made on the life of the Queen, just before leaving the palace for the Church of Atocha, where the royal infant was to be baptized. The

Court procession was passing along the quadrangular gallery, hung with the priceless tapestries only displayed on important occasions, when Manuel Martin Merino, a priest of a parish of Madrid, suddenly darted forward from the spectators lining the way, with the halberdier guard. The petition in the cleric's hand and his garb of a cleric led to his step forward being unmolested, and the Queen turned to him, prepared to take the paper. But the next moment the other hand of the assassin appeared from under his cloak with a dagger, which he swiftly aimed at the royal mother. Fortunately, the Queen's corset turned aside the murderous weapon, and, although blood spurted from her bodice, the wound was not very deep; but she was at once put to bed and placed under the care of the royal physicians.

The royal infant was promptly seized from the arms of its mother at the moment of the attack, by an officer of the Royal Guard, and for this presence of mind the soldier was afterwards given the title of the Marquis of Amparo.

With regard to the assailant, the Queen said to her Ministers: "You have often vexed me by turning a deaf ear to my pleas of mercy for criminals, but I wish this man to be punished immediately." And, with the outraged feeling of the object of such a dastardly deed, Isabella turned to the would-be murderer, and said: "What have I ever done to offend you, that you should have attacked me thus?"

During the trial in the succeeding days the Queen softened to the criminal, and said to her advisers: "No, no! don't kill him for what he did to me!"

However, justice delivered the man to the hangman five days after his deed.

The efforts to discover Merino's accomplices were fruitless, and it was thought that the deed had been prompted more by the demagogue party than by the Carlists.

The cool, cynical manner of the cleric never left him even at the moment of his execution.

When the priest's hair was cut for the last time, he said to the barber: "Don't cut much, or I shall catch cold."

The doomed man's request to say a few words from the scaffold was refused. When asked what he had wished to say, he replied: "Nothing much. I pity you all for having to stay in this world of corruption and misery."

The ovation which the Queen had when she finally went to the Church of Atocha to present the infant surpasses description. Flowers strewed the way, and tears of joy showed the sympathy of the people with the Queen in her capacity as mother, and at her escape from the attempt on her life.

From 1852 to 1854 Isabella failed to please her subjects, and the outburst of loyalty which had followed the attempt on her life gradually waned. Curiously indifferent to what was for her personal interest, as well as for the welfare of the country, Isabella turned a deaf ear to the advice of her Ministers to dissolve a Cabinet which was under the leadership of the Count of San Luis, who was known to be the tool of Queen Maria Cristina, now so much hated by the Spaniards. Miraflores wrote a letter to Isabella, advising the return of Espartero, the Count of Valencia, but the letter never reached its destination.

Remonstrances which had been made upon the Government were now directed straight to the Throne.

"You see," said her advisers, "how the persons whom you have overwhelmed with honours and favours speak against you!"

The Generals O'Donnell and Dulce finally took an active part against the Ministry, supported by the Queen-mother and Rianzares.

The Count of San Luis was a man of fine bearing and charming manners. He had been conspicuous in his early days for his banquets and gallantries, but he had also been known for many a generous deed to his friends; and it was noticeable that when the tide of favour left him he was deserted by all those to whom he had been of service.

The birth of another royal infant in 1854 excited little or no interest in the capital, where discontent with the reigning powers was so evident. General Dulce was accused in the presence of the Queen and San Luis of having conspired against the Throne.

This the officer indignantly denied on the spot, declaring that never could he have believed in the perfidy which had prompted the report.

At last the storm of revolution broke over Madrid, and the parties of the Generals O'Donnell and Dulce came into collision with those of the Government. Insulting cries against the Queen-mother filled the streets, and during the three days' uproar the house of Maria Cristina, in the Calle de las Rejas, was sacked, as well as those of her partisans. The furniture was burned in the street, and Maria Cristina took refuge in the royal palace.

After the Pronunciamento of Vicalvaro and O'Donnell to the troops, it was evident that the soldiers of the Escorial would also revolt against the Government.

It was then that Isabella was filled with the noble impulse to go alone to the barracks of the mutinous regiments and reason personally with them. With her face aglow with confidence in her soldiers and in herself, she said: "I am sure that the generals will come back with me then to Madrid, and the soldiers will return to their barracks shouting 'Vivas' for their Queen."

But this step, which would have appealed with irresistible force to the subjects, was opposed by the Ministers, who objected to a course which would have robbed them of their portfolios by the Sovereign coming to an understanding with those who were opposed to their opinions.

At this time Isabella received from the Infanta Josefa, daughter of the Infanta Louisa Carlota and Francisco de Paula, a letter which showed that the Princess had inherited her mother's hatred of the Queen-mother, Maria Cristina; for she wrote:

"Your Majesty should distrust the artificial and partial counsels of the Queen-mother. This lady, to whom you owe your birth, is sacrificing you to her insatiable greed of gold. Beyond your life you do not owe anything to Maria Cristina. She has done nothing for Spain that you should give her submission and obedience in your conduct as Queen. Hardly had Your Majesty's father gone down to his grave than his widow gave you the pernicious example of an impure love, which began in a scandal, and ended,

130

ten years later, in a morganatic marriage, to the incalculable harm of the country.

"Maria Cristina is lax in the principles of morality, which ought to be the foundation of the education of Princes, and she knew not how to inculcate them in the mind of Your Majesty. Whilst you were a child, she did nothing but accumulate money and arrange for her future booty.

"The disinterestedness and the generous sentiments which enrich Your Majesty's heart, and the high tendencies which have shone in your mind, and which have only been suffocated by the pettiness of your entourage, are exclusively a gift from Heaven, and under favourable circumstances they would have developed into great and glorious deeds. When the time arrived for the marriage of Your Majesty—an event of such import to your destiny—Your Majesty knows that the Queen-mother only used her influence to make you marry a man whose sole merit lay in his power of ministering to her omnivorous nature. Never did a mother behave in such a self-interested way in what concerned her daughter's domestic happiness! And now she continues the soul of the Government, counselling Your Majesty for her own ends, and with utter disregard of the wishes of the people."

This letter, which gives an idea of the dissensions of the Royal Family, and the expression of feeling against Maria Cristina, was shared by the people. Indeed, the hatred of the Queen-mother was publicly shown after she took refuge in the royal palace. The Plaza de los Ministros resounded with the cries from the townsfolk of "Death to Cristina!" A storm of stones broke all the windows of the palace. The soldiers fired on the people. The palace gate of El Principe had to be guarded by two cannon commanding the Plaza de Oriente. Twelve guns were stationed in the great courtyard called the Plaza de las Armas, and all the cavalry at Madrid was summoned to the defence of the royal abode; and during the siege there was serious anxiety that the provisions would not last long.

Queen Isabella sought to encourage and support her mother, but she saw that the stream of public hatred was now too strong to be stemmed.

The arrival of Espartero in Madrid, on July 29, raised the siege of the palace, and the people, delighted at the sight of their favourite leader, gave a loyal ovation to Queen Isabella when she appeared at a window of the palace.

The days from July 17 to August 28 were fraught with anxiety for the Queen of Spain. The cries for the dismissal of the Queen-mother, and for her trial for the appropriation of State moneys, could no longer be silenced, and the day came when the royal lady found that her personal safety demanded her departure from the country. So, accompanied by a mounted escort, Maria Cristina submitted to the decision of Espartero, as the mouthpiece of the people, and she finally bade farewell to her weeping daughter at the palace door, and left the country, never more to return.

Espartero made a crusade against the undue priestly influence at Court. The weak-minded King was quite under the power of "the bleeding nun," as Patrocinio was called, and his constant visits to her apartments in the palace were said to have been in search of spiritual counsel, with which she was supposed to be miraculously endowed by reason of the wounds in her forehead and hands, which refused to be healed, as they were said to be illustrative of those of the Saviour. The Queen and all the Royal Family became hysterically hypnotized by this phenomenon.

But Espartero soon put an end to the matter by having the lady put under the authoritative care of a doctor, who had her hands tied so as to prevent her irritating the wounds; and thus in a short time the supposed miracle was over, and the power of the religieuse and her brother, the Archbishop Claret, was at an end.

Espartero had O'Donnell as his Minister of War. Dissensions broke out again in the Cabinet, and O'Donnell reaped the success of his camarilla influence at the midnight Council meeting held before the Queen in July, 1856. For when Espartero found that his measures for the new Constitution were rejected, he offered his resignation; and then, to his surprise, the Queen, by a prearranged concert, turned to his colleague with her sweetest smile, saying, "I am sure you won't abandon me, will you?" and he was sworn in as Prime Minister the following day.

But O'Donnell had a powerful rival for favour at the palace in the person of Narvaez, a General of some fame, whose alert, dapper little figure, said to have been improved by corsets, made him popular at Court as a dancer.

This officer was extremely arrogant, and noting that the grandees, by right of their special prerogative, stood covered in the royal presence during the ceremony of the King washing the feet of the poor, and feeding them in the historical Hall of Columns, he promptly put his own cocked hat on his head, and bade his officers do the same.

O'Donnell, who was of a heavier, clumsier build than his rival, suffered much at the sight of the success of Narvaez in the arts of society. One day at a state ball at the palace the two Generals stood in readiness to conduct the Queen through the mazes of the rigodon. As Prime Minister, O'Donnell considered that the distinction of taking Isabella's hand for the figures was his by right, but Isabella could not resist the temptation of having for a partner a man distinguished as a follower of Terpsichore, and she therefore singled out Narvaez as her partner.

In a fury at what he considered a public slight, O'Donnell gave in his resignation the next day as President of the Council, and General Narvaez was chosen to fill the vacant place.

It was well known at Court that the British Ambassador, Bulwer Lytton, was working against the Court of Spain in England, and consequently he was an object of great aversion to the military leader of the Government.

Irritated at the Englishman's assumption of authority, Narvaez said one day to Bulwer Lytton that Spain did not interfere with the affairs of Queen Victoria like England did with those of Isabella II. To this remark the British diplomat returned that Victoria did not owe her throne to foreign intervention, as Isabella did.

One day Narvaez was in his bureau in a great state of irritation about some action of the British Ambassador, when Bulwer Lytton was announced. He drew a chair close to Narvaez, and, although the Spaniard pushed his back, drew his seat still closer. Upon this Narvaez jumped up in his excitable manner, and then, wishing to seat himself again, he missed the place and found himself lower than he wished.

Upon this the Ambassador made some remark which added fuel to the fire of the General's wrath, and, advancing to the Englishman, he made him rise from his seat, took him by the neck, and kicked him so that he nearly fell to the ground. The Ambassador took his papers for England that day, and this incident doubtless added to the bitterness with which Bulwer reported on the affairs of Spain.

The incident just related, of this last interview of Sir Bulwer Lytton with the Spanish Premier, was evidently never reported in all its bearings, but enough was known for it to be seen that the Ambassador was apt to embroil matters. For in "The Letters of Queen Victoria," vol. ii., p. 207, Her Majesty writes:

"May 23, 1848.

"The sending away of Sir H. Bulwer* is a serious affair, which will add to our many embarrassments. The Queen, however, is not surprised at it, from the tenor of the last accounts of Madrid, and from the fact that Sir H. Bulwer has, for the last three years, been sporting with political intrigues. He invariably boasted of being in the confidence of every conspiracy, though he was taking care not to be personally mixed up in them; and, after their various failures, generally harboured the chief actors in his house under the plea of humanity. At every crisis he gave us to understand that he had to choose between a revolution and a palace intrigue, and not long ago he wrote to Lord Palmerston that if the Monarchy with the Montpensier succession was inconvenient to us, he could get up a Republic."

But Isabella's realm was still torn by insurrections. In January, 1860, the Prefect of the Police reported that a rebellion was being prepared in Spain against the throne by the Carlist party, under Don Carlos Luis de Bourbon y de Braganza, Count of

---

* "Lord Palmerston had written a letter to Bulwer (which the latter showed to the Spanish Premier) lecturing the Spanish Queen on her choice of a Minister. This assumption of superiority, as Sir Robert Peel calls it, led to a peremptory order to leave Spain in twenty-four hours."

Montemolin. When justice was prepared to take its course against the insurrectionists, Don Carlos wrote to Isabella, saying:

"I am certain that your compassionate heart, which has always shown pity for the unfortunate, will not fail to have mercy on your cousins, and not deny the pardon that we crave."

This mercy was also eloquently pleaded for by the unhappy mother of the delinquents. So, obedient to the impulse of her kind heart, Isabella said to the weeping parent: "Be at rest; your son shall not die."

However, the Carlist family soon forgot the clemency of the Queen, and the letter of Juan de Bourbon, son of Don Carlos, Ferdinand's brother, showed that the spirit of animosity burnt as powerfully as ever in the breast of the claimant to the throne.

"Twenty-seven years you have reigned," ran the Prince's letter to his royal cousin, "and you must confess that the hand of God has not helped you. I know the country; I know equally well that your heart is good, and that you do good when you can, and you regret the evils which afflict Spain. But you try in vain. You cannot fight against Providence, which never wills that evil should prosper. Be assured, dear cousin, that God did not choose you to make the happiness of Spain, and that Divine Providence has denied you the lot of being a great Queen. Descend, Isabella—descend from the throne! Show yourself great in this matter, and take the place to which you have a claim in my family as my dear cousin, and as having occupied the throne for so many years, and do not expose yourself to final disaster and bring ruin on the family."

XII

COURT INTRIGUES
1864–1868

On November 28, 1857, "the birth of Alfonso XII.," as Martin Hume says, "added another thong to the whip which the King-Consort could hold over the Queen for his personal and political ends, and it also had the apparently incongruous effect of sending Captain Puig Moltó into exile."

Of course there were the usual rejoicings at the birth of a Prince, but things were far from satisfactory at the Court. The Queen had now a taste of personal power and a higher notion of her own political ability. The Congress was in slavish servitude to the palace, and, acting in accordance with this sentiment, it had managed to get rid of the men in the Senate who had been working for the constitutional privileges of the country which would have led to the indispensable protection of the prerogative of a true suffrage; and freed from these patriots, the press was silenced and Parliament was suspended.

The return of Maria Cristina, the Queen's mother, was another step which added to the unpopularity of Isabella II. Once more wearied out with waiting for the realization of constitutional rights, the people's exasperation was voiced by the soldiers at the barracks of San Gil, within view of the royal palace of Madrid. O'Donnell at once took steps for the suppression of the insurrection.

The cries of "Viva Prim!" "Viva la Libertad!" showed that the spirit of republicanism was rampant.

Swiftly as O'Donnell went to the scene of action, Narvaez was before him, and so the Prime Minister had the mortification of seeing his rival carried into the palace to be tended for the slight wound he had received in the conflict.

The rebellion was soon quelled, and the insurgents were shot; but disinterested advisers of the Queen might have shown her that such émeutes proved that the fire of discontent was smouldering, and with a strong Government for the constitutional rights for which the country was clamouring the revolution of 1868 would have been avoided.

On the day following the San Gil insurrection a man of influence at the Court went to plead pardon for two of the insurgents from Her Majesty herself.

The interview was characteristic of the kind-heartedness of the Queen.

After waiting for half an hour in the antechamber, the gentleman was shown into the royal presence.

"You have been quite lost," said Isabel graciously, as her visitor bent over her hand. "It is a thousand years since you have been to see me."

Whilst excusing himself with courtly grace, Tarfe noticed that during the two years in which he had been absent from the palace the Queen had grown much stouter, and had thus lost some of her queenly dignity. She seemed distrait and troubled, and the red lids of her limpid blue eyes gave her an expression of weariness. They were, moreover, the eyes of a woman who had been brought in contact with the encyclopædic array of the various forms of the despoilers of innocence.

The petitioner submitted his plea for mercy for his friends by saying that his request was backed by a letter from the holy Mother, begging her to write two letters to General Hoyos for their release. To the delight of the intercessor, the Sovereign at once wrote the letters. When this was done, the surprise of the courtier was increased when the Queen, who was generally mañanista, said in a quick, nervous tone: "Do not delay giving these letters; do not wait till to-morrow; do it to-day!"

Before leaving the royal presence, Tarfe ventured to say that O'Donnell was much upset by the events of the preceding day,

137

and the Queen replied in a tone curiously devoid of feeling: "Yes, I like O'Donnell very much." This she said three times in the same passionless voice, and then, seeing that he was dismissed, Tarfe took leave of Her Majesty; and after fulfilling the mission to Hoyos, he went to see O'Donnell at his palace of Buenavista.

The General declined to believe the reports of his friends, of the intrigues which were to compass his fall.

The victor at Tetuan was more able to repel the open advance of an enemy than the underhand plots of a palace.

But when Ortiz de Pinedo suddenly came in, and said, "Gonzalez Brabo has left San Juan de Luz to-day, and he is coming to form a Ministry with Narvaez," the General was somewhat taken aback.

On the following morning, after finishing a long despatch for the royal signature, he repaired to the palace, and, anxious to know the real state of affairs, he submitted to Her Majesty the list of appointments to the Senate-house, many of which had been suggested by Isabel herself.

To the surprise of the Minister, the list was rejected by the Queen in a cold, disdainful way, so O'Donnell found himself forced to offer his resignation. This was accepted with the usual meaningless smiles and compliments.

Then O'Donnell returned to his house, where his friends were waiting for him. His face betrayed his rage and mortification, and, throwing his gloves on the table with an angry gesture, he exclaimed:

"I have been dismissed just as you would dismiss one of your servants."

"My General," exclaimed one of the partisans of the ex-Minister, "the camarilla delayed the change of Ministry for two days after the mutiny; why was that? And Ayala returned because it was better for Narvaez that we should have the odium of shooting the insurgents. Now he can take his place in Parliament with all the airs of clemency."

O'Donnell, who could not deny the truth of this remark, took General Serrano by the arm into another room, but they could plainly hear their indignant followers saying: "Eso, señora, es imposible!"

The Marquis of Miraflores says that a General Pierrad, the head of the Pronunciamento, told a chief of the halberdiers that he had better tell the Queen that there were no means of putting down meetings, and this for two reasons: Prim and his friends only wanted a change in the power by a disciplined Pronunciamento, but the artillery, through some strange influence, would not recognize military chiefs. He who said this was to have been shot down by them; he saw them drunk and faithless to their commands. This communication was made to the Queen. In 1867 an important interview took place in the Palace of Madrid between Isabel II. and her sister, the Duchess of Montpensier.

It will be remembered that, after the adventures of the royal couple in the revolution of 1848, the Duke and Duchess retired to Seville, where they lived in the Palace of San Telmo with all the state dignity of sovereigns. The Queen had made the Duke an Infante of Spain, and he had also been appointed Captain-General.

The Duke decided to take his wife to Madrid to counsel her sister to adopt a more liberal policy. The Duchess was expecting another child, but she was advised not to postpone her visit to the royal palace of Madrid. The interview was far from satisfactory, for Isabella had no intention of allowing Montpensier to have an active part in the Government. So the Princess returned to Seville, and Isabella afterwards wrote her a letter, in which she expressed displeasure at her aims. This letter received an angry reply, first from the husband, and then from the wife. So a coldness grew up between the sisters, and, indeed, Isabella's want of confidence in Montpensier was proved by the subsequent events in 1868, when Prim himself rejected the Duke's offer to raise forces in his favour.

During all this time the little Prince of Asturias, who was nine years old when the insurrection broke out in the barracks of San Gil for Prim, was pursuing his education in the palace. The style of the Prince's education is given in the remark of the royal child's playmate to his father, when he had been to spend a day at the palace.

"Papa," said the boy, "Alfonso does not know anything. He is taught nothing but religion and drilling. After the religious lesson, which was very dull," the child continued, "Alfonso was given a spear and a sword, and he waved them about so much that Juanito and I were afraid he would hurt us."

A record was kept of the little Prince's doings during the day. His frequent colds, his coughs, his acts of devotion, his appetite at meals, his games, his toys, his little tempers, his deeds of obedience, were all entered in the register as signs of his temperament and as indications of his future character as a man.

The Prince's apartments were dreary. The windows were high up in the thick walls, the ceilings were low, and, as a grandee says when speaking of this fact, it seemed strange that the light and air so essential for a child should be insufficiently supplied to a future King. General Pavia, who was gentleman-in-waiting to Alfonso, only shrugged his shoulders at this remark, but Señor Morphy ventured to say: "That is our opinion, but she who commands, commands."

When the grandee was introduced to the little Prince, he returned the salutation with the manner of one accustomed to it, but with a pretty smile which was very attractive.

"Yes," said his attendant, "His Royal Highness is better to-day. He only has a little cough now, but the doctor says he is not to be tired with lessons to-day; he is only to rest."

"Last night," said the General, "His Highness asked for his lead soldiers to play with in bed. He did not want to say his prayers. So I had to fetch the new prayer-book which Her Majesty sent a few days ago, and I read the prayers whilst he repeated them after me. So in this way he said his prayers, but not willingly."

Hereupon Alfonso protested, saying: "But this morning, Marquis, I said my prayers without your reading anything."

"Yes, yes," returned the gentleman; "but Your Highness did not want to get up, so I had to read stories to you until the doctor came."

A few pages from the diary of the young Prince of Asturias gives some insight into the dreary daily life of the delicate child:

"October 1, 1866.—His Highness breakfasted at 11 o'clock. At 1 o'clock he had drilling till 1.40. At 2 o'clock a writing lesson with Señor Castilla; at 3 o'clock religion with Señor Fernandez;

4.30, rice soup as usual; 4.50 he went up to the rooms of Her Majesty to go for a drive with her.

"October 4.—His Highness played about till 2.15. He had no lessons to-day, as being Her Majesty's saint's day. At 2.43 he went up to the Queen's apartments to assist at the reception. He wore the uniform of a sergeant, with the Cross of Pelayo. The ceremony over at 6.15, when His Highness came down with Señor Novaliches, as a boot hurt him (not the Marquis, but His Highness). The said Marquis took off the boot, and carefully examined the foot, but he found nothing to account for the pain. Mention is made of this circumstance as the Chief of the Chamber of His Highness thinks it fitting to do so....

"October 6.—My Lord Prince lunched at 12 o'clock. I gave him his lessons. He went to the Church of Our Lady of Atocha. He went to bed at 10 o'clock, and slept ten hours. He took some chocolate, made his confession at 9.30, and Father Fernandez celebrated Mass.

"October 9.—He breakfasted with appetite. He had his lessons at the marked hours, and he was somewhat restless. At 4 o'clock he took some soup, and went out for a walk with the Mayordomo, Señor Marquis de Novaliches, Professor Sanchez, and Juanito. He had supper at 8 o'clock, and played till 10 o'clock with Juanito, but left off when he knocked his left leg against a table. He slept from 10 o'clock till 9 o'clock in the morning. He got up at 9.30 without feeling any pain in his leg from the blow. He did his orisons, assisted at the Mass in his room; he went out for a walk with his Mayordomo, returned at 11 o'clock, and assisted at the Mass with Their Majesties and the Princesses; and at 11.45 he had his hair cut."

As Perez Galdos says in his works, the long hours of religious instruction every day would have qualified the little Prince for the Council of Trent. When any Bishops came to visit Isabella, they were sent to the apartments of her little son; and thus Morphy writes in the register: "I gave the lesson to His Highness in the presence of the Bishops of Avila, Guadix, Taragona, and of other dioceses whose names I do not remember." And Losa wrote: "He opened his eyes at 8.30; he dressed and gave thanks to God; he took his chocolate with appetite, and at 10 o'clock had his religion lesson in the presence of the Cardinal of Burgos, who was pleased with his progress, and noted that His Highness was 'magnificent in everything.'"

Courtiers who were true of heart saw with apprehension the artificial character of the Prince's education.

"Ah!" said a man who would gladly have been frank with the Queen, but he felt he was powerless against her crowd of flatterers, "Alfonso is a very intelligent child. He has qualities of heart and mind which would give us a King worthy of the people, were they only properly cultivated; but we shall never see this ideal realized, because he is being brought up like an idiot. Instead of educating the boy, they are stultifying him; instead of opening his eyes to science, life, and nature, they blind them so that his sensitive soul remains in darkness and ignorance."

The same courtier implored the Prince's educators to give the lad a chance. "Take him out of this atmosphere of priests and nuns, and devotional books by Father Claret. If you want Alfonso to be a great King, let him breathe the pure air of fine deeds. Take him away from the gloomy atmosphere of the royal palace; let him inhale the fresh breezes of liberty. His talents will develop, and he will become a different boy."

It was indeed true the little Prince was in an unnatural atmosphere in the palace, where the tunic of the nun Patrocinio had become an object of worship, and where the King, in his stuffy apartments, gave himself over to the study of relics which were brought to him at a high price by the priestly folk, who made harvest out of his credibility.

The situation of Queen Isabella is graphically given by the historian Galdos in the reflections of a loyal courtier whilst having, with his wife, an audience of Isabella II.:

"Oh, your poor Majesty!" he said to himself. "The etiquette invented by the set-up gentlemen of the Court to shut you off from the national sentiment prevents me telling you the truth, because it would hurt you to hear it. Even those on the most intimate terms with you shut you out from the truth, and they come to you full of lies. So, kind-hearted Isabella, you receive the homage of my gilded untruths. All that I have said to you this afternoon is an offering of floral decorations, the only ones received on royal altars.... You, who are more inclined to the ordinary and the plebeian than other Kings—you let the truth come to you in external decorative, and verbal matters, but in things of public consequence you like nothing but lies, because you are educated in it, and falsity is the religious cloak, or rather the transparent veil, which you like to throw over your political and non-political errors. Oh, poor neglected, ill-fated Queen...!"

The reflections of the courtier were here interrupted by Isabella saying to his wife: "Maria Ignacia, I want to give you the ribbon of Maria Luisa.... I shall never forgive myself for not having done it before. I have been very neglectful—eh?"

The Marchioness was eloquent in her thanks, and Beramendi could only say: "Señora, the kindness of Your Majesty is unbounded.... How can we express our gratitude to Your Majesty?"

But the Marquis said to himself: "We take it, because even as you accept our lying homage, so we receive these signs of vanity. King and people we deceive each other; we give you painted rags of flattery, which look like flowers, and you bestow honours on us which take the place of real affection."

Isabella continued: "I must give you a title of Count or Viscount, which your son can take when he comes of age."

The Marquis's wife returned: "Our Queen is always so good; that is why the Spaniards love her so."

"Ah, no, no!" exclaimed Isabella in a melancholy tone, "they do not love me as they did.... And many really hate me, and yet God knows I have not changed in my love for the Spaniards.... But things have got all wrong.... I don't know how it is ... it is through the heated passions of one and the other. But, Beramendi, it is not my fault."

"No, indeed," returned the courtier; "you have not caused this embroiled state of affairs. It is the work of the statesmen, who are moved by ambition and egoism."

143

This indeed was true, for even as Serrano used the Queen's favour to his own ends, and had his debts twice paid by Her Majesty, he was the first to lead the country against her.

"Do you think that matters will improve, and that passions will calm down?" asked Isabella anxiously.

"Oh, señora, I hope that the Government will confirm your authority, and that those that are in rebellion will recognize their error."

"That is what they all say," said Isabella, with a little satirical smile. "We shall see how things will turn out. I trust in God, and I don't believe He will forsake me."

"Ah!" said Beramendi to himself, whilst his royal mistress continued in the same strain of religious trust to his wife, "do not invoke the true God whilst you prostrate yourself before the false one. This god of thine is an idol made of superstition, and decked in the trappings of flattery; he will not come to your aid, because he is not God. I pity you, blind, generous, misled Sovereign.... Those who loved you so much now merely pity you.... You have been silly enough to turn the love of the Spaniards to commiseration, if not to hatred. I see your goodness, your affection, but these gifts are not sufficient to rule a nation. The Spanish people have got tired of looking for the fruit of your good heart."

When Isabella gave the sign of dismissal of the courtier and his wife by rising to her feet, he said to himself sadly:

"Good-bye, Queen Isabella; you have spoilt your life. Your reign began with the smiles of all the good fairies, but you have changed them into devils, which drag you to perdition.... As your ears are never allowed to hear the truth, I cannot tell you that you will reign until O'Donnell will permit the Generals to second Prim's plans. Oh, poor Queen! you would think me mad if I said such a thing to you; you would think I was a rebel and a personal enemy, and you would run in terror to consult with your devilish nuns and the odious set which has raised a high wall between Isabella II. and the love of Spain. Good-bye, lady of the sad destiny; may God save your descendants, as He cannot save you!"

The good-heartedness of the Queen was, indeed, seen by all

about her, and there are people still at the Palace of Madrid who remember seeing Her Majesty take off her bracelets and give them to the beggars which infest the royal courtyard. All the best impulses of Isabella were turned to her own ruin for the want of true patriots, who by supporting the constitutional rights of the nation would have secured the sovereignty to the Queen. The self-interested conduct of the generals and statesmen, whose command in the camarilla of the palace meant rule over the heart of Her Majesty, tended naturally only to the overthrow of personal rivals, and to the neglect of the welfare of the land.

Prim therefore became the hope of the nation. With his return to the capital, thought the people, crushed down by taxation and deprived of constitutional liberty, there will be an end to the camarilla, Narvaez, and Patrocinio, and we shall have the pure fresh air of disinterested policy.

The death of O'Donnell at Biarritz relieved Narvaez of the fear of his rival's return, but the General had the mortification of seeing his royal mistress utterly in the hands of Marfori, who had been raised from the position of Intendente of the Palace to the position of supreme personal favour.

When the Queen heard of O'Donnell's death, she is reported to have said: "He determined not to be Minister with me again, and now he can never be."

The Queen now committed the suicidal act of making Gonzalez Brabo Prime Minister in the place of Narvaez. The poor lady seemed quite to have lost her head, and there was no one to put her on the right path, surrounded as she was with harpies.

According to a letter from Pius IX., found in the Princess's prayer-book in the royal palace after the Queen had taken flight, the Pope counselled the marriage of the Infanta Isabella with a Neapolitan Prince. Even whilst the fêtes of the marriage were going on, Gonzalez Brabo was concerting with the revolutionary Generals, and the name of "Prim and Liberty!" was heard on all sides, and messengers were sent to consult with the leader of the Republican party in London.

The supporters of the Montpensier party hoped that the dethronement of Isabella would mean the acceptance of the Duchess of Montpensier as Queen, and her husband as Prince-Consort. But this idea was soon nipped by Monsieur de Persigny, the President of the Privy Council of the Emperor of the French, saying to Olozaga, who was then Spanish Ambassador at Paris, that he would never consent to the crown of Spain being on the head of either the Duke or the Duchess of Montpensier.

After the historic day of September 29, 1868, when Prim made his successful coup at Cadiz, the Royal Family fled to San Sebastian.

The haste with which the flight was made could be seen in the collections of jewels and money which had been thrust into bags which were after all left behind.

In the Hôtel d'Angleterre of the seaside resort Isabella still seemed to expect a miracle to take place in her favour. A throne does not fall every day, and a crowd hovered about the hotel to see how the Queen would accept her overthrow.

A murmur of satisfaction broke out among the bystanders when the loyal-hearted Marquis de Beramendi was seen entering the hotel. "That is a good thing," they said, "for Isabella will listen to his advice, which is certain to be wise."

The courtier's remarks to the Lady-in-Waiting were short and to the point.

"I have come to tell you," he said, "that, if the Queen keeps to the good idea of abdicating, certain infatuated people ought to be kept from opposing it. I have had direct news from Serrano, and he says that, if Doña Isabella will abdicate in favour of Don Alfonso, he will save the dynasty, and she herself will be saved. The Duke of Torres will not put obstacles in the way of this course."

"Better than that," returned the Lady-in-Waiting, in a voice which a cold rendered almost inaudible, "I thought that Her Majesty had the same idea, 'that she had better go to Logroño, and abdicate in favour of the Prince of Asturias in the presence of Espartero.'"

"That's admirable!" said Beramendi.

"And then, after abdicating, the Queen will depart immediately for France, leaving the new King in the power of the Regent Espartero."

"Admirable! splendid!" cried Beramendi; "but there is not a minute to lose."

"The departure will be arranged this evening."

"But, my God, I fear delays will be fatal; I am afraid that some bad friend, some plotting courtier of the camarilla, will spoil this saving step——"

"Well, I must go upstairs now," returned the lady. "The Señora, Don Francisco, and Roncali, are busy with manifestoes for the nation."

"And Spain will say, 'Manifestoes to me!' Now is the time to show the country fine deeds, and not empty rhetoric."

On the following morning, when Beramendi went to the hotel, he came upon Marfori; and although he had had little to do with this nephew of Narvaez since royal favouritism had raised him to such undue importance, he said, in a tone of assumed respect: "So Her Majesty is going direct to France? Something was said about her travelling to Logroño?"

Upon this Marfori frowned angrily, saying: "You don't understand, my dear Marquis, that it would be very humiliating for the Queen of Spain to ask protection from a General, although he bear the name of Espartero. All concert with Progressists is dangerous. The Queen is leaving Spain under the conviction that she will soon be recalled by her people."

"I knew it was useless to say more. Don Carlos Marfori was busy giving orders to the servants. I regarded him with resentment, because he was the personification of the evil influence which brought the Queen to her ruin.

"His Arab type of handsomeness, with his large mouth and heavy jaw, was eloquent of sensuality, and his obesity robbed him of the attraction which he had possessed in earlier days. He was impetuous, overbearing, and wanting in the courtesy common to a superior education."

The Marquis was then taken into the presence of the Queen, and as he bent over her hand she whispered: "You know we have

147

given up the idea of going to Logroño. No more humiliations! I am going away so as not to aggravate matters, and to prevent bloodshed; but I shall be recalled, shall I not?"

"I had to console Her Majesty with one of the usual Court lies, and the Royal Family soon took its departure, the Queen leaning on the arm of Don Francisco, the little Infantas with their Ladies-in-Waiting, and the Prince of Asturias, in a blue velvet suit, led by Señora de Tacon. The poor little fellow looked pale and sad; his great eyes seemed to express the royal and domestic sadness of the scene, and nothing was now wanting but the order for departure."

Marfori was always much disliked by people at Court. It was in the summer of 1867. Many courtiers and ladies of high rank were promenading in the beautiful gardens of La Granja. The soft, well-kept turf of the shady alleys by the countless sparkling fountains set off the beauty of the dresses, when, with his usual courtly grace, General Narvaez advanced to meet the Countess of Campo Alange.

This illustrious lady, whose salons in Madrid were graced by the highest in the land, was soon to give a ball.

"I have received your invitation," said the General, after he had greeted the Countess.

"It is almost the first that I have sent," returned the lady.

"I have just met Marfori," said the Duke of Valencia, "and he tells me he has not received his."

"Neither will he," replied the lady sharply.

"And why, being a Minister?" queried the General in surprise, knowing how the slight to the Queen's favourite would be resented at Court.

"Simply because Cabinet Councils are not held at my house," returned the lady caustically, firm in her decision to show her dislike of the man.

General Narvaez, whose dapper figure and perfect dancing made him always a welcome guest at the Spanish Court, was still unmarried when he had to withdraw to Paris as an exile. He had always been fond of feminine society, but, gay butterfly as he was, he did not fix his affections upon any one lady.

The beautiful Leocadia Zamora had been once the object of the officer's attention, and, indeed, the charming way she accompanied herself on the harp fascinated other admirers beside the Count of Valencia. She was a constant visitor in the salons of the Countess of Montijo, where the lovely Eugénie shone with the brilliance and charm which were so soon to be transported to the Court of France.

But fate did not reserve the joy of a happy marriage for the lovely Leocadia, and the sweet spirit, disillusioned by an unhappy love, retired to a convent in Oviedo, where she passed the rest of her life performing the duties of a Lady Abbess.

It was said that it was the gallant Don Salvador de Castro who had taken Leocadia's heart captive, when she was young; and, indeed, it is not surprising if this report be true, for he was a typical courtier of his time, and when he was home from his duties as Ambassador in Italy he seemed to dwarf all the attractions of the lady's other admirers. Leocadia was, in truth, a star of the Court of Spain, and the beautiful picture by Frederick Madrazo shows the perfection of her charms, with no other ornament than a white rose to adorn her simple white dress. Salvador de Castro was honoured by the friendship of King Francis II. and Queen Maria Sophia when the Italian Revolution robbed them of the throne of the Two Sicilies, and he was able to render them marked services and prove himself as loyal a friend as he was perfect a gentleman. After the capitulation of Gaeta, the King and Queen rewarded his loyalty by granting him the title of Prince of Santa Lucia, with the gift of the beautiful palace on the banks of the Tiber which is known by the name of the Farnesina, whilst the gardens were sold to the Emperor Napoleon. The place was deserted, and so near to its ruin that sheep and goats fed in its grounds, and the custodian took his meals in the beautiful hall of the frescoes of Sodon.

It was in this palace that Michael Angelo painted a head on the wall, which is known by the name of "The Visiting Card," as he left it as a sign of his call on Raphael when the artist was out.

The Prince of Santa Lucia had the palatial dwelling restored, and he gave magnificent entertainments in this palace, of which it was not destined that the lovely Leocadia should be mistress. Indeed, the lady abandoned all thoughts of love and pomp when she entered a convent in Oviedo, where she ended her days as Lady Abbess; whilst the daughter of her old admirer wedded the Marquis of Bey, and made a mark in Court society of Madrid.

But to return to the gallant little General. His affections were at last taken captive by another friend of the young Empress of the French, the beautiful daughter of the Count of Tacher. The Empress Josephine had belonged to this family, and her parents, the Duke and Duchess de Tacher de la Pogerie, were much beloved by Queen Marie Amélie, wife of King Louis Philippe.

It was General de Cordova, who had played such an important part during the Regency of Queen Maria Cristina, who first took him to the house of the Tachers. When Narvaez paid a second visit to the palace on the Boulevard Courcelles, he found that nobody was at home; and he was waiting in the drawing-room for the return of the lady of the house, when the daughter came in, looking beautiful in a white dress, but with her face tied up.

"Are you ill?" asked the General, with concern.

"Yes," she returned; "I have a swelled face."

"How sorry I am!" said the soldier sympathetically, "for I came this afternoon in the hope of hearing you sing."

"And so you shall," returned the girl kindly. "You shall not go away disappointed." And, taking the bandage from her face, she sang song after song to the fascinated General.

The progress of the courtship was swift, and the marriage was celebrated with great magnificence in the palatial abode of Queen Maria Cristina in Paris, with the attendance of representatives of the most distinguished families of France and Spain.

When General Narvaez returned to Madrid he became Prime Minister of Spain.

Unfortunately, the marriage did not prove a happy one, and, indeed, it would have been difficult for anyone to live peacefully with the irascible Spaniard. This irascibility was seen at the funeral of General Manso de Zuñiga, who had died in the expedition against Prim, in the mountains of Toledo. General Narvaez was chief mourner on the occasion, as the deceased officer had been husband of Doña Valentina Bouligni, a lady of great importance at this epoch, with whom he was connected; and the Bishop of Pharsalia was master of the ceremonies.

At a certain point in the function the order was given to kneel. But, probably absorbed in some knotty State question, the Duke of Valencia still stood. Upon this the Bishop quickly approached the grandee, and said:

"Kneel down, kneel down!"

"But I don't want to kneel," returned the General petulantly, and so he remained standing for the rest of the service.

When she came to Madrid as the wife of the great General, the Duchess of Valencia was appointed Lady-in-Waiting to Queen Isabella, and she never failed in her loyalty to the dynasty which was in power when she came to the country of her adoption by marriage.

Many years later she was in an hotel in Switzerland, where she purposed making a long stay, when Don Carlos happened to come to the same hotel, accompanied by his secretary. As the Duchess of Valencia was unacquainted with the Pretender to the throne of Spain, she wondered who the imperious-looking new arrival could be, who was greeted so respectfully by everybody. Her curiosity was soon satisfied, for the gentleman's secretary presented himself before her to say that the Duke of Madrid begged the honour to pay his respects to her.

The message filled the Duchess with dismay, for, although she held the Princes of the blood in great respect, she had no intention of receiving one who disputed the throne with the reigning Queen.

So, summoning all her dignity to her aid, she said, in a tone of icy politeness:

"Tell the Duke of Madrid that I am very sorry not to have the honour of receiving his visit, but to-morrow I leave for Paris."

And in effect the lady left the hotel on the morrow, and thus the meeting of one of the oldest and most valued Ladies-in-Waiting with Don Carlos was avoided.

Isabella certainly never expected that she would be dethroned, for a few weeks before the revolution of September, 1868, the celebrated General Tacon, Duke of the Union of Cuba, announced the forthcoming marriage of his daughter Carolina with the Marquis Villadarías, of the première noblesse, and a perfect type of a Spanish grandee, and she said: "I congratulate her sincerely on her engagement; but," she added sadly, "for myself I am sorry, as I shall see her no more at Court." The Queen here referred to the well-known Carlist opinions of the Marquis Villadarías, which would have made it impossible to receive the Marchioness at the palace if she had remained there.

So Isabella II. was dethroned in 1868, and she can truly be said to have been the victim of circumstances. From the moment King Ferdinand died his daughter had been the object of intrigue and ambition. Whilst our Queen Victoria was carefully educated and drilled in high principles, Isabella was the prey of those who wished to rise to power by her favour. Ministers made love to the Sovereign instead of discussing the welfare of the nation; flowery speeches on patriotism meant merely the gratification of the orator's vanity to be remarked by Her Majesty. Personal advancement was the end and aim of those in the Government, and thus poor Isabella's susceptibilities were worked upon to an awful extent.

It is well known that General Serrano, who might have been thought to have the welfare of his country at heart, gained an undue influence over the Queen by means of her affections, and fomented to a great extent the matrimonial differences between her and her husband. Generous to a degree, Isabella paid the debts of this courtier twice, and yet it was this same General who was the first to have her hurled from the royal palace.

When the great Canning visited Madrid, Bulwer Lytton showed him at a Court ball the many women who were the favourites of the Ministers, and there was, indeed, hardly a statesman who would not sacrifice principles to the pleas of his mistress. It was at this Court, steeped in immorality, that Isabella was brought up with little or no knowledge of right and wrong, and even in her marriage she was a victim to the intrigues and ambitions of other

Courts of Europe as well as those of her own. She was, in fact, a scapegoat of the nation.

Harassed and in desperation at being pressed on to a miserable marriage destitute of all that could justify it, Isabella, after one of those long and fruitless discussions with her mother, once addressed a letter to our Queen Victoria; but in a pure Court like that of England little idea could be formed of the stagnant atmosphere of the Spanish palace from which the poor young Queen sent forth her plaint. Beyond the Court raged the stormy discontent of the country, which had been thwarted for more than thirty years of the fulfilment of its constitutional rights promised by Ferdinand VII. as the condition of his return to the throne of Spain.

Whilst Queen Victoria was daily increasing in the knowledge of constitutional rights which are the base of a Sovereign's power, poor Isabella's Prime Ministers resigned at any moment in pique or jealousy of some other politician, and the people grew daily more discontented at finding the Parliament was a farce, and it meant neither the progress of the land nor the protection of the people.

Bulwer Lytton was constantly sending despatches to England about the shortcomings of Isabella II. as a woman, but he seemed to lay no stress on the cause of her failure as a Queen. Under proper conditions Isabella doubtless would have been a good woman and a great Queen, but choked with the weeds of intrigue she was lost. Undisciplined and uneducated, the poor Queen fell a victim to what, if properly directed, would have been virtues instead of vices.

The marriage to which Isabella was forced by intrigue was, of course, the greatest evil which could have befallen such an impulsive, warm-hearted girl, who knew no more how to turn a deaf ear to a claimant for her favour than to keep her purse shut to the plea of an unfortunate beggar.

The Right Hon. Henry Lytton Bulwer wrote a little later from the British Embassy at Madrid to the Court of St. James's, saying that he "looked at the Queen's conduct as the moral result of the alliance she had been more or less compelled to contract, and he regarded her rather with interest and pity than blame or reproach."

153

Isabel's natural intuition of our Queen Victoria's good heart prompted her letters to her. They were sent by a private hand, and who knows what evils might have been prevented in the Court of Spain if the long journey, so formidable in those days, had not placed the sister-Queens so far apart?

Espartero's plea for Isabel to marry Don Enrique de Assisi, the man of her heart, met no support in a Court torn with intrigue, and the sad, bad story of Isabel doubtless had its source in the tragedy of an unhappy marriage. At the plea of a persistent wooer, who knew that the Queen had the right of dissolving a Ministry, a Government would fall; and as the station of her favourites became lower and lower, as time went on the ill-regulated Sovereign had a Government as undependable as her friends.

Treachery was the keynote of the Court of Spain, and some of the leaders of the revolution were those who had used the Sovereign's ignorance and foolhardiness to their own ends. In such an atmosphere of untruth and treachery such men as Espartero, Prim, etc., could play no enduring part. Hardly had Espartero swept the Court clean of the Regency of Queen Maria Cristina than his fall was encompassed by O'Donnell, his rival. The flagrant falsification of the Parliamentary election returns— which is still the cankerworm of the country—was the check to all progress. Count San Luis made a primitive effort for the reform of the elections; he suggested that the names of the candidates as deputies should be put in a bag, and drawn out by a child blindfolded, for the law of chance seemed to him better than the custom of deception.

Isabella's acts of generosity are still quoted with admiration at the royal palace of Madrid by those who served her as Queen.

Four hundred girls owed their marriage dots to Isabella, and it was the fathers of these four hundred royally endowed brides who treacherously worked for her expulsion.

One day, hearing the story of the penury of a clever man of letters, Isabella commanded 20,000 francs to be sent to him. The administrator of her finances, thinking the Queen could hardly know how much money this sum represented, had twenty notes of 1,000 francs each changed into small money, and put out on a table by which she had to pass.

"What is all this money for?" asked Isabella, when she saw it spread out to view.

"It is the money for the man of letters, and this shows Your Majesty how large is the sum of 20,000 francs."

"So much the better," was the prompt reply; and the courtier saw it was not by proving the amount of the boon that he could check his Sovereign in her generous actions.

A Court official at Madrid, who has been sixty years in office at the palace, told me he often saw Isabella take off her bracelets, and give them to the beggars who pressed upon her as she crossed the courtyard of the royal domain.

"And who could help loving her?" said the old courtier, with tears in his eyes; "I know I could not."

Caught in the darkness of ignorance and intrigue, Isabella was naturally enraged at the revolution. When her son Alfonso was nearly made captive by the Carlists at Lucar, she said: "I would rather my Alfonso be a prisoner of the Carlists than a captive of the revolutionists."

Isabella had a faithful friend in the Marquis of Grizalba, and he said to Croze:*

"It is the loss of faith which causes our woes; the charm of death has been destroyed with the hope of a hereafter. But Spain will die like a gentleman."

From September 19, 1868, to 1870 there is no history of the Court of Spain, as there was no King, and it was not known if there ever would be one again. Isabella lived, as we know, in Paris, and her son pursued his education in Vienna, in the Theresan College, and later at Sandhurst. The young ex-Prince was devoted to society and to gaiety, and, seeing how his mother was fêted in Paris, he was often heard to say:

"I should rather like to be a dethroned King and live in Paris with plenty of money."

In Spain, meanwhile, Serrano, Duke de la Torre, was enjoying

* The author of "La Vie intime d'Alfonse XIII."

155

his long-sought-for ambition of being supreme in the country, whilst General Prim was President of the Council of Ministers. The Duchess of la Torre made an ineffectual attempt to gather a Court around her at La Granja; but a palace made after the essentially royal abode of Versailles, with its countless well-kept alleys and its many panoramas of fountains adorned with allegorical scenes and figures, did not lend itself to anything but the stately entourage of a royal Court.

Whilst the Republican party grew in power in the Parliament, the Generals who had made the revolution sighed after a monarchy.

The Duke of Montpensier, the brother-in-law of the ex-Queen, might have had a good chance as candidate to the throne, and he was supported by Topete and the three Liberal Generals; but Spain could not forget his treachery and ingratitude to Isabella by joining with her enemies against her, and he found he could gain no real support from the country. And this coldness became more marked after the tragedy in which he was the chief actor made a dreadful stain on Court history.

It will be remembered that Prince Henry of Bourbon, the brother of the ex-King, whom Isabella had personally preferred to the husband she was finally obliged to accept, and who married, in 1849, Helena, daughter of the Count of Castellvi, had been removed from his position of a General of the army, to which he had been appointed by his cousin, and expatriated for a writing which was very insulting to the Queen.

Having thus associated himself with republicanism, Prince Henry became the source of many disloyal publications against the Queen and her Ministers, and when the blow was struck for the dethronement of Isabella, he openly welcomed the revolution.

The final opinions which caused the tragic ending to his life were expressed in an article entitled "The Montpensiers," and this so enraged the candidate to the throne that he called out the author of the pamphlet in a duel, and a wave of horror swept over the Court of Spain when the ex-King's brother thus met his death at the hand of the Duke of Montpensier.

The funeral of the Prince was solemnized with all the insignia of his rank as Lieutenant-Colonel and the owner of the Collar of Charles III., and with the rites due to a Freemason of high office. He was buried in the Escorial, and it is said that his remains will be finally removed from the simple niche where they now lie to the imposing tomb of "the Infants."

Another tragedy befell the family of the ex-Queen of Spain in December, 1871. On May 13, 1868, the Infanta Isabella, the eldest daughter of Queen Isabella II., married Count Frederick Girgenti, who created a most favourable impression in the country by the valiant way he fought in the Battle of Alcolea under the Marquis of Novaliches.

But the brave young Prince was subject to epileptic fits, and one day in December, 1871, to the horror of his wife, he shot himself in Lucerne. The poor man lived for some hours, tended by his sorrowing wife. But neither love nor science could avail in such a case, and the Infanta Isabella found herself a widow at the age of twenty. However, the Infanta never allowed sorrow to kill her sympathy for her compatriots, and to go to Spain is to find that no philanthropic scheme or project is considered complete without the patronage of the Infanta Isabella.

XIII.

THE COURT OF SPAIN UNDER ITALIAN SWAY

In February, 1869, Serrano was chosen head of the Executive Government, and in June of the same year Serrano, Duke de la Torre, was appointed Regent until a King should be elected.

To General Prim, whose ideal had always been that of Liberty, it was not surprising that, in seeking a Sovereign who, it was hoped, would steer the country through the shoals of self-interest and stagnation, set up by an autocrat monarchy, his eyes should turn to Prince Amadeus of Savoy, whose father had led such a splendid struggle for the freedom of the country from the despotism of clericalism. A deputation, formed by deputies who subsequently became Ministers of Alfonso XII., presided over by Ruiz Zorilla, who was later a pronounced republican, were thus sent to Italy to submit the offer of the throne of Spain to the Prince of Savoy. Their mission to the Prince over, they proceeded to the bedroom of his young wife, who had recently been confined, and there conveyed to her in due form the invitation to become Queen of Spain.

The claim of the Italian Prince to the throne rested on the royal decree of Philip V. of Spain, which formed the integral part of the Treaty of Utrecht, November 5, 1712. This decree set forth the claim to the throne of Spain through failure of legitimate line by the Duke of Savoy, and through failure of the male line by Prince Amadeus of Carignano and his sons, as descendants of the Infanta Catharine, daughter of Philip II. When the question of the claims to the throne of Spain was put to the vote, it was found that Amadeus registered 199, Espartero 8, Alfonso 2, and for a Republic 63.

Castelar used all his eloquence against the Italian candidate. "Who are these wretched Dukes of Savoy," he said, "that run like hungry dogs in the wake of the coach of our Kings?"

Courage was a great characteristic of young Prince Amadeus. When only twenty-one, in 1866, he saved a wounded soldier's life by carrying him out of danger on his own mule, in one of the skirmishes during the struggle for Italy's liberty.

The young man's calmness in the hour of danger was shown in 1867, when the boiler burst on the ship on which he was returning to Italy, after attending the function of the opening of the Suez Canal. The Count of Castiglione was killed, and the panic on board threatened more disaster. But Amadeus was cool and collected. He calmed the people and insisted on the sailors' return to their several duties, and the ship was successfully brought back.

Fortunately, the young Prince was allowed to marry the lady of his choice, who proved a devoted friend and companion in all the vicissitudes of their lives.

When Signor Francisco Cassini, the President of the Chamber of Deputies, told King Victor Emmanuel whom his son wished to marry, the royal father said: "Do the young people love each other?"

"They idolize each other," returned the statesman.

"Then very well; they shall be married," was the reply. "It is not for me to stand in opposition to the sentiment of my son."

So the royal couple were married, and thus fate led to Princess Maria del Pozzo becoming Queen of Spain.

Naturally, Amadeus was not attracted by all he heard of the country over which he was called to reign. However, when his father said, "Of course, it is very hot in Spain at this time, and by going there you would also run the risk of a disagreeable adventure, and perhaps even get a bit of lead in your ribs," the natural courage of the Prince was stimulated, and he declared he would accept the invitation to the throne, come what may.

As the new King of Spain's wife had not recovered sufficiently from her recent confinement to travel, her husband went alone to Spain. Before starting for his new country, Amadeus said to his friends:

"I go to fulfil an impossible mission. Spain, now divided into various parties, will unite against a foreign King, and I shall soon be obliged to return the crown they offered me."

However, the Italian Prince knew he had a valiant supporter in General Prim, who used all his oratory and influence to get the sympathy of his countrymen on the side of the new-comer. But, as we know, it was not the fate of the pioneer of Liberty to see the realization of the scheme which he had hoped would be for the welfare of the country, and on December 30, 1870, the day on which Amadeus landed on Spanish soil, Prim was foully murdered by Spaniards.

Long inquiry and investigation never revealed convincingly the hand that shot the General in the street. It was supposed by some to have been a partisan of an unsuccessful candidate to the throne; others think it was a gipsy, who did it as a deed of outlawry. Be that as it may, strong suspicion fell upon Señor Paul y Angulo, who expressed his indignation strongly in the prologue to his paper on "Revolutionary Truths":

"The sacrifices that I have made for my country have been no light matters, and all I have in return is to find myself obliged to leave my poor country, to be the victim of vile calumniators, and to have to fly from persecution as if I were some horrible criminal."

Prim's death was accompanied with much suffering, for some of his fingers were so seriously injured by the shot, it was thought that their amputation would save his life. But the operation was in vain, and the General died in two days, just as Amadeus landed at Carthagena.

When the sad news reached the new King, that his ardent supporter had fallen a martyr to his cause, he said:

"Gentlemen, my duty is clear: I must go on to Madrid."

Arrived at the Spanish capital on January 2, 1871, where a fall of snow added gloom to the occasion, Amadeus at once repaired to the Church of Atocha, to pay his respects to the remains of the man to whom he mainly owed the throne of Spain.

As the young King gazed at the corpse of the great leader, who

160

had inspired trust and confidence in all with whom he came in contact, he prayed for strength to be able to fulfil the hopes which the Spaniard had directed to himself. With Prim, the pioneer of Liberty in Spain, young Amadeus, who had fought for the same cause in his own country, had always felt in sympathy.

Those who had suffered for their religious opinions had looked to the great soldier as the herald of a new era. Juan Cabrera, the leader of the Protestant movement, who had fled to Gibraltar for fear of imprisonment, and there led a life of exile and hardship, hastened to meet Prim after the coup which put Spain practically in his hands.

"May I return to my country?" asked Cabrera, when he saw him at Gibraltar.

"Yes, yes, my man," replied the General, whilst fixing his keen eyes on the Protestant's face, worn with study and anxiety, "you can go back to Spain now with your Bible under your arm."

And this the preacher of the reformed faith found to be true, for Spain had no longer to fear the active persecution of those who resisted the introduction of the Bible into their land.

As Amadeus gazed at the features of the General, set in death, he sighed deeply in sorrow at his loss, and when he arrived at the royal palace, the magnificent setting of so many scenes of struggle for supremacy in the country, he sat down wearily, and said:

"I feel sure that my loyalty will not be able to save Spain from the fury of contending factions."

When the new King took up his abode in the fine domain, with Prim dead, he felt as if he were starting for a voyage on a ship of which the rudder was lost, for he knew not whom to trust or to whom to turn for counsel.

But Amadeus was not a man to let himself be enervated by fears and doubts for the future, although the first few weeks of his residence in the palace were additionally anxious from the fact of his wife being ill at Alassio. For the new young Queen of Spain had not been able to accompany her husband to Spain, as she was not sufficiently recovered from her confinement; and when, in her desire to join Amadeus in the new sphere of influence, the

161

journey was made too soon for her health, she was for some time ill at Alassio.

At last the new Queen was able to undertake the ten days' journey by sea to Alicante, where she was received with great delight by the young King.

The bright spring day which saw the arrival at Alicante of Queen Maria Victoria seemed to augur well for the success of the young couple. A thrill of pride passed through the young wife when she saw her husband come out to meet her in a white-and-gold launch, his face bright with hope, and looking every inch a King. As the bright barque cut through the sunlit waters, with Amadeus accompanied by his Ministers, who had come to welcome her in state, she stepped to the prow with pretty words of greeting on her lips, and when she was finally taken off from the Italian ship to set foot on Spanish soil, a storm of cheers burst from the throats of the Italian sailors, to be echoed by those from the Spanish crews and sight-seers anxious to welcome the new Sovereign. The bright and intelligent young wife did indeed seem to bring sunshine to Spain, and in the opening of the Senate there was a sincerity in the royal speech which found an echo in the hearts of those who really wished for the welfare of the country.

"When my feet touched Spanish soil," said Amadeus, in a voice which penetrated to every part of the house, "I determined to merge my ideas, my sentiments, and my interests, in those of the nation who elected me as its head, and whose independent character would never submit to foreign and illegitimate intrigues. My sons will have the good fortune to receive their first impressions of life here; their first language will be Spanish; their education will be in accordance with the customs of the nation; they will learn to think and feel as you think and feel; and we shall unite with imperishable bonds our own fate with your fate."

But no patriotic sentiments could entirely extinguish the sparks of smouldering resentment that a foreigner should be set over Spain.

The pride of the Castilians was wounded, and no salve of sympathy could prevent the canker caused by such a hurt. Everything the Italian King and Queen did was purposely misinterpreted. He was dubbed "King Macaroni," and this mocking appellation expressed the resentment of the Court and country.

The very democratic simplicity of the young couple was an offence to a land which revels in old-world ceremony and stately Court etiquette, and the clerical party never let the people forget that it was Victor Emmanuel, the father of their new King, who had ousted the Pope from his position of political supremacy.

Of course Isabella was very indignant when she heard who had been elected as ruler at the Court of Spain, and she expressed her feelings in a torrent of speech.

"The revolution continues," she said, whilst her eyes blazed with indignation, "and it has just disavowed the rights of my son, who is to-day your legitimate King according to all the Spanish constitutions, by calling to the throne of St. Ferdinand a foreigner, whose merits, however great, cannot entitle him to be your Sovereign, in the face of the rights of a whole dynasty, which is the only one that has in its favour the legitimacy which has been consecrated by the lapse of ages and by constitutions which it has been a signal folly to disavow."

Of course the Bourbon party echoed these sentiments of its ex-Queen, and Amadeus felt the want of unity which has ever been the main defect of the country.

People who came into contact with Amadeus at the Court of Spain admired the sense of his opinions, although the form of their utterance was not in accordance with that adopted by former rulers at the palace; for the King had many habits of a nervous man. One of these was to take hold of a chair when he was talking, and twist first one of his long legs, and then the other, in and out of the woodwork as he turned it about before him.

As simplicity was a very marked trait in the young royal couple's tastes, they rejected the idea of establishing themselves in the magnificent apartments used by the ex-Sovereigns, and chose a simple suite of somewhat small rooms commanding a beautiful view of the Casa de Campo, and there the King passed the happiest hours of the day with his wife and children. The young Queen's fine intelligence rendered her an able confidante for her consort's

163

State difficulties, and she was generally present at the discussions with the Ministers.

Sunday generally saw an intellectual gathering round the royal dinner-table, but the admiration of the select few who began to appreciate the gifts and aims of the young couple did not, unfortunately, represent the feeling of the country, and it required all the charity and philosophy of King Amadeus and Queen Maria Victoria to ignore the half-concealed sneers of those at Court who mocked at the foreigners and their simple, superior tastes.

Indeed, the Alfonsists never lost an opportunity of testifying their allegiance to the Bourbon dynasty, and, as they studiously avoided the royal palace from whence it had been expelled, the Court society of Madrid presented a strange medley of people who were so little conversant with the customs of such centres that Amadeus began to doubt if Madrid had any really good society.

A certain Señor B., who was subsequently a Minister during the Regency, was invited to a function at the palace. So he went to a first-rate shirt-maker and ordered a shirt for the occasion. The shirt came with the fine embroidered cambric frill set out over blue tissue-paper. So, thinking the blue paper was meant to be worn with the shirt, Señor B. strutted into the royal presence quite proud of his attire—paper and all.

So naturally Don Amadeus was constantly saying: "But there is no society in Madrid." This remark was repeated in one of the salons of the aristocracy on the eve of the funeral of Blanca Osma, the Marchioness of Povar, mother of the present Duke of Arion, who had been renowned for her beauty and elegance, and, stung at this slight to their circles, somebody said: "Well, to-morrow Amadeus shall see whether there be any good society in Madrid, for we will all parade in front of the windows of the palace after the funeral." And so they did, and thus the demonstration of sympathy for the family of Osma and Malpica became one of political importance.

February 10, 1872, was celebrated at the palace of the Dukes of Bailen by a magnificent ball. The minuet was danced by ladies in most beautiful Pompadour dresses, trimmed with handsome lace, and their hair powdered in the style of the last régime, and the gentlemen showed their high degree in dress and dignity. This minuet was repeated in the Palace of the Plaza del Angel by request of the mother of the Empress Eugénie, and society kept alive the feeling for the ex-régime by the same sort of fêtes until the day dawned for the restoration, which doubtless these gatherings aided, for the little rooms adjoining the salons were the scene of many councils in the cause of the Bourbons.

One day this feeling of antagonism was expressed in a more patent and painful form.

It was a hot evening, which the King and Queen had spent listening to the music in the gardens of the Buen Retiro. The royal couple was returning to the palace by the Arenal, when suddenly a vehicle opposed the passage of the carriage by crossing just in front of it. The coachman checked the horses and cleverly prevented a collision, and just then a shot was directed towards the royal party.

Upon this the King sprang boldly to his feet, exclaiming:

"Here is the King! Fire at him, not at the others!"

But no further attempts were made at assassination, and the retinue reached the palace in safety, where the young Queen sought to still her tremors of anxiety by the sight of her brave young husband standing sound and well before her.

To the King the late hours of the Court were particularly disagreeable. At work from six o'clock in the morning, he rang at eight o'clock for breakfast; astonishment was on the lackey's face when answering the summons; he heard that it had never been customary for their ex-Majesties to be served before eleven o'clock. So Amadeus, wishing to avoid any friction by insisting on earlier hours, adopted the habit of going to a café for his early meal after long application to State matters had made him conscious of the necessity of breaking his fast.

Thus the maids, who sally forth in Madrid with baskets on their arms to be filled with necessaries for the household, would often return and regale the ears of their mistresses with how they had brushed against His Majesty as they did their business in the market-place. In one of these peregrinations Amadeus noticed

165

that Castelar, the leader of the Republican party, raised his hat to him. Surprised at this sign of respect from the enemy, the young man stopped, and said he wondered that anybody of Castelar's opinions should salute royalty, to which the great orator replied, with all the grace and charm of an accomplished Castilian:

"My salute was not to royalty, sire, but to the bravest man in Christendom."

And it was this bravery which aroused the admiration of Spain. However, no quality could overcome the country's rooted prejudice against "the foreigner," and when Amadeus had taken his seat on the throne in the magnificent crimson-and-gold setting of the state salon of the palace, it was not to take real possession of his subjects' hearts. There was no antagonism against the Italian King, but utter indifference for him, which was much more difficult to deal with. He was unknown to the Spaniards, a mere guest, and the necessity of forming a Court for his wife was attended with the difficulty of the ladies of high degree being Alfonsists or Carlists, and thus many of them considered themselves superior to the lady on the throne.

The ladies of the last régime openly showed the Italian royal couple that their loyalty was still directed to the Spanish ex-Sovereigns, by constantly presenting themselves in the Buen Retiro, and other resorts where they drove or walked, in the white lace mantillas and other characteristics of costume especially Spanish.

As a counterfoil to these signs of disrespect to those in power, the ladies who were followers of King Amadeus and his wife arranged a cortège formed of women of the town, who were all dressed like the Spanish doñas of high degree, and they were accompanied by a noisy, bullying sort of fellow who obviously represented the King's Chamberlain, the Duke of Sexto.

Thus the feeling of the Court of Spain at this epoch was manifested in a series of spiteful acts unworthy of people of high position.

The Court ladies showed little sympathy with the philanthropic aims of Queen Maria Victoria. The existing Home for the

Children of Laundresses is still a standing proof that the sight of the thousands of women on their knees by the side of the River Manzanares, washing linen, had evoked a feeling of pity in the heart of the young royal mother.

The King found it impossible to take any action for good in his adopted country. The want of sympathy, and suspicion, which met every suggestion of the young King, allied with the confusion reigning in every department of the Government, made progress unattainable, and the King, having nothing to do with his time in a serious way, was soon found to be an easy prey to the seductions of designing Spanish women, and it was not known till some time afterwards that the Government had to interfere in ridding the Court of an adventuress who managed to get into the Court circle.

As Queen Maria Victoria wrote to a valued friend in Italy, she seemed wanting in the essential to make her a good Queen of Spain, and that was the desire to remain in the country.

Sensitive as the young Sovereign was, she was ever conscious of the half-concealed looks of scorn of those about her, who wondered that she preferred the simple customs of a happy domestic life to the pomp and etiquette of an old Court régime. The Countess della Alinma and the Marquis of Ulugares sympathized with Their Majesties' tastes, but these two friends could not stop the whispers of discontent and disapprobation reaching them from the large circles of the great palace.

Much of the rigidity of Court etiquette was abandoned during the short reign of Amadeus and Maria Victoria. The custom of courtiers prostrating themselves on their knees before Their Majesties was abandoned, and, thanks to the good sense of Alfonso XII., it was never more resumed.

Queen Maria Victoria created an Order which was called by her name, but it lapsed after her departure from the palace.

We read in "Cosas del Año 1873" (Things of the Year 1873), by Carlos Frontaura, that many open insults had been levelled at the Italian Sovereigns during the last few weeks of their reign. At the Court reception which is always customary on New Year's Day in Spain, the Conservative deputies were conspicuous by their

167

absence, and Generals Serrano, Concha, Infante, Rivero, Allende, Zabala and Hoyos, Topete, Malcampo, Martinez Espinosa, and the ex-Ministers Rios, Rosas, etc., all excused themselves from attending the banquet which took place in the evening.

The Countess of Heredia-Spinola gave a magnificent ball in her house in Calle Fernando el Santo, and all the guests wore the fleur-de-lis as a sign of their devotion to the Bourbon family.

Society at the Court of Spain was very different in the year 1872 from what it had been during the late dynasty.

As Napoleon I. said, "You may confer titles and dignities, but you cannot give that particular cachet which goes with real Court society."

The Countess of Campo Alange always said, "Did So-and-so learn the minuet when he was young?" For if the answer to this question were in the negative, it showed that the courtier only belonged to the new dynasty.

The Marquis of San Rafael was then Prime Minister, but when the Marchioness wished to enter the Queen's presence she was not allowed to pass, whereas an arrogant lady of the old aristocracy quickly forced her way in. The Prime Minister was advised to report this slight to Amadeus himself. When the King heard of the matter, he only shrugged his shoulders, and said, "Let them fight it out."

The King and Queen felt that their days in Spain were numbered, and it only wanted some incident to put the match to the train of discontent.

The ostensible cause of the break of the King with the Government was the appointment to the command of the artillery of Hidalgo, who five years before had been in command of the company which had made the insurrection in the barracks of San Gil in 1866. The King himself did not favour this appointment, but when Ruiz Zorilla showed him a vote of confidence in the course carried by the Congress, Amadeus thought it time to resign the crown which meant nothing but mortification to himself and his wife. So on that evening (February 11, 1873) the republic was proclaimed, and six o'clock the following morning saw the sad exit from Spanish Court life of the Italians who had been so fruitlessly summoned to its circle.

Queen Maria Victoria had also been wounded in her susceptibilities as a mother. When her second child was born to her about a fortnight before the proclamation of the republic, the young Sovereigns naturally expected that the Ministry, Diplomatic Corps, military dignitaries, and clerical leaders, would be ready to greet the baby Prince according to the Court etiquette of the country. But the representatives of the country did not feel sufficient interest in the birth of "the little foreigner" to hasten to pay him their respects; and although the red and yellow flags waved triumphantly above the royal palace, it was several hours before there gathered in the audience chamber an assembly sufficiently large and august to receive the presentation of the son of Amadeus and Maria Victoria.

It was hardly a fortnight later when the die was cast, and the Italians decided to abandon the throne of Spain.

The personal attendants of the Queen wept as they saw her carried to the entrance of the palace still weak and ill from her recent confinement. The dethroned young King took the frail form of his wife in his arms when she was taken from the litter at the foot of the grand staircase, and, after placing her in the carriage waiting in the archway, proudly saluted the Guard and stepped in by her side.

In a departure arranged so hurriedly, all the necessary comforts were forgotten, and the royal invalid was faint for want of nourishment, which was only attainable after hours of travelling. Amadeus was grateful indeed for the soup he was at last able to procure at a little railway-station on the line, and he boldly met the remarks and curious looks of the people who crowded to see the royal fugitive as he bore the cup from the restaurant to his wife.

Once in Portugal, Amadeus had nothing more to fear for the personal safety of the family, and it was from thence they soon sailed quietly for Italy.

XIV

SOME TRUTHS ABOUT THE REPUBLIC
1873–1874

We have an interregnum in the history of the Court of Spain during the republic which held rule from February 11, 1873, until the restoration of the monarchy on December 30, 1874; but those readers, who like to have some idea of what was passing in Spain whilst the palace was empty, may be interested in the following particulars, drawn from a book entitled "Contemporaneous Truths," by His Excellency Vicente Lafuente. These truths were republished by Colonel Figuerola Ferretti* in 1898, with an able prologue from the officer's pen, to show those malcontents who wished to return to this form of government how baneful it was for the welfare of the land.

Queen Maria Cristina graciously accepted the book from the Colonel, who was then a Chamberlain at her Court, and it doubtless served to disperse the false ideas as to the nature of a Spanish republic which had arisen in the minds of those who were absent from the country whilst it held sway.

Twenty-five years had elapsed since Spain adopted the republic, but, as Figuerola Ferretti reminds his readers, that time had not obliterated the horrors of that period from those who belonged to that time.

Those who were inclined to regard a republic as an ideal form of government were reminded that the fatal night of February 11, 1873, saw the opening of the Pandora box, whence issued

---

* This Spaniard is connected on his mother's side with Pope Pius IX. (Mastai-Ferretti), whilst his father was Figuerola, the patriot of Cuba.

all sorts of moral and political calamities, which spread like a black cloud over the Spanish nation in both worlds. With the enthronement of moral and material disorder, licence and anarchy came from all sides, to the increase of impiety and corruption of customs, the ruin of families, the debasement of the public credit, the demoralization of the forces on sea and land, the loss of honour and national dignity, and the peril of the independence and integrity of the country both in the Peninsula and in America.

Such is the picture of the republic from the night of February 11, 1873, until the morning of January 3, 1874, when it was dissolved by the coup of General Pavia. This opinion is no mere expression of party rancour, for, as it is founded on the facts and events recorded in the Gazette and the Journal of the Sessions of the Cortes, which were noted day by day, they became, under the pen of the historian Lafuente, the true history which, according to Cicero, is "the light of truth and the master of life."

A few quotations from this diary of facts, which Ferretti republished as an antidote to the anti-dynastic feelings which were aroused by the loss of Cuba, give some idea of the effect of the republic on Spain:

"February 16, 1873.—Assassinations in Montilla under shocking circumstances. Eight houses sacked and burnt; Señor Robobo assassinated and quartered. Abolition of the oath of loyalty in the army.

"February 20 and 21.—During these days the theatre of Barcelona was the scene of dreadful military orgies and acts of immorality and barbarism. The column of Cabrinati rebelled in Santa Coloma de Farnés, at the instigation of the republicans, and the cry of 'Down with the officers!' was heard all over Catalonia.

"February 24.—There was a general Carlist rising in Navarre, and a call to arms of all men between twenty and forty years of age.

"February 28.—The neighbourhood of Madrid, in view of the prevailing want of discipline and the ease with which dwellings could be invaded, began organizing armed bands.

"March 15.—The battalion of 'the Cazadores of Madrid' committed unspeakable horrors in Falset, and several companies of Catalonia began a course of pillage and immorality.

"March 17.—General Hidalgo harangued the savage soldiers of Falset, but he was so hissed that he was obliged to retire, like almost all the other officers.

"March 18.—A great meeting was held at San Isidro, where the public commemorated what they called 'the glories of the Commune of Paris,' which they were evidently seeking to imitate."

The record of March closes with the mention of the occupation of the churches of Barcelona as barracks and theatres.

April 3 we read: "The republicans of Manresa invade and profane a church, take possession of the library and rooms of the seminary, and the town-hall of Tarragona.

"May 13.—An electoral meeting in Barcelona; the popular Mayor Buxó is wounded by a stone. The voluntary troops of Madrid knock down and wound the chaplain of the hospital, insult the officials who seek to release him, and commit various robberies and assassinations, so that the troops have to be called out against them.

"June 3.—In Madrid and other places the procession of the Corpus Christi could not take place on account of the uproars in the streets. Orgies in the churches of Belen and San José at Barcelona, and indecent balls, in which the mysteries of our redemption were mocked at.

"June 16.—Horrible assassinations at Bande (Orense). Sixty unhappy beings of all ages and both sexes fell victims to this savagery."

After three days' fighting the international incendiaries and assassins were expelled from Seville, leaving the city stained with blood and injured by fire.

"September 23.—General Don Manuel Pavia was appointed Governor of Madrid."

Carlism was rapidly gaining ground during these months. There were 8,000 Carlists in Aragon and Valencia, and as many more in Catalonia, 12,000 in Navarre, and more than that number

172

in the Basque provinces, thus making more than 40,000 Carlists in all Spain.

"November 7.—Señor Castelar, the President of the Republic, was daily losing power in the Congress, where neither eloquence nor good sense seemed to have any sway over the turbulent spirits."

When the Corporation of the city became disaffected from the Government, it seemed to the Governor of Madrid that it was time for him to assert the power of military rule.

So on December 2, when the chamber of the Congress was nothing but a scene of riot and disorder, each deputy striving by his loud voice and violent actions to overpower his fellow, the cultured Castelar, the head of the republic, whose orations would have reflected honour on the Areopagus of old, was met by a vote of want of confidence.

Then was the time for General Pavia's action. Arthur Houghton, correspondent to The Times at Madrid, gives, in his "French History of the Restoration of the Bourbons," the account of this coup in the General's own words; for, favoured by the soldiers' friendship, Mr. Houghton had the opportunity of hearing the story first-hand, and the smart General, looking spruce and trim in his well-cut black frock, would often talk to the Englishman, when he met him in the salons of Madrid, of the way he took matters into his own hand when the republican Parliament could not manage the Congress.

"No, no," said the former Governor of Madrid, "I admitted nobody into my counsel, but, under the stress of circumstances, I took all the responsibility upon myself. When I heard how the Assembly had given voice to a vote of want of confidence in Castelar, I thought the hour had come; and as the session the next day increased in force and disorder, whilst the hours of early dawn succeeded those of the evening and the night in fruitless and violent discussion, I called a company of the Civil Guard, and another of the Cazadores, and, to their surprise, I led them to the square in front of the Congress, and stationed them all round the building. Then, entering the Parliament with a few picked men,

173

I surprised the deputies by ordering them to leave the House. A few shots were fired in the corridor on those who sought to defy the military order, so the members did not long resist, and by four o'clock in the morning I found myself in complete command of the House. I called a Committee, with the power to form a Ministry, of which General Serrano was once more elected President, and thus ensued the second period of the republic."

This brilliant and successful coup reminds one of that of our Oliver Cromwell when he freed the country of a particular Government; but in this case of military sway in Spain General Pavia acted from no aims of self-interest, but only for the restoration of order, which it was his duty as Governor of the city to preserve.

During the second period of the republic, which lasted from January 4, 1874, till December 30 of the same year, Serrano had his hands weighted with two civil wars—the never-ceasing one of Carlism in the Peninsula, as well as that of Cuba—and, as Francisco Paréja de Alarcon says, in the criticism which he publishes in the above-mentioned work on this period, the Government formed under Serrano proved unable to restore order and save Spain from the dishonour which was threatening it.

So when the Ministers heard of the rising at Sagunto, on December 29, 1874, for the restoration of the monarchy, they knew that the movement was really supported by leading military men, who had been inspired thereto by the ladies of the land, who resented the irreligion and disorder of the republic; and, as they saw that resistance would only lead to another disastrous civil war, they resigned their posts peacefully.

It was thus that the son of Isabella II. was raised to the throne. And Alarcon says: "The hypocritical banner of 'the country's honour' was set aside; for had it not meant the support of a foreign monarchy, destitute of prestige; and then an unbridled, antisocial, impious, and anarchical republic, which was a blot on the history of our unhappy Spain in these latter days, which have been so full of misfortunes under the government of the ambitious parties which harrowed and exploited under different names and banners?"

174

The Circulo Hispano Ultramarino in Barcelona, agitating continually for the restoration of Alfonso XII., was a strong agent in the monarchical movement. Figuerola Ferretti worked strenuously as secretary of the society, and this officer is the possessor of the only escutcheon signed by Alfonso XII., in which he paid tribute to the Colonel's valiant conduct in the Cuban War of 1872.

It is interesting to see that the opinion of the republic published in "Contemporaneous Truths" by this Ferretti was echoed by the great leader of the party himself, for Señor Castelar writes: "There were days during that summer of 1874 in which our Spain seemed completely ruined. The idea of legality was so lost that anybody could assume power, and notify the fact to the Cortes, and those whose office it was to make and keep the laws were in a perpetual ferment against them.

"It was no question then, as before, of one Ministry replacing another, nor one form of government substituting another; but a country was divided into a thousand parts, like the Kalifat of Cordova after its fall, and the provinces were inundated by the most out-of-the-way ideas and principles."

When the great republican speaks in such a derogatory way of the republic of which he was the leader, it is not strange that public opinion turned to the restoration of the Bourbons as the salvation of the country. Society clamoured for such balls and entertainments as had formerly taken place at Court, or which had been patronized by the palace, and the dreary disorder wearied both politicians and patriots.

The house of the Dukes of Heredia-Spinola never ceased to be the scene of the reunion of Alfonsists, and as General Martinez Campos played his daily game of tresillo at their table, many expressions of hope for the return of the ex-Queen's son fell upon his ears; whilst the Countess of Tacon, who had been Lady-in-Waiting to the little Prince of Asturias as a child, was loud in her opinions. It is interesting to note that this lady subsequently filled the same office for the restored King's little daughter, the Princess of Asturias, Doña Maria de las Mercedes.

From a social point of view the salon of the old Countess of Montijo ranked foremost in Madrid, and it assembled within its walls the frequenters of Court society in the reign of Isabella. Scenes from "Don Quixote" were given with great success at the Countess's little theatre; and the year of the restoration was marked by a very successful dramatic representation, in which some of the members of the old nobility took part.

Moreover, the services held every Friday in the private chapel of the mansion, where great preachers made remarkable orations, were a protest against the irreligion of the period. On these occasions ladies of Court society, among whom may be noted Clara Hunt, wife of one of the diplomats of the English Embassy—who was quite a notable singer—gave proofs of their talent.

The niece of the Count of Nava de Tajo was another of the distinguished ladies who frequented the salon of the Countess of Montijo. The Count was varied in his interests. One afternoon he paid a series of visits, beginning with the Pope's Nuncio, going on to the house of Canovas, then to Roque Barcia, who was asking for subscriptions for his famous dictionary, and ending with the unhappy Lopez Bago, who was seeking support for his Review of the Salons, of which only three or four numbers were ever published.

XV.

THE REVIVAL OF COURT LIFE IN SPAIN UNDER
ALFONSO XII
1874–1884

The foregoing brief sketch of the political and social life in Spain during the republic will have given some idea of the joy which filled Spanish hearts at seeing the Bourbons once more on the throne of Spain in the person of Alfonso XII. Madrid indeed was wild with joy when the little Prince whom we saw at eleven years of age, in his blue velvet suit and lace collar, leaving his country as an exile, with his mother and family, re-entered the royal palace as a young man eighteen years old in January, 1875, having wisely passed through Catalonia, which Martinez Campos had gained over to the cause, and pleased the people by saying: "I wish to be King of all Spaniards."

As Isabella had abdicated in favour of her son on June 26, 1870, there was no impediment to his taking the oath of coronation soon after he was summoned to the Spanish capital. Of a good figure, gentlemanly, and well cultured, Alfonso added the art of good dressing to his other attractions, and the excellent taste and cut of his clothes led to his being called "the Beau Brummell of Spain."

The Countess of Campo Alange, who had assisted at the ceremony, in Paris, of Isabella's abdication in favour of her son, was one of the first to pay her respects to Alfonso XII. on his return as King to the Court of Spain. She went in a beautiful costume of crushed-strawberry-coloured satin, and she carried in her hand a snuff-box decorated with a picture of the entry of Charles IV. into

Badajoz, and it was with a graceful speech that the Countess drew the King's attention to the miniature.

"What a memory you have, Marchioness!"

"Oh, facts and people remain in my mind when they are forgotten by others," returned the lady; and the affectionate look she cast at the King reminded him of her fidelity to his family.

In his youthful exuberance of spirits, the young King was always ready to join in any frolic, although he was not lacking in serious and intelligent application to matters of State.

It was the Monday preceding Shrove Tuesday, and Alfonso had remarked somewhat regretfully that the rollicking spirit of the season seemed somewhat subdued. This the Duke of Tamanes determined to remedy, so, when the Cabinet was assembling for a royal audience, he swiftly emptied a bag of flour over the head of the Minister of War, who gravely sat down to business in his transformed condition, much to the amusement of Alfonso.

The young King was always genial and affable, and anxious to avoid too much ceremonial etiquette when it might cause discomfort to those who followed it.

One day he came unexpectedly into the Archæological Museum of Madrid with an Austrian Prince. There he found two men studying with their hats on; for all those who use public institutions in Madrid know that the cold is intense during the winter in these buildings. At the entrance of Alfonso the students promptly bared their heads.

"Don't do that," said the young King kindly; "put your hats on again, or I shall have to take off mine."

Alfonso was a bright and attractive figure in Spanish Court society. His gift of making verses, either gay or sentimental, as the occasion warranted, was always attractive, and he slackened the stiff rules of Court life as much as possible.

The Ilustracion Española y Americana publishes an excellent account of the historic ball given by the restored monarch:

"The festivities which celebrated the restoration of King Alfonso XII. in the feudal mansions of Spain finally saw their culmination in the magnificent ball given at the royal palace by the young

178

monarch and his widowed sister, the Infanta Isabella, the heir to the throne, on January 15, 1877.

"The state apartments were illuminated by millions of candles in the crystal chandeliers; the double-winged splendid staircase— guarded at the foot by the historic white marble lions, and lined with the Royal Guard of the Halberdiers in their high black-cloth leggings, slashed scarlet cutaway coats, tricorn white-banded hats, and their glittering Toledan steel halberds, at attention— was crowded with thousands of guests in gorgeous uniforms and lovely toilettes, who were radiant at this opportunity of once more greeting royalty at a great fête.

"The King, with his sister, looked smiling and happy, and their genial words of welcome warmed the hearts of the guests.

"The fine ballroom was soon filled with the stream of people in gorgeous array; the large mirrors on the wall reflected the dancing of the stately rigodons, so that they could be seen from the entrance of the room even by those who could not obtain a place within its precincts.

"A magnificent supper was served, and so perfect was the arrangement that 3,000 people were able to partake of it without confusion.

"To the royalties who gave this ball it offered little real enjoyment, for the strict Court etiquette only allowed them to dance a few rigodons according to the protocol, and to pass through some of the illuminated salons, where they greeted those privileged to approach them."

In his anxiety to make acquaintance with his kingdom, Alfonso went this year to Barcelona, Granada, Malaga, Seville, Asturias, Galicia, etc., and he took his place as the head of the grandees of Spain when, with all due pomp and ceremony, he was made Grand Master of the Orders of Santiago, Alcantara, Calatrava, and Montesa.

It was on December 8 in this year that the Duke of Sexto went to Seville to formally ask for the hand of Doña Maria Mercedes, the seventeen-year-old daughter of the Duke and Duchess of Montpensier, in marriage for her cousin Alfonso XII.

The royal suitor had long been attracted to this charming girl, and during the years of his exile many were the happy days he spent with his cousin in his vacations from Sandhurst at Vichy. When walking out together in the watering-place, the thoughts of the young people would sometimes wander to the possible future, and the young cadet, whose purse was occasionally very attenuated, would regretfully turn away from some pretty present he would gladly have bought for his cousin, saying: "It is rather dear; but never mind, I will buy it when I am King."

The account of the delicate mission of the Duke of Sexto, the Marquis de la Frontera, the Chamberlain, and Don Fernando Mendoza, Secretary of the Etiquette and Mayordomo of the Royal Palace, is given in the publication mentioned below.* The Duke and Duchess of Montpensier were in the white salon of their palace when they received the request for the hand of their daughter in marriage to the reigning King of Spain; and they were well pleased with the suggested alliance, as they trusted that the hope of Louis Philippe, that his descendant should sit upon the throne of Spain, would soon now be fulfilled.

When Alfonso followed the favourable reception of his request by a visit to Seville, all went merrily enough in the royal circle.

A magnificent Court ball was given at the Palace of San Telmo on December 26, to celebrate the royal engagement. The first rigodon was led off by the King with his fiancée, looking fascinating, gowned in white and glistening with jewels; the Infanta Doña Luisa Fernanda danced with the Duke of Sexto, and Alfonso excited much admiration by the able way he conducted the cotillon.

However, the Princess of Mercedes had not been the only girl friend young Alfonso had had during his exile. For when he could not go to the Montpensiers at Vichy, the ex-King liked to visit the Austrian Archduke and Duchess at Biarritz, as he found their daughter Maria Cristina très bonne camarade, and well able to hold her own with him in a game of tennis or billiards. Maria Cristina seems to have been attracted by Alfonso, for when his

* "The Wooing and Marriage of Alfonso XII."

180

marriage was announced with Mercedes of Montpensier, she joined the rich and noble Chapter of Prague, of which she accepted the responsible office of Lady Abbess, with an annual income of 20,000 marks.

The marriage of Mercedes and Alfonso took place on January 23 with all befitting ceremony. The Patriarch of the Indias blessed the union in the Church of Atocha. The ex-King Francisco was best man, and the Infanta Isabella represented her grandmother, Queen Maria Cristina, as the chief lady at the ceremony.

The retinue of the palace, the grandees, the fine caparisoned horses with their bright-liveried lackeys, the gorgeous coaches with their magnificent trappings, all made a striking show as they swept through the Spanish capital from the church to the Court.

But a note of horror was struck when a sudden awful sound was heard, and a woman fell dead struck by a bomb; but no other fatality occurred, and cheers filled the air as the troops of the capital filed before the palace, where the Royal Family witnessed the review from the windows.

The genial character of the young King was seen in a letter to an Archduke, a college friend, shortly before the death of his beloved Mercedes. This friend, with all due respect to Alfonso as King, mentioned the fact of his marriage with a young Princess of Spain. To this communication the King replied that he never forgot college friends, whom he preferred in many cases to later ones.

"I forbid you to address me as 'Majesty'; treat me as you treated me in the Teresiano. When you marry, come to Madrid with your wife, whom I shall at once regard as a friend. Mercedes is very kind; we will hunt, and we will chat about old times, and so your honeymoon will be spent as happily as mine was...."

But a telegram soon followed this bright and happy letter. It ran thus:

"My dear Frederick,

"Queen Mercedes is dead. May God give you in your marriage the happiness which He has denied me! In your approaching days of joy remember the woe of your friend.

"Alfonso."

It may be mentioned that Queen Isabella wrote to Madrid to signify her displeasure at her son's marriage, for the fact that the daughter of Montpensier, who had intrigued to succeed her on the throne, became Queen of Spain was rather a bitter pill to swallow.

However, all animosity on that score ceased at the death of the beautiful and lovable Queen, who had had undisputed sway in the heart of her young husband, and whose intelligence and good feeling at the age of eighteen had promised so much good for the country. There were not lacking those who attributed the dreadful event to the enemies of the Montpensiers, but others said it was due to a chill. During the sufferings of the last few hours the young husband sat in sorrow by the bedside, and the much-loved wife strove between her attacks of pain to comfort him with the hope of meeting in a future world.

At last all was over, and the poor young Queen was laid out in state on a low couch in the stately Hall of Columns. This Hall of Columns was often used for state banquets, but, after being the scene of the last sad functions in honour of his beloved wife, Alfonso had a new banqueting-hall built, and the salon of such sad memories has never since been used for any but solemn ceremonies, such as the washing the feet and feeding the beggars by royalty on Maunday Thursday, the Chapter of one of the grand military Orders, etc.

The corpse of the young Queen was dressed in the white garb and black cape of a nun of the Convent of Don Juan de Alarcon; the lower part of her face was covered with a white gauze handkerchief; her beautiful white hands, which looked like wax, were crossed on her bosom; and her face, which had been so admired a few short weeks before—when, according to the custom of Spain, she passed through the streets on foot on Holy Thursday, to make her visits to the churches in company with her husband and the Court—looked drawn with pain and fever as it lay in the light of countless candles.

The public defiled sadly through the mortuary chapel, and many were the Masses celebrated by the Church dignitaries on the altar erected at the end of the hall.

On the day of the funeral the royal cortège solemnly passed down the soldier-lined streets to the station. The sound of the horses' hoofs was deadened by the tan with which the roads were strewn, and the silence was only broken by the piercing note of an occasional clarion or the dull tattoo of the muffled drums. Grandees, Gentlemen-in-Waiting, mace-bearers, and officers, all with crape badges, preceded the catafalque, before which was borne the standard of the Sisterhood of the Royal House, followed by the cross and the clerics in their vestments. Finally came the band of the halberdiers, whose soblike strains of a funeral march was in tune with the occasion.

At last, for the first time in history, the remains of a Queen were placed on a railway-train for the Escorial, and so the coffin of Mercedes left the station amid the booming of the cannon and the strains of the Royal March played for the last time in her honour.

A short time after the death of the Queen, Alfonso was the object of a regicidal attempt as he was passing No. 93 of the Calle Mayor, on his way from the station to the royal palace after a visit to Asturias. The criminal was a young fellow, twenty years of age, from Tarragona, named Juan Oliva Montcousi, and he was caught with the pistol in his hand before he had time to discharge it. The young King was enthusiastically acclaimed when he calmly pursued his way home as if nothing had happened.

Alfonso's three younger sisters, Doña Pilar, Doña Paz, and Doña Eulalia, were often seen at this time in a quiet carriage making excursions together, so when the news of the death of Doña Pilar spread through the capital it gave quite a shock to Spain.

It was said that the death of the Infanta Doña Pilar was indirectly due to a shock received during the review held in honour of the Prince of Austria. This Prince was known to have made a favourable impression on the Infanta, and if she had lived it would probably have resulted in a marriage. But, unfortunately, as the artillery carriages in the military function were passing down the Alcalá, one blew up and killed several soldiers on the spot. Perhaps for a moment the Infanta feared that the honoured guest was among the killed and wounded. Be that as it may, she and other members of the Royal Family were upset in the carriage, and she died six weeks later.

Talk of the second marriage of the King followed very soon after the death of Queen Mercedes, as a direct heir to the throne was so essential to the country, and all eyes turned to Maria Cristina Enriqueta Reniera, daughter of Charles Ferdinand, Archduke of Austria, as the future Queen of Spain. The Duke of Bailen went to Vienna to ask the Emperor Joseph of Austria for the hand of his daughter, the Archduchess Maria Cristina, for his Sovereign, King Alfonso of Spain.

On August 22 Alfonso arrived at Arcachon, incognito, under the title of the Marquis of Covadonga, to claim in person the hand of the Archduchess.

Alfonso had reason to expect he would be favoured by Maria Cristina, as she had always seemed to enjoy his society when he came to visit her family, as a young cadet from Sandhurst. The royal wooer gave expression to his poetic feeling when he found himself on such a delicate mission at the beautiful spot which had been so frequented by our poet Shelley. People in the place seemed at once to recognize the royal visitor, especially as he wore his arm in a sling, from the effect of a carriage accident which had been noised abroad.

Anxious for the interview which was to decide his fate, Alfonso took a basket pony-carriage from Monaco to Arcachon, and, in company with the Duke of Tetuan and the Spanish Ambassador from France, he soon found himself at the Villa Bellegarde, the abode of the Archdukes of Austria.

When the young King passed into the salon, where he was soon welcomed by Maria Cristina, his eyes fell upon the portrait of Mercedes, whom he had lost a few short months before, and he soon found that his bride-elect was in sympathy with his sorrow for his loss, for, in a voice trembling with emotion, she said:

"My dearest desire is to resemble Mercedes in all things, and even if I am to succeed her I can never dare hope to supplant her."

Such a sympathetic speech could but unseal the heart of the widowed King, and, having succeeded in his wooing, Alfonso could hardly tear himself from the side of the young Archduchess, with whom he could talk so freely of the wife he had lost.

On August 29 the young King finally left Arcachon; the Archduchess accompanied him as far as Bordeaux, and the royal marriage was fixed for November 29.

When the Archduke and Duchess and their daughter arrived at the Casa de Campo on November 23, they were met by the King, his three sisters, and the royal retinue, who accompanied them to the Palace of the Pardo, where the marriage settlement was signed on the 28th.

The bride-elect won all hearts by her delicate and sympathetic behaviour on the occasion, for, turning to the Patriarch of the Indias, she said, in a voice broken with feeling: "Pray that I may make the King happy, for it is a difficult task to succeed a Queen who was a saint, and who will always live in the affections of the King and the people of Spain;" and here she drew a miniature of Mercedes from her bosom, and gazed at it with respectful admiration.

This ceremony took place in the banqueting-hall of Ferdinand VII., and, to the delight of the Spanish people, it was graced by the presence of the ex-Queen, Isabella II.

"The great Isabella is coming!" was the cry that rang through the capital, and the dethroned Queen was moved at the enthusiasm of her quondam subjects as she passed through the city, for she saw that there was more fidelity in her people of low degree than there had been gratitude in the hearts of the great whom she had overwhelmed with favours.

The wedding ceremony took place in the Church of Atocha, and hardly was the service concluded when the King's bride went and knelt at the feet of Isabella and kissed her hand. It was a tribute of gratitude to her royal mother-in-law, for it was a fact that the influence of his mother had led the young King to take his new bride from the House of Austria. Isabella had signified her disapproval of the union with the Montpensiers by not being present at that wedding, but this marriage she favoured from the beginning.

A few days after the royal marriage an attempt was made on the lives of the young couple, by a man named Francisco Otero Gonzalez, as they arrived at the chief entrance to the royal palace; but, fortunately, although the bullet almost grazed the forehead and neck of the King and Queen, they escaped unwounded.

Queen Maria Cristina is a very accomplished woman, and she soon set herself to learn the language of her adopted country. In her eagerness to master the tongue, she often turned to King Alfonso to supply her with the word she required, and, in fun, he would often supply her with some expression which she saw, by the looks of her entourage, was hardly fitting for a lady. Maria Cristina proved she had made great progress in Spanish when she was able, with all the gracious courtesy for which she was noted, to ask of a certain academician, who was complaining of the hatred of Sagasta, would he not do better to use the word inquina than inquinia?

The affection with which the Queen inspired the young King was seen in his daily letters to the Court when journeys on State business obliged him to absent himself from Madrid.

"I have just put your carnation in water," he would write; and the many other allusions to their little domestic joys showed that the heart of the King was with the Queen in his absence.

The Queen had to contend with national jealousy at Court when she intimated her wish that her Austrian physician, Dr. Riedel, should attend her in her forthcoming accouchement. Court etiquette was not, however, to be set aside even by the chief lady in the land, so the matter was finally settled by the doctors of both countries presiding jointly over the event. Thus the little Princess of Asturias made her entry into the world, on September 11, 1880, with her right hand held by the Austrian physician, Dr. Riedel, and her left in the grasp of the Court doctor of Spain.

The young King proudly presented his little daughter to the Prime Minister and his Cabinet, the Court officials, and the military diplomats and clerical dignitaries, assembled in the antechamber, as she lay in a nest of costly lace on the historic silver tray.

On September 14 the baptism of the infant Princess of Asturias was celebrated with all the pomp usual to the occasion. The galleries were hung with the historic tapestries, representing Bible scenes. The Royal Guard, in their classic dress and with their shining halberds, formed a line on either side of the gallery between the people and the royal procession.

First came the Gentlemen-in-Waiting, de casa y boca (of the house and the mouth), their gold or silver keys signifying the respective offices of attendance; then came four mace-bearers, grandees of Spain, the men-at-arms with the royal arms, all the Infantes and Infantas in full Court dress, with their ladies and gentlemen in attendance; the seven gentlemen of the Chamber— the Marquis of Salamanca, the Dukes of Almenara and Valencia, Count Villanueva de Perales, the Marquis of Sotomayor, the Marquis of Benamejis de Sistallo, and the Count of Superunda— all passed in gorgeous dress and with stately step, bearing respectively the salt, cut lemon, cruse of oil, piece of cotton-wool, the cake, the white cape, and the water of Jordan, which all had their part to play in the baptismal service.

The royal infant itself was carried between Isabel II., who was godmother, and the Pope's Nuncio, who represented His Holiness as godfather. Then followed the proud young father, accompanied by his military suite, and the procession ended with the band of the halberdiers, playing a cheerful march from an opera. By the wish of the Queen, the infant Princess was named, after her predecessor, Mercedes.

It was in 1882 the King and Queen paid a visit to the Duke and Duchess of Montpensier at their beautiful Palace of Sanlucar de Barrameda, and the Queen won the hearts of her host and hostess by her charming manners and the admiration with which she always spoke of their daughter, the late wife of Alfonso.

On November 12, 1882, the Infanta Maria Teresa was born, and two days later she was baptized with the customary ceremony.

On April 2, 1883, the King's sister, Doña de la Paz, was married very quietly to Prince Lewis Ferdinand of Bavaria. The Prince is a very able surgeon, and when he comes to Madrid he delights in going to the military hospital and exhibiting his scientific skill on some soldier-patient.

The newly wedded pair laid the foundation-stone of the Cathedral of the Almudena, and, according to the custom, the Princess de la Paz placed in the casket a poem from her own pen to the Virgin of the Almudena. The departure of the Infanta de la Paz left the Infanta Eulalia with no companion in her musical and artistic tastes, for the sisters had worked, played, painted, and poetized, together.

In September, 1883, Alfonso XII. went to France and Germany. True to his old friends, the King went to see the Warden of the Teresian College at his private house. As he was not at home, Alfonso asked for a pencil and paper to write him a note, which he handed to the servant. When she saw that the letter ran,

"I came to pay a debt of gratitude by coming to see you. I shall be going to the Teresian College in two hours.

Alfonso, King of Spain"

she fell on her knees and entreated forgiveness for her stupidity in having asked the royal visitor into the kitchen.

But Alfonso, with his usual kindness, expressed interest in this, the first kitchen he had ever seen. He asked many questions about the utensils, and showed great curiosity about the use of a ceramic vessel, which, according to the description he subsequently gave and the sketch he made of it to show the Court officials, proved to be an egg-poacher.

The enthusiastic reception accorded to Alfonso at Homburg excited the ire of the French, and so antagonistic was the exhibition of public feeling as the young King was crossing Paris alone that he informed the President of the Republic that he would recall his Ambassador at once. This prompt act brought the necessary apology, and the King of Spain subsequently attended the banquet given in his honour at the Elysée, at which the Minister of War was absent, as the President of France had asked him to send in his resignation.

The news of this contretemps reached Spain, and when the Queen returned from La Granja to Madrid she was at first quite alarmed at the enthusiasm shown by the people at the station. She clasped her children to her breast, and seemed to think she was on the brink of a revolution. But her fears were soon stilled when somebody shouted: "Señora, the Spanish people are only protesting against the recent events in Paris."

The return of the King from France saw an ovation of equal enthusiasm, and, in defiance of all Court etiquette, the people pressed up the staircases and into the galleries of the palace, crying: "Viva el Rey y la Reina!"

It was on Maunday Thursday, 1884, that the Court went for the last time in state to make the customary visits on foot to the chief churches of the capital. There was the usual service in the morning in the chapel of the palace, the washing of the beggars' feet and feeding them, and the solemn, imposing public procession at three o'clock in the afternoon. The streets were strewed with tan to soften the cobbled stones to the feet of the ladies, whose high-heeled velvet shoes rather impeded their walk. The streets were lined with troops, and the Plazas de Oriente, Mayor, and La Encarnacion, were respectively filled with the regiment of the Princess of Pavia and the artillery.

First came a mounted company of the Civil Guard; then a long line of kettle-drummers, the grooms and all the officials of the Court, all in full dress; then the six men-at-arms with their embroidered vestments, the Chamberlains, gentiles hombres, the grandees of Spain, the King's military retinue, etc.

Their Majesties walked between the lines of halberdiers, followed by the Patriarch of the Indias, the Ministers of the Crown, the chiefs of the palace, the Ladies-in-Waiting, and the Aides-de-Camp of the King and Queen.

A Captain of the Guard and about thirty lackeys carried the historic sedan-chairs, and notable among them were those of the Dukes of Granada, Osuna, and Villahermosa, ornamented with beautiful paintings.

The procession ended with a company of halberdiers and a squadron of the royal escort.

Don Alfonso walked with martial step, his head in the air, and smiling pleasantly to all the friends he saw. He was in the uniform of Captain-General, with the Order of the Golden Fleece and other decorations.

In this final public visit to "the Virgins," the Queen wore a white velvet robe embroidered with gold and ornamented with sapphire buttons, and her necklace and bracelets were of the same precious stones. She wore the Orders of Maria Luisa and the starred Cross of Austria. The dress of the Infanta Isabella was of pale blue velvet embroidered with flowers, and all the dresses and mantles of the royal ladies were of equal magnificence, with tiaras of jewels and feathers and mantillas on their heads, and, as all the ladies of the Court also had their places in the procession in splendid attire, one can imagine it was a superb show; but it was not one to be seen again in the public streets.

The health of the King was now beginning to give anxiety at Court, and loyal subjects regretted that people in high places did not use their influence to stimulate the King in his good desires for the welfare of the land, instead of pandering to his fancies with adulation and flattery.

Charming ladies literally forced their way into the palace, and one day Queen Maria Cristina gave a well-deserved* box on the ears to the Duke of Sexto, when she came upon him introducing a dancer of light character to His Majesty. It is noteworthy that one of the first acts of the Queen as a widow was to ask this Duke to resign his post at the palace.

It was to such flattering courtiers that Maria Cristina owed the shadows which crossed the happiness of her married life, for under good influence Alfonso would always have been true to Maria Cristina, as the King loved and venerated her above all women; but when politicians encouraged the escapades of an attractive young Sovereign the wife's influence was weakened. Queen Maria Cristina was deeply offended when she found that her husband's connection with this Elena Sanz was a well-known fact, two sons being born to the singer.

It was then that it was seen that the Queen was no mere weak woman who would submit calmly to what might be termed los costumbres (custom) of the Court; and when she found that the King had a rendezvous with a señorita in the Casa de Campo, the

* "La Vie intime d'Alfonse XII.," par Croze.

magnificent wide-stretching park beyond the palace, she declared she would leave Spain and go back to Austria.

Nothing but the strong pleas and arguments of those about her, including Alfonso XII., persuaded her to stay at the Spanish Court, and it was certainly due to this illustrious lady that a higher morality there became customary. For, as nobody ever was able to breathe a word against her honour, she subsequently exercised her right, as Queen-Regent, of sweeping the Court clean of those who smirched its purity.

Moreover, those who had expected Alfonso XII. to save Spain by the introduction of a pure and unmystified suffrage, such as he had seen in England when studying at Sandhurst, were disappointed in their hopes; for Canovas, the leader of the Conservatives, openly said at Court: "I have come to continue the history of Spain"— which meant the history when the voice of the people is not heard; and Sagasta, the head of the Liberals, acted in the same spirit, although he did not express himself so openly.

Canovas, the leader of the Conservatives, and Sagasta, the chief of the Liberals, used all their eloquence at the Court of Spain to persuade Alfonso XII. that sincere elections in Spain would lead to the Carlists attaining a majority in the Congress. So the King, not seeing that the leaders of both parties wished to prevent the realization of a true Parliamentary representation, because it would lose them their patronage of deputies' seats, ended by signing the Pacto del Pardo. This document, endorsed by the King at the country palace, was simply an arrangement between Canovas and Sagasta, by which each was insured an equal period as Prime Minister, so that their respective partisans could feel that their patrons had the same amount of influence.

And yet Alfonso XII., who was overborne by what he considered the experience of the two leaders, had the welfare of his country at heart, for he said to Ernest Daudet: "I am Sovereign, and as long as I am King of Spain I will never allow a Ministry to be overthrown by an intrigue in the palace, as it has frequently happened hitherto. If the country wants a Liberal Government, it shall have it; but, before talking of liberty, Spain herself must have both liberty and stability.

As to those who say I am not accessible to truth, it is because they have not tried to show it to me. The country is difficult to manage; it is impatient, and cannot see, as I do, that its condition requires prudence and management. We have remade the army; we have not had a manifesto for three years. We have a standing army of 80,000 men, and we have been able to send 20,000 to Cuba. The insurrection of Cuba is a great wound, and it must be healed before we can cure the other evils." But the King was never allowed to take the sure means of healing these wounds; he was never permitted to say: "I wish to respect the people and their votes, and by the Law of the Universal Suffrage they can go to the polls."

With the loss of the love of his life, the young Queen Mercedes, Alfonso seemed to become enervated, and self-interested courtiers found that they could use the King's pocket for the protection of needy ladies of all ranks.

Canovas and Sagasta were both aware of this abuse, and, indeed, both these Ministers were themselves under the influence of certain ladies, who used their power over these Ministers to their own pecuniary advantage; for they themselves were liberally rewarded for the titles which they persuaded these politicians to ask the King to grant.

The Queen's ignorance of Spanish when she first came to Madrid made it more difficult to contravene the influence of the camarillas, which wove their nets round the young husband, whose real wish for the welfare of the country would have made him a willing disciple of good advice.

Moreover, flattering courtiers carefully concealed from the King the sad results which would inevitably follow his course of self-indulgence, and the palace became a constant scene of camarillas and intrigues which could but be disastrous to the land.

Even Nakens (whose protection of the anarchist Morral, after the bomb tragedy of the royal marriage morn of May 30, 1906, led to his being imprisoned for nearly two years) pays tribute to the wish of the young King to act for the welfare of the kingdom, for, in a collection of his articles published when he was in gaol,* we

* "Muestras de mi Estilo," Nakens.

read an appeal to Alfonso to consider his own good with regard to his health, and not to listen to self-interested advisers.

"Nobody," says the writer in this appeal, "has the courage to warn you of the impending evil. When the doctors order you change of climate, the Government opposes the course for reasons of State. 'Reasons of State' imperil the life of a man! And a man to whom we owe so much!

"Therefore, even as a republican, I beg you, as the occupier of the throne, to look to your health, if it be only to overthrow some iniquitous plan, or some unworthy object which is contingent on your illness; and if scientists think it well for you to pass the winter in some other place in Spain, or abroad, follow their counsel, and not that of interested politicians, in sacrificing your life to their ambitions."

It was certainly true that the King was overborne by the intrigues of the politicians in the palace. Even in such a little social matter as that of wishing to go in costume to a fancy ball, the King could not have his own way, for Canovas showed such aversion to Alfonso donning fancy attire for the occasion that he had to abandon the idea and wear his ordinary dress.

If such influence had been used to the prevention of the King favouring a danseuse like Elena Sanz, which brought so much sorrow and so many complications in the Royal Family, his life might certainly have been prolonged. It was true that the doctors advised the King's wintering in Andalusia, but "State reasons" led to the failing Sovereign being exposed to the colder climate and sharp winds of the Palace of the Pardo, where politicians could use their influence with the invalid, and remind him continually that he alone was the arbiter of parties.

Alfonso was only twenty-seven years of age when he felt he was doomed to an early death; but his natural energy led him to take horse exercise, despatch business with his Ministers every day, and, in spite of daily increasing weakness, to do as much as possible.

If his longing for the sea-breezes of San Sebastian had been gratified, his life might have been prolonged; but politicians gave little heed to the plea, and their authority was paramount.

On November 24, 1894, the royal invalid was seized with faintness when he came in from a walk. Queen Maria Cristina, Queen Isabella, and the Duchess of Montpensier, were called to his side. Seeing his wife by him when he recovered consciousness, the King embraced her, and the alarming symptoms vanished for a time; but the following day he was seized with another fainting fit, which proved fatal.

We read in La Ilustracion Española of this date, that when Queen Maria Cristina was told by Dr. Riedel that all was over, she fell weeping at the head of the bed of her unhappy husband, whilst covering his hand with kisses.

Cardinal Benavides performed the sacred office of the occasion. The doctor could not suppress his emotion, and hid his face, covered with tears, in his hands; and Count Morphy, the King's faithful secretary, went sorrowfully to announce the sad news to the Queen-mother and the rest of the Royal Family.

At nine o'clock the next morning the little daughters came to embrace their father for the last time. The Queen, with only the assistance of Dr. Camison, prepared the body of her husband for burial, and she assisted at the obsequies in the Escorial with her little daughter, the Queen of Spain. Arrived at the historic monastery, the Augustine Brothers came to meet the sad cortège, in their black vestments and holding lighted torches, and, headed by the Prior and the Principal, the procession passed to the burial-place of the Kings.

The iron seemed to enter the soul of Maria Cristina when the Chief of the Palace cried before the catafalque: "Señor, señor, señor!"

Solemn silence reigned. "Then our Sovereign really is no more," said the Chamberlain. He broke his wand of office, whilst the drums of the halberdiers, the bells of the cathedral, and the booming of the cannon, added to the solemnity of the occasion. The Bishop of Madrid officiated at the final office, after the coffin was finally carried with countless candles down into the Pantheon, which he had entered ten years before in all the exuberance and with all the illusions of youth.

Then the unhappy widowed Queen returned to Madrid, there to pass the sad months till the child should be born who might prove the future King of Spain.

It was an impressive sight to see the Queen, with her orphaned little girls, take the solemn oath of Regency. Putting her hand on the Gospels, which the President held open, she said:

"I swear by God to be faithful to the heir of the Crown during the minority, and to guarantee the Constitution and the laws. May God help me and be my Defence; and if I fail, may He require it of me!"

Then the Queen sat down with her little girls, and the Prime Minister made the following formula:

"The Parliament has heard the solemn oath just made by Her Majesty the Queen-Regent, to be faithful to the legitimate successor of Don Alfonso XII., and to guard the Constitution and its laws."

The marriage of the Infanta Eulalia with Don Antonio, son of the Duke and Duchess of Montpensier, in 1886, was the next interesting function at the Court of Spain.

The Montpensiers seized this fresh opportunity of becoming connected with the Spanish Royal Family, and Doña Eulalia augmented their riches by a large sum of money; but it seemed as if fate wished to warn the Infanta that the marriage would not be happy, for it was postponed through the illness and death of her brother, and she was weeping as she came out of the royal chapel on her wedding-day. And, indeed, it was not long before the Infanta found her husband was utterly unworthy of her, and she now lives apart from him.

The Infanta Eulalia was a great loss to the Court of Spain, where her bright intelligence and charming ways had made her presence like sunshine. She was twenty-two years of age when she married, very pretty and high-spirited, an expert in riding and driving, and a lover of all kinds of activity.

Her father, Don Francisco, and the Duke of Montpensier—who, we know, killed Don Enrique, her uncle, in a duel—supported her at the altar; and Queen Isabella, the Comtesse de Paris, the Queen-Regent and her little daughters, were also at the ceremony.

This Infanta is often seen at the Court of Spain, with her son Alfonso. It was she who warned Alfonso XIII., when he presented his new-born son to the assembled Ministers, that the infant might catch cold if exposed too long; and at the royal baptism on June 2, 1907, she looked striking in her long train of scarlet velvet, with the satin front sewn with jewels, and with scarlet plumes surmounting her tiara of diamonds.

Even those who had not been in favour of Alfonso were rapidly gained over to the Bourbons when they saw the difficult position of the Queen-Regent. All the chivalry of the Spaniards was aroused to support the young widowed mother in her trying task.

When a lady of the Court condoled one day with the royal widow, and expressed wonder that she could so valiantly seek to steer the ship of State whilst suffering the pain of loss, and not knowing how fate would settle the question of the future Sovereign of Spain, Maria Cristina looked up at the speaker, and said with a smile in which courage seemed to conquer sorrow:

"But, Duchess, everything is easy when one has hope."

The character of Alfonso XII. is sympathetically drawn by Don José Fernandez Bremon. He says:

"He was affable and extremely simple in his manner, and opposed to strict etiquette and Court ceremonies; much given to riding, hunting, shooting, and all physical exercises. His favourite study was that of the relation of science with war. He was an adept of poetry, and he much liked public applause. His facility in speaking and his flow of language inspired confidence in his auditors and in those whom he received in audience. His affability gave people more the idea that they were speaking with the emigrant from Vienna than the King of Spain. He was short, but well-proportioned and slender. His eyes were expressive, and he was what the Spaniards call very simpatico. He liked starting discussions on daring theories. He was very prudent in the Council Chamber. He was clever, and he sometimes spoke as if he felt himself taken captive in the gilded cave of government."

XVI.

THE PALACE AND POLITICS DURING THE
REGENCY OF QUEEN MARIA CRISTINA
1894–1902

The country was certainly in a very unsettled condition at the commencement of the Regency, and the difficulties of administration were increased by the insurrections in Cuba and the Philippines, which were unquestionably due to the corruption of the Government of the mother-country.

The recently published "History of the Regency," by Señor Juan Ortega Rubio, which I had the privilege of studying in the library of the royal palace at Madrid, throws much light on the state of affairs at this period; for the author ably sets forth in the prologue the political condition of the country during the Regency.

"There were certainly plenty of vehement politicians and eloquent orators," says the writer, "but we can scarcely cite one true statesman. Favouritism was never more dominant and prevalent than it was at this time. And favourites whose advancement was due to adulation and daring, if not to insolence, gave no support to industrious men, and much less so to those who were firm and energetic.

"The army, professorate, Church, and, indeed, all the professions, were regarded as schools of politics, and were in the greatest state of decadence.

"No respect could be accorded to flattering courtiers or to an ignorant people. If the beautiful sun of religious tolerance shone upon the whole of Europe, Spain would be the one country condemned to dwell in the shades of fanaticism.

"It is necessary to raise the moral sense of the Spanish people. If this be necessary in all moments of history, it is more than ever indispensable now that despair is taking possession of all hearts, doubt of all spirits, egoism of all consciences, and positivism of all men.

"From the sixteenth century Spain has been gradually going down. We do not lose hope, but we think, like the Roman Plato, that the sun of education will gradually pierce the clouds of ignorance, slavery, doubt, and sophistry, and the dawn of justice, order, and faith, will break over our land."

Thirty prelates came to condole with the Queen on the death of the King, and the Church always made a great claim on the attention of the Queen-Regent in consideration of her former position in the religious house in Austria.

It was said that, if the Pope left his magnificent home at the Vatican, he would come and take up his abode in Spain; but, as the Figaro said:

"The Government of the Queen-Regent will thus put itself completely under the power of Leo XIII., who will be treated like a Sovereign; and he will, they say, be given the Palace of Aranjuez for his residence."

When the Queen-Regent asked Canovas whom she ought to appoint President of the Ministry, he promptly said, "Sagasta"; but the Congress was a fictitious Congress, for, as Martin Hume says when referring to the Parliament in the earlier part of the century:

"There was not then, and never has been since, any sincerity or reality in the pretended antagonism of the political parties."

The lack of sincerity in the political opinions, even of those devoted to the monarchy, is shown by Rubio in the speech of Martinez Campos to Silvela; for he said:

"I am neither a Liberal nor a Conservative. I made myself a Liberal because I thought the King wanted the Liberals to come in, and now I am a Conservative because the Queen wanted to give the power to the Conservatives."

The politicians in the camarillas at the palace always brought forward the phantom of Carlism to scare the Sovereigns from

198

fulfilling their desire of promoting true Parliamentary elections, and true patriots sought to show King Alfonso XII., Queen Maria Cristina, and, later, Alfonso XIII., that those who tried to prevent the country from enjoying this constitutional privilege of going to the polls were only anxious to preserve their own patronage in the nomination of the deputies, and that the monarchy would be adored by the nation if it favoured the reform which had been promised in the days of Ferdinand VII.

The Queen-Regent Maria Cristina was told that the public offices were in the hands of patrons, and it was well known that a recorder in the law courts of Barcelona was blind, but he owed his place to being the brother of the cacique (or influential person) who supported Canovas in Catalonia; and there was also a magistrate in Madrid who could not see, but he, too, had his patron.

The Queen lent a willing ear to the plea of the Chamberlain for reform in these matters, and an inquiry was instituted about the blind recorder at Barcelona. But so powerful is patronage that, although the recorder had been seen to have his hand guided to sign the necessary documents, it was declared that he was not blind; and the informer of the abuse nearly lost his life at the hand of a relative of the man in power who had allowed such a state of things, for he was struck by a sabre at the back of the head, and prostrated senseless to the ground.

Naturally, the wounded man wished to call out his assailant for such an insult, but the Queen-Regent, who sent daily for news of the injured man, begged him, as a favour to herself, to abstain from further steps.

To this request the officer was obliged to accede, on the condition, which was confirmed, that the assailant should formulate a full apology for his deed, and this was done.

It is difficult for foreigners to realize the power of the cacique in Spain. He is always the most influential person in the district, and the appointment of Judges, Alcalde (Mayor), Governor, and deputy, are all in his hands. The man he suggests as representative of the district in the Congress is sure to be elected, and when the Ministers wish a certain person to have a place in Parliament, the name has only to be sent to the cacique who supports that Minister.

Caciquism cripples Spain, and the collection of magnificent speeches and articles published in a large work under the title of "Oligarchy and Caciquism" shows that every man of importance in Spain can give his testimony against the evil which crushes the country; but, eloquent as they are on the matter, the Ministers do not take a step to do away with a system which advances their own ends.

So, as Martin Hume says, "No attempt is made, or, indeed, can be made under present circumstances, to trample out the evil that is sapping Spain's vigour—empleomania; no bold politician dares to look facts in the face and speak the whole truth. And so the evil circle is complete; dishonest Governments are faced in sham battle by dishonest oppositions, and Parliamentary institutions, instead of being a public check upon abuses, are simply a mask behind which a large number of politicians may carry on their nefarious trade with impunity."

And when it is remembered that, according to the law of Spain, it is the King alone who has the right of appointing a Ministry, it is he who has to bear the onus of what goes wrong.

An amusing story is told of a Señor Comas, who was a cacique of Sagasta's. The gentleman had been bidden to an audience of Her Majesty at half-past six. He arrived at the palace punctually, as he had promised to return to dinner with his grandchildren. Some hours elapsed in the antechamber; diplomats came and went, and many others who, according to the strict Court etiquette, were to take precedence of the politician.

At last he became impatient, and the thought of his grandchildren waiting so long for his return overcame all politeness; he took up his coat, put it on, and, to the astonishment of the Court officials, he prepared to depart.

"You are going, sir?" said the lackey at the door.

"Certainly," was the reply; "it is dinner-time, and my grandchildren are waiting for me."

"But what shall we say to the grandee?" said the servant, raising his hands to heaven, and referring to the grandee in attendance on the King.

"Tell 'the great one' (el grande)," returned Comas, "that 'the little one' has gone off."

And so he did.

The remark was repeated at Court, and the following day the Queen-Regent received the cacique with demonstrations of respect.

Queen Maria Cristina always encouraged those who really wished to counsel her for the welfare of Spain. When, therefore, somebody was loyal and disinterested enough to present a programme to Her Majesty which would do away with the abuses of the Government by introducing a true Parliamentary representation, she pressed the paper to her bosom, crying: "Yes, yes, it is true, it is true, and I will do it!"

But politicians would not support a course which limited their exclusivism, and so things went on in the same fatal way.

To the surprise of the Court, Castelar, the great republican leader, made at this time a great speech in which he showed that the advanced opinions of his partisans were not incompatible with monarchy, for he said:

"When our fanaticism made us think that monarchy was incompatible with public liberty, we did not understand the monarchical principles of England, Sweden, or Norway. But now I can tell you that a monarchy should be a Liberal monarchy."

And the orator went on to say that a Liberal monarchy is a democratic monarchy in so far as the universal suffrage became an accomplished fact, for a democratic monarchy is the formula of this generation.

Of course this speech, which certainly showed that the leader of republicanism had considerably modified his views, called forth much remark, and gossip in the press even went so far as to associate the name of a "charming royal widow" with that of the great orator.

But Sagasta set the matter right by saying, in one of his speeches, that "those who spread such reports were strangely ignorant of the temple of the soul of the august lady, and that no credence was to be given to the stories."

More sincere than the monarchists, Castelar made a strong protest against the mode of Parliamentary elections, for he said: "The census is a lie, votes do not exist, and scrutineers destroy what there are."

This statement of facts could not be refuted, and the Central Union gave voice to the opinion that "municipal elections, like all others, should be the result of universal opinion, and that the indirect intervention of the Ministers was deserving of censure."

Such expressions of opinion show that there was a deeply rooted feeling of the falsity of the Spanish Parliamentary system, but it required politicians to be patriots to reform them.

The corruptions in the Spanish colonies were, indeed, a standing proof of the evil wrought by the Parliamentary system of patronage, as it introduced people to places of importance in the colonies who were utterly unfit for them. The Marquis of Salamanca made a vehement protest against these abuses in the colonies, which were estranging them from the mother-country; and Maura, as Minister of Foreign Affairs, made one of his first marks as an orator by setting forth before the Congress the evils of the dishonest actions of those whose advance had been due to their patrons instead of their patriotism.

Canovas declared in the Congress that "he was very anxious that the Great Antilles should elect its own representatives, so that its voice could be heard in the national Congress"; but, unfortunately, the statesman did nothing to promote such an advisable course, and the leaders of the political groups held to the power which they gained from the patronage of the colonial posts.

Canovas, who now called himself the "Liberal-Conservative," in his fear that his Liberal rival should gain more partisans than himself, went on to say that "the Government recognizes the necessity of introducing great reforms in the administrative and financial affairs of the island of Cuba, for the political posts ought to be filled by the sons of the colony"; and he ended by saying: "When the triumph of our arms is an accomplished fact, and when the rebellion is suppressed, these reforms will be realized in a wide and generous spirit."

But unfortunately the triumph of the Spanish arms could not be accomplished, for they were led against insuperable difficulties, and it was an injustice of the mother-country to expect that her forces could prove victorious against the forces of a continent like that of America.

It required a strong hand to save the Spanish Court from the overbearing of one whose father had adopted revolutionary ideas.

It was the Duke of Seville, the eldest son of the late Don Enrique, who, when in command of the Guard at the palace, entered the antechamber of Maria Cristina's apartments one day, and demanded an interview. The Gentleman-in-Waiting said that Her Majesty had just returned tired from a walk, and had given orders that she could not receive anybody. But the Duke insisted, uttering disrespectful remarks as to what he could do if he were driven to desperation. These words were repeated to the Captain-General, who commanded the division to which the Duke of Seville belonged, and he was summoned before a court-martial.

The Minister of War made a speech, in which he said: "When the whole nation vies in showing respect and sympathy to a lady who claims protection in her dignity and her misfortunes as a widow, it is deplorable when a person of the family of the Bourbons shows such disrespect, which has such a bad effect on all, and which can only be explained as a momentary aberration of reason."

The trial led to the Duke of Seville being condemned to eight years of imprisonment.

The Queen-Regent was always far more concerned about matters of the State than about those of her own comfort, and the Court was certainly wanting in good service at this time, and Her Majesty caught a severe chill one cold day, because the fur cloak she had asked for was not forthcoming, when she had to go out in an open carriage to attend an important function.

And it can be said with truth that the luxuries of a Court did not include the necessary one of having fresh eggs for breakfast. A Chamberlain having noted the sweet patience with which the

Queen bore the daily vexation of finding the eggs musty, finally ventured to present her with a little egg-boiler and some fresh eggs. The gifts were accepted with the Queen's usual grace, and with the assurance that she would now be able to enjoy an egg in her own apartment, like one of her subjects.

In the evening Maria Cristina played dominoes, listened to music, or conversed with the greatest affability with those present, whilst trying to forget for a time the cares of the State.

It was now that Catalonia began to show signs of insisting on a true suffrage, and Ferretti saw that it would be much better for the monarchy to satisfy this natural desire for a voice at the polls than for it to be enforced, as it subsequently was, to the misrepresentation of the Region in Madrid. So the Colonel wrote to press the matter on the consideration of Señor Canovas de Castillo. But the Prime Minister's insight was not willing to read the signs of the times, for he wrote the following letter, which I translate from the original:

"February 4, 1887.

"To Colonel Señor Don Luis de Figuerola Ferretti.

"My dear and honoured Sir,

"In reply to your letter of the 1st instant, stating that I gladly note the regionalist tendencies of Catalonia are fortunately unauthorized by sensible people, and it seems that the effervescence of the first moments is passing off, I think it best not to publish anything that has reference to the matter.

"However, I thank you very much for your efforts in the cause of order, and I beg to remain,

"Yours very sincerely,

"A. Canovas del Castillo."

Thus the statesman wilfully shut his eyes to the importance of the movement, which they vainly hoped was a mere passing feeling.

But, sure in his presage of the signs of the times, Ferretti strove to show the Queen-Regent that the politicians turned a deaf ear to the will of the Catalonians, because they wished to keep the patronage of the seats of the deputies in their own hands; for if deputies were elected at the polls there would be an end of patronage, and people fitted for the representation of the respective centres would be elected by the constituents themselves.

Moreover, the dreadful abuses in the colonies from this same source of patronage made the Cubans raise their voices high on the matter. Martinez Campos had seen things as they were in Cuba in 1878, and he found that Spain could only put an end to the Cuban War by promising the Cubans the autonomy for which they craved. But when the General returned to Spain he was unable to keep the promise made in the name of his Government, as the Parliament did not wish to abandon the fruitful field of patronage.

It was some time before Martinez Campos received any reward for his loyalty in proclaiming the restoration of Alfonso XII. in 1874. Politicians told how Alfonso XII. refused any title as a sign of gratitude, and as time went on disappointment was expressed at the seeming neglect of the officer. It was then that a Chamberlain at Court ventured to say to the Queen-Regent: "Your Majesty will have been told that Martinez Campos has refused a title for himself; but may it be suggested that a title be offered to his sons?" And thus Maria Cristina, who was always ready to render justice, conferred the title of the Duke of Leo d'Urgel on the eldest son, and that of the Marquis of Bastan on the second one. Moreover, after the death of the great soldier, the Queen-Regent made his widow a grandee of Spain.

The enthusiasm shown in the spring of 1907, when a statue was unveiled to the memory of the ardent Monarchist, showed that neither the Royal Family nor the country had forgotten his services to the throne.

The failure of the country to keep the promises of Martinez Campos to the colonies in 1878 was felt in 1897; but politicians in the palace still represented matters, and the Queen-Regent was under the impression that autonomy would mean Separatism. It was then that a Chamberlain showed Her Majesty a letter from a cousin in Cuba, the mother of more than one leader of the insurrection, for in this letter the mother said that she would willingly sacrifice her sons for the autonomy which would save the island from ruin, through the abuses and corruptions of the Government at home. And with the grant of the autonomy America would have no further excuse to interfere in the matter.

With a true Parliamentary representation in Spain, such an important State matter could not have been left in the hands of a man like Sagasta, who, like other politicians, used the intrigues of the palace for a perversion of the truth. The deputies, if they had been real patriots instead of being merely the tools of those in power, would have risen as one man against the refusal of the autonomy; the good sense of the Queen-Regent would have been satisfied, and the prestige of Spain and her colonies would have been saved. And to those who think this statement exaggerated, I must say that as Maura, the present Prime Minister, permitted me to address him some questions on the policy of Spain, I asked the great statesman if it were true that the abuses in the Governmental departments caused the loss of Cuba, and he replied emphatically in the affirmative. This confirmed the report in the country, for it is well known that, as Minister of Foreign Affairs at the time, Maura lifted up his voice in the Congress for the reform of the evils which threatened and finally caused the loss of the colonies.

Moreover, Maura boldly took up his stand for the much-required suffrage for Spain, when he said in the Congress:

"A country cannot maintain its loyalty to the Crown in the integrity of its national being, if it cannot count on the will and the hearts of the inhabitants."

When the country was filled with anxiety at the sudden serious illness of the little King, the stocks fell, the Carlists began to make themselves conspicuous again, and evil threatened the land with the shadow overhanging the Court, and the anxious royal mother was constantly heard to cry:

"Oh, child of my heart! My God, do not take him from me!"

But it was not in idle tears that the royal mother spent her time by the baby boy's bedside. Everything that the knowledge of hygiene and her love as a parent could suggest was brought into use, and finally Maria Cristina had the triumph both as a Queen and a mother to report the child out of danger.

Castelar wrote to Sagasta at this time, saying:

"I am very anxious for you to convey my respects to Her Majesty, and tell her that I have inquired after her august son, the King, twice every day; and please do not forget to add how sincerely I congratulate her on his restoration to health."

It was, indeed, quite due to the rare intelligence of the Queen-Regent and her knowledge of the laws of hygiene that little Alfonso XIII. was saved for Spain.

It was by such proofs of her intelligence that Maria Cristina gradually asserted her just sway at Court. It had been a great struggle in the first years of her widowhood to gain this sway, for she was liable to be set aside as a stranger in a foreign country, of which the language was unknown to her, and she could not help knowing that derogatory remarks were made about her even by her royal relations. Her very name was against her, as Spaniards associated it with that of the mother of Isabel II., who was said to have exploited the land to her own ends. The Duke of Seville, Prince Henry of Bourbon, was heard to say, in the presence of the Royal Guard, in 1886: "Of course, the Regency cannot be entrusted to a foreign Princess." But he found afterwards he was wrong in the estimate he had formed of the Austrian lady.

Whilst Alfonso XII. had been alive, Maria Cristina did not feel she was merely a stranger in a foreign land, and she was often compared to a ray of sunshine, so bright and joyous was she at Court. For, always active, merry, and happy, her six years of married life had passed without heed of the cares of the State, so it was a surprise to the Spaniards to find that she was possessed of such diplomatic power.

Moreover, the Queen-Regent's intelligent care of her child during his illness was a practical lesson to those around her; for, fond mothers as Spanish women are, the laws of hygiene play little part in their education.

The little Prince, Alfonso XIII., was indeed a charming child, and soon gave proofs of his affection for those about him, whilst being the despair of his governess, Señora Tacon, by the way he set the strict laws of Spanish Court etiquette at defiance.

"Ah, Juanito! bon petit Juan!" he would call out to the distinguished General Juan de Cordova, Marquis of Sotomayor; and the Duke of Bivona he dubbed "Xiquena." Señora Tacon strove to prevent this familiar style of address by saying:

"But, Sire, Your Majesty must recollect that the gentleman to whom you are speaking is the Duke of Bivona."

"The Duke of Bivona!" returned the little King mockingly. "That's all very well, but I know it is Xiquena. Are you not Xiquena?" he continued, addressing the grandee. Then, seeing a smile on the solemn countenance of the Duke, he continued: "You see, this lady is always giving different names to people. She says that my Juanito is General Juan de Cordova, Marquis of Sotomayor. Don't be silly!" he added, turning to Señora Tacon. "That is my Xiquena, and the other is my Juanito—so there!"

The King's childish way of settling things developed as he grew into a lad into the power of forming logical conclusions which would have done credit to any statesman.

A Chamberlain one day ventured to suggest to the Queen-Regent that it would be good for the kingdom if a royal visit could be paid to Barcelona; for if the King did not go to Barcelona, it was not a question of Catalonia separating itself from the rest of Spain, but of the Court separating itself from Catalonia. The courtier's idea was repeated to the young King by his mother as he came into the room.

"Yes, yes," returned Alfonso, with his prompt acceptance of a good suggestion. "If we do not go to Catalonia, it is just as if a prelate did not visit one part of his diocese, which would mean separation from that district."

It was in 1898 that the terrible débâcle of Cuba realized the worst fears of patriots. The Queen, who had been so badly advised in the Council by Sagasta, was overwhelmed with grief. The army and navy, and even the throne of Spain, were loudly attacked, instead of the Government which had brought them the disaster.

It was then that Figuerola Ferretti had the clever idea of having a great illustration placarded about the streets of Madrid, headed by a representation of Mercier's picture of an angel carrying a wounded man, with the device "Gloria Victis." For glory was due to the men who had suffered nobly and hopelessly in the struggle to which politicians had provoked the colonies by their maladministration; and leaflets, setting forth the same idea, were distributed broadcast by thousands in the streets of Madrid.

This daring protest for the prestige of the Spanish army and navy doubtless stemmed the tide of public opinion, and the Queen-Regent congratulated the chamberlain on his loyal course.

Castelar, in an article he published in La Nouvelle Revue, put all the blame of Spain's misfortunes on Maria Cristina, even going so far as to compare her with Marie Antoinette, who was so fatal to France. But one must recollect that, as Rubio says, Castelar said in the Congress: "'I am an historical republican, an invincible republican, a republican all my life by conviction and by conscience, and he who doubts my republicanism offends and calumniates me, and for this reason I do not wish to be anybody in any monarchy.'"

But General Blanco declares, with greater justice, that the blame of the Cuban disaster should rest on the shoulders of Sagasta; and El Liberal of that date says:

"Señor Sagasta is the one, and the only one, responsible for the terrible misfortunes which assail our country.

"It was he who advised the Queen-Regent to persist in the course which led Cuba to seek the intervention of America; and when the royal lady seemed ready to listen to the wisdom of patriots who pleaded for the autonomy of the colony, he would present himself at Court, and there once more persuade the Sovereign to his false view of the matter."

As Rubio says in his able "History of the Regency":

"When Sagasta, Romero Robledo, Silvela, and Gamazo spoke in the House on this burning question, their speeches seemed more like essays in polemics in an athenæum than discussions in an assembly of legislators on a matter entailing the salvation or the ruin of the country."

To those who preferred to be true patriots to flattering courtiers the state of affairs was desperate, for they felt indignant at the Queen-Regent being persuaded to a course for which, as Sovereign, she would have to bear the chief share of the blame; and Ferretti, who years before had served under General Blanco at Saint Domingo, and had keenly felt the loss of prestige to the Spanish army when he had to obey orders and lead the last company from the island, fought hard to prevent a similar disaster in Cuba in 1898.

In August, 1897, a shudder ran through Spain when Canovas fell by the hand of an Italian anarchist, and the fact was still more shocking as the republican Nakens had been told by the perpetrator that the deed would take place, and he did nothing to warn the statesman.

For ten years Canovas had been the foremost figure in the Congress and the Court of Spain. The prominent part he had taken in the restoration had placed what we should call the "strawberry-leaves" on the brow of his wife; and when, after the tragedy of Santa Aguedas, the widow followed her husband's corpse into their palace in the Castellane, it was to retire definitely from the banquets, reunions, and great functions in which she had always shone so successfully and conspicuously as the wife of the Prime Minister of Spain.

After the death of Canovas, Silvela came forward as the leader of the Conservatives, for the camarillas and intrigues of the followers of Canovas had hitherto barred his way to high preferment in the Parliament.

It was known that the Queen-Regent was inclined to patronize General Polavieja, and there were also Villaverde, Romero Robledo, and numerous other politicians who all had their partisans, and sought by camarillas in the palace to gain power for their partisans.

The Queen-Regent often used her charm as a woman to captivate those opposed to the monarchy, and this power, exercised with all the rigidity of a lady of strict morality, had its due effect on General Cazola. It was well known that this officer enjoyed great prestige in the army, and as he was republican in his opinions, he could have become a sort of Oliver Cromwell in Spain. He was the only man Canovas stood in fear of, and Sagasta did not breathe freely till death removed him from his path.

Maria Cristina was quite aware that he admired her, and when she heard that the General had given voice to one of his speeches, which might prove fatal to the loyalty of the army, she sent for the officer, and with all the charm of her manner she let him see that she was conscious of the power he could exercise against the dynasty if he wished. Touched with the evident anxiety of the Queen, all the chivalry of the gallant General was called into play, and, putting his hand on his heart, he soothed the fear of the Sovereign by saying: "Do not be afraid. Your Majesty is sacred in my eyes."

Such conquests were a satisfaction to Maria Cristina, both as Queen and woman; and when one noted the great personal influence of the widowed lady, one could only wish she had given herself more scope for its exercise, and had not submitted herself so freely to priestly guidance.

Some dissatisfaction was caused among the Liberals by the Queen's appointment of a Bishop especially for the palace, where the Prelate of Madrid had officiated formally. As he had no diocese, the Pope gave him the title of Bishop of Alcalá and Sion, and this appointment meant the institution of forty Canons at the Court. The duties of these Canons was specified as that of drawing the curtains in the royal boxes of the chapel, but now there are no curtains to draw.

It was whispered by the partisans of Silvela that Polavieja was favoured by the clergy, and with him in power the Queen-Regent and the country would be given over to the clerical party. Canovas had allowed the lady in power to be called the "priestess," and Sagasta had repeated to the Queen-Regent reports which were circulated as to Señora Canovas boasting of having more power than the Queen herself.

Finally, after the death of Canovas, and a short term of power of General Azcarraga, Silvela was put at the helm of affairs. But the camarillas at Court again led to the fall of the Ministry, for Silvela's choice of Loño as Minister of War was opposed by the choice of Polavieja by the Sovereign.

Thus, when Figuerola Ferretti saw that the impending death

of Sagasta would lead to the Liberal party being cut up into as many groups as that of the Conservatives, so that the country would on both sides be a prey to the intrigues at Court of the partisans of the respective groups, he ventured, in view of the very superior intelligence manifested by the young King, after he had attained his majority, to represent to His Majesty that true Parliamentary elections were the only means of solving the problem of government, and for this he could exercise his royal prerogative of forming a Provisional Government. The King seemed to listen to this proposal with approval, and, indeed, if this election of the deputies by public vote had been promoted in the capital, it could never have been used by republicans as a cloak for Separatism.

The petition for this step was drawn up in the names of the widows and orphans of those who had fallen in the Cuban War. It was sent in proof to the secretaries of the King and the Queen-Regent. But the patriot had not counted on the antagonism of those in power; and albeit Loygorry, the follower of Lopez Dominguez, spoke eloquently in favour of the idea in the Senate, Moret, the Minister of the Interior, stopped its course by forbidding the Prefecture of the Police to affix the necessary seal to the document; and it was doubtless through such political influence in the palace that the Chamberlain found that further influence with the King was prevented by his removal from Court.

The cordial reception of the Colonel by Alfonso XIII., when he saw him in London in 1905, was cheering to the patriot, and it seems more than probable that the King is unaware of the Court intrigue by which his valued adviser was removed from his side.

It was in 1905—only a fortnight before his death—that I had the privilege of seeing Don Francisco Silvela, who had spent so much time and effort in the service of his country.

"I am utterly weary of politics," said the statesman, lifting his tired eyes to my face. "It is a fruitless task, and no one is safe from the intrigues at Court. No, no; I am going to give up my spare time to literature now, which will be far more profitable. And, indeed, it seems like pouring water into a tank with a hole in it to expend efforts on the country which is unsupported by a true suffrage."

It is thus that Alfonso, in 1906, had to appoint seven different Governments in the space of fourteen months, and it would sometimes require more than supernatural power to detect the real cause of the fall of a Cabinet in Spain.

XVII.

ALFONSO XIII

May 17, 1886, the day on which Spain hailed the birth of their baby Sovereign, Alfonso XIII., is always kept as a fête-day in Spain. Shortly after Señor Sagasta had proclaimed the news to the assembly of Ministers and grandees of the realm, the Duchess of Medina de las Torres appeared in the antechamber, bearing in her arms a basket that contained the royal infant. Wrapped in cotton-wool, the infant King received the homage of his Ministers.

Five days later Madrid was en fête for the baptism of the royal child. Wearing a robe of the richest English lace, and the broad velvet sash, embroidered with fleurs-de-lis, that his father had worn at his baptism, the royal infant was borne on a silver salver, draped with costly coverings, through the lines of officers, statesmen, and Court ladies, into the chapel of the palace, where at a solemn service he received the names of Alfonso León Fernando Maria Santiago Isidro Pascual Antony.

The second birthday of the baby King was celebrated by a review in the Prado. The Queen was on horseback, dressed in black, without any ornaments. The Minister of War was on her left hand, and the Duchess of Medina behind her. Her horse was startled by the quantity of flowers thrown before the royal rider, but, being an excellent horsewoman, the Queen controlled the animal, and no mischance happened.

Aided by the Duchess of Medina de las Torres, the Señora Tacon, and an excellent nurse, Queen Cristina devoted herself entirely to the care of her child. His rooms were in close proximity to her own private apartments, and "Puby" (a German pet-name), as she called him, learned from an infant to look for the loving good-night visit of his mother, who, seating herself at the head of the blue silk curtained cot, would hush her boy to sleep. Her soothing caresses grew, as time passed on, to be tender counsel to the child.

Unwilling to sacrifice his physical health to his mental progress, the Queen waited till her son was seven years old before planning for him a course of serious study. With an hour's steady instruction daily, the young monarch soon learnt to read and write with ease. It is interesting to know that he was never allowed to use a word without being thoroughly acquainted with its meaning. By this means he acquired an intelligent interest in things about him.

It was at the seaside resort of San Sebastian, in the beautiful palace of Miramar, that the royal child's second course of instruction commenced. Don Regino Zaragoza was his tutor for geography and history. About this time also he began rapidly to gain ground in French and Latin. But the quick intelligence of the lad did not impair the mischievousness natural to his age. I was told by the King's Chamberlain that once, when he was about eight years old, streams of water were seen running down the corridor from the bath-room of the royal palace. The door of the apartment was found to be locked, and it was only when the Queen herself insisted on its being opened that the young delinquent was discovered enjoying what he called "a naval battle in high seas," the ships being logs abstracted from the wood baskets, and the high seas the overflowing bath.

The same courtier told me that once, when staying at the Casa de Campo (the country place near Madrid), the boy escaped from his governors to climb up on to the roof of a building, which he had remarked as the resort of some roosters.

It must be remembered that the young King's courses of instruction were always those of the Universities and institutes of the kingdom. He usually wore the uniform of a cadet of the Military Academy, except when, on a visit to a man-of-war, he adopted the naval dress. That his tutors found him a docile pupil can be gathered from the following anecdote: When one day a professor stood waiting for his royal pupil to be seated, he laughingly shook his head, saying: "No; you are the master, and I am the pupil. It is for you to be seated first."

Queen Cristina overcame her son's difficulty with German by composing a small grammar for him, which enabled him to master the rules of the language in a simple and amusing form. His inquiring turn of mind and his desire to thoroughly understand many subjects were early made apparent by his leaning towards natural science, chemistry, etc.

The King's love for all that is military dates from his earliest childhood, when his great delight was to watch the change of the royal palace Guard from his nursery window. His boy regiment is now almost historical. Many of its members still talk of their delight at its promotion to the dignity of a Mauser gun of a most professional calibre. Their young Captain's power of resource and command was evidenced in the way he carried the day in a wager made with his child soldiers that they should not on the morrow meet the admiring eyes of their parents at that part of the royal palace where the Foreign Office then had its bureaux. The following day the young battalion approached the palace. The little subalterns, about to glance at the windows, thought they had won the bet, when lo! in clear sharp young tones there rang out the command: "Vista à la derecha!" (Look to the right!). Not an eye was turned towards the palace windows, and the royal commander scored.

Early rising has, of course, been always an essential part of the young King's programme, or he would not have time for such pursuits as photography (developing his own plates, and in this he excels), swimming, bicycling, music, painting, etc., as well as his graver studies.

During his minority Alfonso XIII. rose at 7 o'clock, and, after a cold bath and some exercise in the gymnasium near his bedroom, he had a light breakfast with his mother and sisters. From 9 to 10 o'clock came a lesson in French from Don Luis Alberto Gayan, or in English from Don Alfonso Merry de Val. At 10 o'clock he went for a ride on horseback until 12 o'clock, when he lunched with the Queen and the Infanta. Then, after a lesson in German or music from Señorita Paula Czerny, or in painting from Don José Pulgar, the King again walked or rode, generally in the company of his mother. At 2 o'clock he had military instruction, and between 3 and 4 o'clock a lesson in universal history, or in fencing with other boys, under Don Pedro Carbonell. From 5.30 to 6.30 came a lesson in political law and administration, and once a week a lesson in general Spanish literature and classics. Dinner was at 7.30, and the remainder of the evening would be passed pleasantly in conversation or in playing duets with his sister Maria Teresa until it was time to retire to rest.

This programme was punctually adhered to, under the direction of Don Aguirre de Lejada, the director of His Majesty's studies, and excepting when the King went to church on a Saturday afternoon at 5 o'clock with his mother and sister, it was rarely relaxed.

It was the royal youth's natural simplicity, combined with his splendid education, that saved him from embarrassing self-consciousness on the great occasion, when on May 17, 1906, he took the Constitutional oath (the Jura), which gave him the full rights of a King, in the Houses of Parliament (Palacio del Congreso), before the brilliant assembly of Princes, Ambassadors, and Ministers assembled for the occasion. The words were simple, but impressive:

"I swear before God upon the Holy Gospels to maintain the Constitution and the laws. If I do so, God will reward me, and if not, He will require it of me."

All present were touched at the young monarch's evident disinclination to take precedence of his mother when leaving the Palacio del Congreso. But the law of etiquette had to be observed: the Regency was over, the reign had commenced; the Queen's power had ceased, the King's sway had commenced, and, as the first person in the realm, he had to precede his mother.

But that very day the King issued a decree to the nation by which the royal mother retained all the privileges of the position she had held as Regent, which permits no one but the possible future wife of the King to take precedence of her. This, the first royal proclamation, shows the devotion of the son to the mother, for as Queen Cristina is out of the line of possible inheritance to the crown, she would otherwise have taken lower rank than her sisters-in-law or her daughters.

As the young Sovereign, after the solemn ceremony in the cathedral, took his place under the white satin canopy, and passed down the aisle, filled with the highest representatives of Church and State, the sun, streaming in Spanish intensity through the heavily carved oaken door of the cathedral, fell upon his face. He looked like some youthful knight of olden days. With his dark head held high and a look of resolution on his features that seemed to bode well for his office, he passed out of the cathedral into the sunshine and air, thrilling with the applause of his people.

The close association of the King of Spain with the Ministry gives play to intrigues at the palace, which cause dissatisfaction in the country, and the King alone has the responsibility for the result.

It was towards the end of 1906 when General Lopez Dominguez, the fifth Prime Minister in less than a year, was the object of a palace intrigue which brought his work to an end, and excited much discontent in the country. The Cabinet had given a vote of confidence in the General, and the officer subsequently reported the matter to the King.

But in the meanwhile the partisans of Moret had been intriguing at the palace, and the Prime Minister's assertion of the confidence shown him was met by a sceptical look from Alfonso, as he drew from his pocket a private letter from Moret, in which he threw doubt on the satisfactory state of Parliamentary affairs. The General, who had grown grey in the service of the King, stared blankly at the treacherous letter.

"Then Your Majesty has not complete confidence in me?" he asked, in astonishment.

The King did not reply, so the Prime Minister took the only possible course in the matter, and promptly offered his resignation.

Thus, Moret had plotted for his return to power, and, indeed, he was asked by the King to take the helm of affairs. This he did; but he was not prepared for the indignation of the Congress at the turn of affairs, and when he went to the Congress to make his opening

218

speech, he was met by such storms of disapproval and with such silent contempt that he abandoned his post in three days.

When Maura permitted me to address him some questions on his policy, I asked if he did not think a pure suffrage would be for the progress of the nation.

"Yes," he replied; "but the intervention of the Government is only to supplement the inertia of the nation."

But the Prime Minister did not seem to take into account the despair of the people at the uselessness of their efforts. Sometimes there is a call to arms against this want of activity, but to such appeals the Spaniard shrugs his shoulders.

"What is the use of my going to the poll, when I know perfectly well that my vote will be either destroyed or burnt?"

"It is, then, the duty of the Government," writes a pioneer in the Press, "to take great precautions for the protection of the polls, and even if necessary to guard them with a military force; for it is in the verity of the elections of these representatives in Parliament that lies the secret of the recovery of the virility of Spain."

Catalonia, as we know, has recovered this virility by insisting on the return of her own deputies, and the enormous enthusiastic meeting held in a great hall of Barcelona on June 29, 1908, to hear the deputies' opinions on a great matter of legislation shows how deep is the public interest in matters of politics, and how much the constituents appreciate their hardly-won privilege of being represented in the Congress by men they trust.

XVIII

PRINCESS VICTORIA EUGENIE
OF BATTENBERG AS QUEEN OF SPAIN
1906

As the Spanish authoress Concepción Gimeno de Flaquer devotes the last chapter of her book, "Mujeres de Regia Estirpe" (Women of Royal Degree), to Queen Victoria Eugénie of Spain, it seems that I should fall short of the mark were I not to publish some of the Spanish impressions of the present English Queen at the Court of Spain.

Señora Flaquer says: "The presence of the beautiful Princess at the royal palace is like a shining star on a dark night, a soft balmy breath of wind in a violent storm, a refreshing dew in hot weather, and a ray of hope in depression."

This description is Spanish in its imagery, and it is interesting to note the more measured language in which Figuerola Ferretti expresses the joy of Spain at the news of the engagement:

"The news is like a fresh spring of hope to us Spaniards, who regard any English girl as a symbol of sincerity and sweetness, and how much more so when that girl is grand-daughter of the great Queen Victoria, whose name is venerated throughout the Peninsula!

"Whilst regarding the entry of Princess Ena into Spanish spheres as the commencement of a new era for the education and progress of our women, who are only waiting for the opportunity to prove their intellectual worth, I must say I might have some fears lest the Princess should be chilled by the restrictions of Spanish Court etiquette, had not King Alfonso already shown himself capable of breaking down the unnecessary barriers which would prevent his future bride continuing the happy outdoor life and the social pleasures which brighten the existence of royal ladies in England.

"'Manners maketh man,' it is said, but it is also true that 'man maketh manners,' and when our monarch follows the natural and noble impulses of his heart, it is always to the making of a manner which expresses good feeling.

"The young Spaniard has marked with great interest King Alfonso's foreign mode of courtship, which oversteps the lines of our customs; and as he follows in the footsteps of the royal fiancé, he will soon see that invigorating motor-car excursions and walks in a garden with the queen of his heart are more conducive to mutual knowledge of character than perpetually thrumming on a guitar outside the lady's window, or only being permitted to whisper words of love in a corner of a room where the rest of the family is assembled.

"To judge from ancient records, the arrival of the young Princess Eleanor of England in 1170 as the bride of Alfonso VIII. of Spain led to a reaction against the strictures of etiquette introduced by the Moors to the extreme limitations of the liberty of our ladies; and it was by the natural assumption of a certain freedom of action that the daughter of young Henry II. passed a happy life of nearly half a century as Queen-Consort in our country. And Princess Ena is not likely to fall short of her English predecessor in her natural love of liberty.

"Readers of Mariana's 'History of Spain' may be struck with the resemblance of the meeting of the young royal lovers on the borders of Spain in 1170 and that of the illustrious couple at Biarritz. The ardent young Alfonso VIII. was charmed with his English Eleanor, even as our Alfonso XIII. admired the Ena of your land; and as Queen Eleanor associated herself with the promotion of learning and letters for men, and supported the foundation of the University of Palencia, our future Queen Ena will doubtless encourage the present movement for the education of girls, which has just culminated in the opening of the Middle-Class College under the committee of ladies of the Ibero-American Society, presided over by Queen Maria Cristina."

The joy foretold by the Spanish courtier was more than realized at the arrival of the English bride. Her bright, sunny smile and ready acknowledgment of the people's evident admiration of their future Queen delighted the people.

But the tragedy of the bomb cast in the bouquet, which caused so much disaster, came like a sudden frost, and nipped the spontaneous joy of the young Queen, and the drives and walks in the city of Madrid became a source of fear instead of joy. It is hard to us here in England to realize what the bomb outrage on her marriage-day was to Queen Victoria of Spain.

Wearers of the Victoria Cross and the D.S.O. have not often gone through such a terrible ordeal. For soldiers on active service are at least prepared for such tragedies, but in the glitter and gaiety of a marriage-day the blow was dealt in the dark.

An officer in the Wad Ras Regiment, who was close to the carriage, told me that he can hardly bear to speak of it even now. The gaily-decorated street was suddenly transformed into the fearful scene of a battle-field. The cries of the dying and the sight of the killed sent many people out of their minds. With the calm courage of a soldier's daughter, Queen Victoria neither swooned nor went into hysterics; but the shock went deep into her soul, and she naturally fears a repetition of the horror when she is in the city.

The people, therefore, are a little disappointed at their greetings not meeting with the quick response of the first days in her new land; and as Spaniards would do anything for a smile, and love to see happiness, this inborn terror, begotten of the tragedy of her wedding-morn, would form a barrier between the English Queen and her people, were they not reminded of the source of the set expression on her face.

In La Granja this is different. The freedom of the country life gives scope again for our Princess's smiles, and the beautiful gardens and the charm of the palace seem far removed from the tragedy of the city.

"Oh, how we adore her when she is like that!" said the simple-hearted, sympathetic Spaniards, as they saw the eager, guileless way the Queen showed her young cousin, Princess Beatrice of

Coburg, her lovely country residence; and after she had passed up the fine staircase of the palace, lined by the halberdiers sounding their drum tattoos of welcome, she appeared at one of the windows to smile on the soldiers as they saluted her in their parade past the palace.

Bouquets are naturally, of course, still looked upon with suspicion at the Spanish Court. When Miss Janotha, the celebrated pianist, wished to leave a beautiful bouquet at the palace as an offering to Princess Henry of Battenberg, when she was in Madrid, the lackey looked at it askance, saying:

"We are not to take bouquets."

Miss Janotha looked regretful, and I was very glad when a superior official stepped forward and said:

"We do not take bouquets, but as it comes with the English lady we know here, it is all right."

This confidence I acknowledged gratefully; the Polish pianist was pleased, and the bouquet was taken.

"The Queen is always her bright, merry self on the yacht," said a distinguished naval officer, when speaking of the shock of the bomb to the young Queen. "She sings, and is as happy as the day is long, for there is no fear of such tragedies on board ship."

One always connects Spain with sunshine, and Queen Victoria was interested at seeing the after-effects of a snow-storm in Madrid. Their Majesties sallied forth in a motor-car to the park of the Retiro. The Queen expressed her admiration at the clever efforts in statuary made of the snow which had fallen in the morning. The newly-appointed Prime Minister, Maura, was easily distinguished as a snow-man, and many other celebrities were recognized in this exhibition of snow-figures made by the street gamins. Great lions in front of the War Office also showed the skill of the officials in turning the snow into form when clearing the pathways, and in the squares and streets there were many presentments, both male and female.

The Infanta Maria Teresa was driving across the Puerta del Sol with her young husband during the inclement weather, when a mule of her carriage slipped on one of the tram-lines, which form a perfect network at this busy centre, and the carriage came to a standstill. The Princess descended from the vehicle, and would have walked home had she not herself slipped on the treacherous footwalk. Fortunately, the etiquette which formerly forbade a commoner to touch royalty even in a time of danger does not now prevail, and a policeman raised the Infanta from the ground, and placed her in a tram, in which the rest of the journey to the palace was made.

An Audience at the Court of Spain.

It was one morning during this short season of snow in 1907 that a charming Spanish lady, Señora doña Carmen Burgos de Seguí, called to ask if I would join her and two or three other members of the well-known Andalusian Centre in their visit to the palace to invite King Alfonso XIII. and Queen Victoria to a forthcoming fête to be held by the Centre at a theatre. All the formalities with reference to the audience had been arranged, and I was pleased to accept the invitation to join the commission.

As a fall of snow precluded the possibility of being able to obtain a carriage or cab—for the cobbled stones of the roads make it unsafe for horses in slippery weather—I put on my snow-shoes and fur cloak, and soon arrived with my companions at the royal palace, which flanks the whole side of the great Plaza de Oriente, and towers majestically above the richly-wooded valley of the River Manzanares.

The white-cloaked sentries, in their three-cornered hats, saluted us respectfully as we passed, and the colonnaded, rich-carpeted staircase soon led us to the gallery which lines the quadrangle of the royal palace.

A sympathetic porter helped me to remove my cloak and overshoes, and as I shook out my dress and donned my white gloves he said:

"Her Majesty will be very pleased to see a compatriot, for since last June she has not seen an English lady."

The ring of the halberds on the floor of the gallery as the historic

224

halberdiers changed guard, and the quick word of command, were the only sounds to break the solemn silence as darkness fell on the courtyard, where snow was falling softly.

A lackey in gold livery now issued from the royal apartments and met us in the gallery. He then conducted us to an imposing doorway leading to the landing of the state double-winged staircase, which is only used on very important occasions. It was in this gallery that the young King and his sister, Maria Teresa, startled Queen Victoria, on her first Shrove Tuesday in Spain, by jumping out at her disguised with masks.

The white marble lions, the blazing lights of the fine chandeliers, the rich carpets, the carved marble rails and handsome walls, looked like a scene in a fairy-tale as we saw it for the first time, and after passing several footmen and officials on the landing we reached an antechamber, where we were asked to wait our turn of audience.

The walls of this salon were hung with rural scenes embroidered on tapestry set in crimson velvet. Large mirrors reached from the floor to the painted ceiling, and reflected the crystal candelabra and the works of art which lined the room, with its crimson-satin-covered furniture on a velvet-pile carpet.

Just before we were summoned to the royal presence, I was told it was contrary to Court etiquette to wear a veil, so I removed it in time to obey the summons of the Court official, who appeared with the papers relating to our visit; and being handed over to the usher, we ran the gauntlet of the eyes of Chamberlain and military men standing about in uniform in every salon, and passed through a large anteroom with green-satin-panelled walls hung with pictures of the royal predecessors of the present King, and thence into a room like a large and splendid ballroom, where a lady was sitting on duty in full Court dress with a companion, and we were finally ushered into the presence of the King and Queen.

The Queen looked fair and regal as she stood in the beautifully decorated French salon in a perfectly-made pale pink dress trimmed with the finest lace, and the King was in the undress uniform of a Captain-General.

225

The Queen looked somewhat sad as she graciously received us, and she must, indeed, have thought that it was another wearisome occasion of speeches and remarks which would be in an unknown tongue to her. According to the etiquette of the Spanish Court, the King and Queen were both standing to receive us in the beautiful little boudoir. Indeed, the room seemed only arranged for such audiences.

My introduction to the King as an Englishwoman at once met with a cordial shake of the hand and a pleasant "How do you do?" after the Queen had gracefully greeted us. As Her Majesty looked pleased to see somebody from her native land, I begged to be allowed to address Her Majesty, and, passing behind the King to her side, I soon had the great delight of hearing her speak with pleasure of the Shakespearian Bazaar in London, where I had last seen her as Princess Ena; and when speaking of my friend, Miss Janotha, she said, "Yes, I have known her since I was so high," holding her hand a little distance from the floor.

In the talk with the Spanish ladies, Alfonso pleased one who has rather advanced opinions by the gusto with which he said, "Yes, there are indeed far too many associations in Spain!" for this remark showed that His Majesty is alive to the evil; and if the clerical party would only allow action to be taken to prevent this overwhelming number of religious associations in Madrid, it would be to the joy of the country.

For these associations ply their trades of printing, chocolate-making, boot-making, needlework, etc., and they undersell the trades of the lay-workers, as they have neither taxes nor rent to pay. This abuse the Government was seeking to remove by bringing in a law for the diminution of such societies, but the camarillas of the palace, instigated by the clerical party, checked the progress which Canalejas, the President of the Congress, was making in this direction, by causing the fall of the Ministry. It was falsely reported at the palace that Canalejas is atheistic and antagonistic to the Church, whereas he told me himself that he is very religious. He has a private chapel in his house, where Mass is celebrated every day. But, as the Minister said, this matter of the associations (of which many are from Belgium, France, and other parts of the Continent) militating against the trade of Spain is a matter of State policy, and has nothing to do with religion.

"And now the King is offended with me, and I have no chance of an explanation with His Majesty," said the ex-Minister, who a short time before had been patted on the back for his zeal for the welfare of the land.

When I looked at the young Queen, so tall, so elegant, and so alone in a foreign land, I felt how difficult it must be to fulfil her rôle to the satisfaction of all parties.

The report that the expected royal heir's layette was to be made entirely in Spain excited much commendation; but when I went to see the things at the best shop in Madrid, I could but note that they were not so fine as I had expected.

"No, no," said the proprietor of the place; "all the best things are made in the convents, and we have only the second and third best. The Queen, I believe, meant to benefit the trade of Madrid, for she was so sweet and gracious when she called here, but the priests gave most of the work to the societies in which they are interested."

Moreover, the King not only expressed himself frankly about the associations at our audience at Court, but he showed a deep interest in the details of the Andalusian fête to which we had come to invite Their Majesties. It is the King's keenness in all matters which captivates those about him.

"What dances will there be?" he asked eagerly. "And will there be songs of the Region?" he queried. To all these questions the Spanish ladies answered, flattered at the interest manifested.

During the talk I was privileged to have with Her Majesty in English, I was charmed with her evident affectionate recollection of things in England, whilst graciously interested in the subjects which had brought me to Spain.

She smiled sweetly when I kissed her hand on leaving, as I said I did not know whether I did it as a Spanish subject or as an English compatriot, but in either case it was an honour I could not forego.

Then, the audience over, we were conducted with the same

pomp and ceremony as before through the stately salons and guarded galleries till we were once more in the free atmosphere of the Plaza de Oriente, environed by the statues of past Spanish Sovereigns, who looked spectral in the moonlight, and met by editors who wished to make copy out of our audience.

The King said we could see the state apartments of the palace on the following day, but, as the weather was bad, I proved to be the only one who appeared the next morning to profit by the royal permission.

There was much discussion in the Chamberlain's office as to the right course to pursue about my visit. The royal permission, which is rarely granted whilst Their Majesties are in residence, had been given to the party of ladies, and only one had come. Was that one to be given the privilege or no? I was amused at hearing the flow of oratory which the subject aroused among those in the office, but directly I suggested myself deferring the visit to another day, the traditional courtesy of the Spaniards gained the day, and with many bows and protestations of pleasure I was escorted past the sentries on guard by a courtly guide, who did the honours of the salons. If I describe these state apartments in the words of Pierre Loti, it will be seen that I do not exaggerate their magnificence, for the French author writes:

"The place is decorated by Velasquez, Bayeu, Tiepolo, Mengs, Luis Lopez, Rubens, Vicente Lopez, Luis Gonzalez, etc. A whole world of splendour seems to unfold, and as one passes through what seems an interminable line of salons, all marked with the particular ideas of the artists employed on them, one is struck by a series of surprises.

"The great frames of the doors are all made of agate or rare marbles, whose colours and veined surface harmonize beautifully with the brocades of the walls.

"The Salon of Charles III. is hung with blue satin starred with silver. Other salons are hung with exquisite old satin, with furniture of the time of Louis XV.; others are hung with an inimitable red embroidered with gold of the time of the Renaissance, or with pale green curiously blended with yellow or saffron colour, or deep

228

blue embossed with yellow, with the stiff but elegant furniture of the Empire period.

"Then there is a salon with the whole ceiling and panels of faience, and when the artist died before completing the work, his wife finished it by inaugurating and superintending the exquisite embroidery of garlands of white and pink roses on panels of grey silk."

There is another salon with the walls covered with cherubs of the white pottery for which the factory of the Retiro was famous—viz., the throne-room, with its ceiling painted by Tiepolo, its crimson-satin-hung walls, its long mirrors, its many crystal chandeliers, its busts of the Roman Emperors on pedestals, and, above all, its magnificent throne with its crimson and gilt chairs. The four steps of the throne are guarded by two large lions of gilt brass, and the royal seats are flanked by figures representing the cardinal virtues; and the banqueting-hall, with its magnificent columns, panels of porphyry and marble, is a perfect picture.

Spanish ladies declare that Victoria of Spain looked every inch a Queen when she first took her seat by her royal Consort. Her diadem-crowned golden hair, beautiful face, and her exquisite toilettes, make a striking feature at the State receptions; and when we consider that it was in an unknown tongue the talk went on, it was wonderful she could preserve her stately and quiet demeanour. Now the Queen has become mistress of the Spanish tongue, her subjects can admire her intellectual as well as her physical charms.

The Court of Spain at Candlemas.

The protocol of the royal Court etiquette at Madrid and the rites of the Roman Catholic Church produce a pageant in the Spanish palace at the Feast of the Purification (commonly called Candlemas) which, in splendour and solemnity, savour more of the Middle Ages than of the present practical period.

The galleries on the first-floor of the magnificent quadrangular Palace of Madrid showed the advent of a great event, for the windows looking on to the spacious colonnaded courtyard were hidden by the fine tapestries of the same character that lined the walls on the opposite sides. Rich carpets covered the floors, and the companies of stalwart halberdiers, the Guard of the palace, were placed at ten o'clock along the corridor, bearing on their shoulders their halberds with the inscription, "Fabrica de Toledo, Alfonso XIII., 1902," which were presented to them when the present King was added to the list of the Sovereigns to whom the corps had the honour to be the bodyguard. Officials of the palace and officers constantly passed to and fro, giving orders and seeing that the soldiers stood in their right places.

The three-cornered hats edged with white, the high black leggings reaching to the white breeches, and the blue coat decorated with scarlet badges bearing the castle and the crowned lion, is the same uniform of the Royal Guard as it was in the early part of the last century, and it reminds one of the pictures of Napoleon, etc., of that time.

A clap of the hands from a Court official announced the opening of a large door leading to the apartments of the Infanta Maria Teresa and her husband, Prince Ferdinand of Bavaria. Bright and happy looked the young Princess as she passed along, with her ready sweet smile for familiar faces, and looking quite pretty in her pale blue dress. The merry eyes of the stalwart, fair young Prince were cast about in cheerful greetings as he swung along in his striking blue and scarlet hussar uniform, with the jacket slung on one shoulder, revealing the richly embroidered sleeves underneath.

There was a pause after the young couple passed to the seats set apart for the Royal Family in the chapel; then the strains of a march from an opera were heard from the band of the Royal Halberdiers in the courtyard below, the halberdiers stood at attention, and the royal procession was seen coming along the gallery.

The gentlemen of the Court, with the badges marking their respective offices, the Chamberlain, all in full dress, with white silk stockings and richly embroidered coats, were followed by the grandees and officers in their striking uniforms. They walked in two single files, so as to leave clear the view of the Royal Family. The Infantas of Bavaria and the Infanta Isabel came with their respective Ladies and Gentlemen in Waiting in full Court dress. The widowed Prince of Asturias was in his place, and lastly came the King in his uniform as Admiral, and wearing the Order of the Golden Fleece and the Collar of Carlos III., and the procession solemnly passed through the guarded portals of the chapel, where the Queen-mother and the young Queen Victoria had already taken their places. For after December 25, 1886, when a special service was held in the royal chapel of the palace, in which the Virgin's protection was petitioned for the young Sovereign, the Court was in gala costume for two days. A reception was held, congratulations received, and from then till the birth of the expected heir Queen Victoria did not sit with the King on the throne in the chapel, but in the royal box on the ground-floor. All eyes were soon turned in admiration to the youthful English Sovereign of Spain, who looked like a beautiful picture in her white mantilla shading her diamond-crowned beautiful hair, and dressed in a rich, soft white Court dress.

The doors of the chapel were soon again flung open, the halberdiers were again called to attention, and the procession issued from the chapel in the same order in which it had entered, only now it was preceded by the Canons of the palace and other clerics in gorgeous vestments, with the Archbishop of Sion in gold-and-white mitre and emblazoned cope; and everybody in the procession carried a long candle, as they solemnly made the tour of the gallery to the tune of the psalm of old in which Simeon declared that the Babe brought to the Temple would be "a Light to lighten the Gentiles."

The King, as he bore his candle, looked ruefully at his sister, as much as to say: "How am I to manage this?" The Infanta smiled pleasantly, and her young husband's eyes twinkled with fun. The evident strain on the dignity of the stately grandees and Chamberlains to carry their lights befittingly gave a touch of humour to the stateliness of the scene, and I overheard a grandee say, when he was asked by one behind him not to walk

231

so slowly: "I can't go any quicker, or I shall spill some grease on the Infanta's train!"

The tour of the galleries made, the procession returned to the chapel, the King went back to his throne, and Queen Victoria of Spain to the royal box, the Chamberlains, grandees, Court ladies, the Infanta Maria Teresa, the Infante Ferdinand, Don Carlos, and the Infantas of Spain, all knelt reverently with their candles, whilst the incense was swung in front of the King after he had partaken of the Holy Sacrament.

Then, when the candles were removed by the Chamberlains, the strains from the beautiful stringed orchestra accompanied the fine voices of the hidden choir, which swelled in harmony in the chants of the occasion. The lofty cupola of the chapel, with its mythical painting supported by the gilt cherubs poised above the marble and porphyry-pillared panels of the walls, were a fitting setting to the scene.

Then the candles were once more handed round, and the glittering company again knelt in prayer. When the torches were finally taken from the worshippers, the assembly all left the chapel in solemn order, each grandee kneeling in turn for a second before the altar, and crossing himself before saluting the Queens in the royal box. The Infanta Maria Teresa, the Infanta Isabel, and the Court ladies, made a low reverence to both the Queens in the royal box before leaving the chapel, and the King, with his characteristic freedom from the fetters of etiquette, disregarded the scarlet mat, and knelt on the carpeted floor for a minute before the altar; and then with his natural grace he made a respectful salute to both his mother and his wife, and left the church, to pass once more with his retinue, and followed by the military, along the tapestry-lined galleries to the royal apartments.

The Court of Spain is especially noted for its cult of symbolism. The events of the Church calendar are presented in a realistic way which is suggestive of the Middle Ages.

I believe the Courts of Spain and Austria are alone in their dramatic representation of Christ's act of washing the feet of the disciples and feeding them on the eve of the Crucifixion.

How the King washes the Feet of the Beggars
and feeds them on Maunday Thursday.

It is only by special invitation from the chief Court Chamberlain that one can witness the King's performance of this religious function on Maunday Thursday. Being the fortunate possessor of this permit, I passed at three o'clock in the afternoon to the Hall of Columns in the palace. There the Court soon assembles in state, the ladies in magnificent dresses, of which the trains are tastefully arranged by the Gentlemen-in-Waiting over the backs of the chairs behind them, and the throng of nobles, Ministers, and officers in their gorgeous uniforms, make a brilliant show.

The King soon appears, attended by the Bishop of Alcalá and Sion, some clerics, and twelve grandees in Court attire. After divesting himself of his sword, Alfonso is girded with a towel by the prelate, and passes to the line of beggars, who sit humbly waiting for the honour which is to be paid them.

These poor men are chosen by lottery about a fortnight preceding the function, and their feet naturally undergo a course of preparation prior to the ceremony, and they are all swathed in the long Spanish cloaks given them for the occasion.

The twelve grandees in attendance have meanwhile knelt in front of the twelve beggars and taken off their shoes, and the forms of these stately personages in this humble position make a sort of screen between the eye of the public and the King's action of passing a towel over the feet of the poor men, which have been sprinkled from the gold ewer of the Bishop who precedes the Sovereign.

The King then passes to the long table, of the form and laid in the style familiar to us in pictures of the Last Supper, and the beggars are handed by their respective grandees to their seats at the board. The poor men on the last occasion were blind, but this in no way affected their calm acceptance of the fact of being the cynosure of a Court in splendid state and the object of their Sovereign's service. Stolid were the faces as the King swiftly passed the items

233

of the long menu before their sightless eyes, and as the smell of the good things was wafted to their nostrils they knew that time would give them a more substantial realization of the dainties.

For the dish of each part of the menu found its way to the baskets for the respective beggars, after being handed by the King to the grandees in attendance. Thus twelve large pieces of salmon, twelve joints of beef, and a dozen dishes of every item, were distributed by the august purveyor.

The menu finished, His Majesty completed the programme by handing also the glasses and cruets to the distinguished retinue, they also finding their way to the poor guests; and finally the King concluded the function by folding up the tablecloth with the zest characteristic of his actions.

The final privilege granted to these beggars on Maunday Thursday is the sight of the state apartments. This benefit seems to be thrown away on those whose affliction deprives them of the appreciation of their splendour, but etiquette must be preserved.

On Good Friday the King exercises his power of pardoning criminals, so he stands in front of the high-altar, and, raising to heaven the gold salver containing the names of the privileged persons, he says: "These I pardon for their crimes, even as I hope God will pardon my sins."

The carving of the lamb on Easter Sunday is quite a religious function at the King's table. The Bishop of Sion has a service of benediction, and the King and Queen take their places in state on this occasion.

One of the most striking ceremonies preceding the birth of a royal infant in the palace is that of transporting the arm of St. John the Baptist, a sash said to have belonged to the Virgin Mary, and other relics, from the chapel to the bedroom of the Queen. The King and the Court all take part in the function, attended with all the ceremony due to the occasion, and so fatiguing is the ritual that in May, 1907, Queen Victoria nearly fainted during the performance. Indeed, so many are the wearisome rites which Queen Victoria had to follow, according to the customs of the Court of Spain, that more than one editor of a democratic paper declared that if he were interested in the royal succession he would see that the authorities did not thus imperil it.

On Saturday afternoon the King and Queen go to hear the Salve in a quiet, simple fashion at the Church of the Buen Suceso. Women who press their hungry children to their bosoms as they gaze up into the face of the young Queen as she sits in the royal box on this occasion wonder if Her Majesty knows what their sufferings are. The rise in the price of bread, which the Spanish Press speaks of as an act of unjustifiable oppression, recently drove the women to desperation, and made them break the windows of the bakers' shops in some quarters of the city. This strong measure was successful, and bread is now at its usual price; for, as a Spanish lady said, "The determination of hardly-driven mothers can accomplish more than the discussions of men."

The poor people who greeted the Queen with such loud acclamations on her arrival in Spain wonder, moreover, if she knows that the liberal gifts bestowed on such festivals as the King's Saint's Day (January 23) to the orphans of the Sacred Heart of Jesus, the Real Associación de Beneficencía Domiciliaría, etc., are devoted to the maintenance of the friars and nuns of these associations rather than to the benefit of the needy.

The Queen's philanthropic spirit is, moreover, only appealed to on behalf of the orphanages and schools in the hands of the clerics, and so she is not in touch with the lay side of her country's efforts.

"If such serious matters as the lessening of the heavy duties on articles of food which go to the support of the friars, and the limitation of the associations which kill our industries, are not soon settled by the Government, they will be settled in the street!" say many thoughtful men in Spain; and it was those who saw the seriousness of the aspect who expressed their disappointment that the English Queen was so gracious in her reception of the deputation which presented the King with a petition, signed by leading ladies of fashion, against the Law of Associations; for these ladies are naturally unable to realize the struggles of their sisters against the monopoly by these associations of many of the industries on which their bread depends, such as chocolate-making, perfume-distilling, embroidery, lace-making, etc.

A bitter smile wreathes the lips of people as they read of the royal sympathy for these organizations, but they say: "What can one expect, when the young Queen is only environed with Spanish ladies, whose support of the clerics smoothes their lives, and with the Spanish priests, who dictate every deed of sympathy to the Sovereigns of Spain?"

In speaking of Queen Victoria, it must be remembered that all opinions expressed are modified by the reminder of the Queen's difficulty of knowing the real circumstances of a strange land of which she had to master the language, and that conventional greetings, gala receptions, and State dinners, do not lead to a true knowledge of the country and its needs.

It is hoped by patriots that the Queen's advent will lead to the adoption of a system of Parliamentary elections in Spain similar to that of England; for, as everybody says, if the deputies of the Congress were elected by the votes of the people instead of by the voice of the Ministers, the country's conventional love would be cemented into real devotion to the dynasty, and the reforms would be enacted which would save the land from stagnation and poverty.

The article published in an English review by a Spaniard, called "Spain's Hopes of a New Era," showed that the English Queen was looked upon as the coming saviour of the country from much that has so far crippled it; and the twenty-four short articles and poems published in the Woman's Agricultural Times from the pens of leading literary and professional ladies, begging their future Sovereign to encourage the lighter branches of agriculture as professions for women, show the hoped-for result of the new reign.

Disappointment has been expressed that this spontaneous act from Spanish women of note, many of whom have influence in the Press, has not so far resulted in any royal act of encouragement in the direction desired; so the people do not know whether their Sovereign is in sympathy with their needs or not. Directly Her Majesty is in touch with the more progressive women of her country the Press will be filled with the fact, and the warm hearts of the people will beat with gratitude, and they will be able to talk about more than the beauty of the Queen's hair and complexion.

The Spanish Court seemed to surpass itself in magnificence in the splendid functions of the christening of the first heir to the throne.

Every seat in the chapel of the royal palace was reserved for those of the highest degree, and the gallery along which the royal procession passed on its way from the royal apartments to the church was crowded by people, who could only gain admittance by tickets from the Chief Chamberlain of the palace.

The magnificent tapestries only used on State occasions were displayed, the halberdiers lined the way, and the ladies, all in mantillas, with their cavaliers in uniform or evening dress, waited in breathless impatience for the advent of the new Prince of Asturias. At last came the announcing hand-clap, and with solemn, stately step the procession came round the angle of the gallery.

First came the mace-bearers, then the ushers, all in double file, then two long lines of Chamberlains in gold-laced coats and white silk stockings, followed by the grandees of Spain in their striking military uniforms and feathered cocked hats. Then came seven grandees carrying the seven salvers with such requisites for the holy ceremony as a salt-cellar, a gold basin and ewer, a cut lemon, a lace towel, a cape, and a large cake. Behind this party came the royal Prince himself, looking really an ideal infant in his beautiful laces. His fair little uncovered head, and sweet, placid, tiny face, and clenched fists were the admiration of all beholders. He was in the arms of the Marquesa de los Llanos, who is the chief of his retinue, and on one side walked the Nuncio, who is the representative of His Holiness, as godfather, and on the other was the Queen-mother, as the godmother. The King looked dignified in his new position, as father. The Infantes and Infantas followed, with their suites. The Infanta Maria Teresa and her husband, Infante Fernando, being only convalescent from measles, were unable to be present. Don Carlos, the widowed husband of the King's late sister, the Infanta Mercedes, led little Prince Alfonso, who was known as the heir to the throne until the birth of his little cousin, and by the way he tripped along and evidently enjoyed the brilliant sight he seemed in no way saddened by his deposition from his former rank.

It was then understood that Don Carlos would marry before long the beautiful daughter of the Princess of Orleans.

The little sister of the ex-heir was led by the hand by the Infanta Isabel, at whose side walked Princess Henry of Battenberg, beautifully robed in grey velvet and ermine. Prince Arthur of Connaught, with Captain Wyndham and the Princes from Russia and Germany, etc., all had their places in the procession. China was also represented. The personal staff of the King was conspicuous, and the halberdier band of music marshalled the glittering throng to the chapel.

The altar was decorated with white flowers. The historic font in which the members of the Royal Family have for centuries been baptized was in the centre of the chapel.

Thirty-six Bishops and four Cardinals officiated. The royal neophyte was very good in the arms of his grandmother, Queen Maria Cristina. The water sprinkled on his brow was from the River Jordan. The christening ceremony over, the King decorated his infant son with the Order of the Golden Fleece, the Order of Isabella the Catholic, and the Collar of Charles III. All the ladies of the Court were in full dress.

Then the procession filed back to the royal apartments in the same order in which it had come. The dresses of the ladies of the nobility were all rich in colour and profuse with splendid jewels. The white satin, gold-embroidered train of the Duchess of Arion set off the beauty of her person.

Amid the many stately personages, the majestic figure of Sir Maurice de Bunsen was conspicuous, and Lady de Bunsen attracted attention by her beauty and her beautiful and yet simple Court dress. The ceremony was, indeed, one not easily to be forgotten as the occasion of a gathering of important personages or their representatives from far and near, and no infant could have taken its prominent part on such an important occasion with greater equanimity than did the beautiful babe—the Prince of Asturias. To sleep and to smile seem easy things to do, but to do them during the solemn, stately functions in which Church and State meet together to do him honour is not always an easy thing for an eight-day-old infant, and by accomplishing this task little Prince Alfonso added to the affection and admiration with which he is regarded.

It is always pleasant to Queen Victoria Eugénie to pass from the pageantry and pomp of the palace of Madrid to the less formal surroundings of the country. It is by no mere figure of speech that it can be said that when they are at the Palace of San Ildefonso, at La Granja, King Alfonso and Queen Victoria Eugénie lead the simple life.

The King rises early in the morning, and takes a long walk or ride—sometimes alone, sometimes attended by one gentleman, and sometimes accompanied by the Queen—or he has a bicycle spin in the grounds.

Not long since, when the King was driving alone with the Queen in a motor, he saw a soldier thrown from his horse, upon which he immediately jumped from his automobile and rushed to the assistance of the poor man.

The King's interest in his soldiers is very marked, and when the bell rang at dinner-time, when he was in consultation one morning with the commanding officer, he went with him to inspect the food, and tasted it himself.

The Prime Minister could hardly hide his surprise, when he arrived from Madrid one day to transact political business, to meet his Sovereign in his shirt-sleeves, the young King having taken off his coat, as it was a hot day for golfing.

King Alfonso and Queen Victoria like to go about unattended together, and the Spanish custom of wearing no hat in the country has been quite adopted by the English Sovereign; and people in the little town are pleased to see the Queen pass by on foot to pay a visit to some friends without anything on her head, but, of course, carrying a parasol. Both the Sovereigns spend hours with their baby son in the beautiful gardens of La Granja. The King will often take him in his arms and carry him about, or if they meet the baby Prince in his little white carriage when they are out walking they stop and fondle and talk to him.

The Queen is beginning to share King Alfonso's interest in golf, and, indeed, she takes her part well in the game, and can easily do the full round over the rough ground without any sign of fatigue.

When the weather is too hot for golf, Her Majesty much enjoys a peaceful afternoon by the river, trout-fishing. In this sport she is quite an expert, and the large basket of fish caught by the Queen and the Duquesa de San Carlos was carried home in triumph on one occasion, and figured on the royal menu for dinner.

In the Court, surrounded by courtiers and people, whose rôle is to please, the Queen may hardly gauge the depth of Spain's devotion to their English Sovereign.

When the people of Galicia presented the island of Cortegada to Alfonso XIII., they said it was also a tribute of sympathy to their Queen. "It will be nice for Her Majesty to be within sight of the English ships as they lie at anchor off the coast," they said. "It will be easy to go to England from there, and she will perhaps be reminded of her Isle of Wight. Then, we hope to see King Edward in the Spanish island home."

The enthusiasm for England is very great since the royal alliance, and for the successful recommendation of any fashion, game, or sport it is only necessary to say it is English.

It is, therefore, hoped that a nearer acquaintance with our Parliamentary system will lead to its adoption in Spain.

As, in face of his overwhelming influence, it is not possible for the people to elect a deputy of either party in opposition to the one chosen or supported by the cacique of the district, the deputies elected by public vote have mostly been republicans. Hence the suffrage is associated with republicanism in Spain, and Catalonia, where this has been successful, is connected with the idea of Separatism. Thus, with the misreport of things in Madrid, it is thought that Catalonia is wanting in Monarchists. But whenever the wisdom of the King leads to a royal visit to Barcelona, the enthusiasm for the royal visitor always proves that the Press has misinterpreted the state of feeling there; and the welcome that will be given to Queen Victoria when she makes the long-looked-for visit to Barcelona will show that Catalonia is also content that an English Queen should reign over them.

At Cortegada the peasants to whom I was introduced made the sign of the cross, for they said they had never seen an Englishwoman before; but they had one for their Queen, and she was welcome in the land.

"Viva la Reina Victoria!" was the cry which floated across the moonlit waters as the peasants returned to the mainland after the celebration of their annual festival on the island which had been offered for the acceptance of the King and the Queen, and, indeed, this cry is echoed throughout the land.

Made in the USA
Las Vegas, NV
25 January 2024

84873045R00146